D1526485

“VAST ENCYCLOPEDIA”

Recent Titles in
Contributions in Drama and Theatre Studies

Confronting Tennessee Williams's *A Streetcar Named Desire:* Essays in Critical Pluralism
Philip C. Kolin, editor

Challenging the Hierarchy: Collective Theatre in the United States
Mark S. Weinberg

The Dawning of American Drama: American Dramatic Criticism, 1746–1915
Jurgen C. Wolter, editor

The Actor Speaks: Actors Discuss Their Experiences and Careers
Joan Jeffri, editor

Richard Wagner and Festival Theatre
Simon Williams

Playwright versus Director: Authorial Intentions and Performance Interpretations
Jeane Luere, editor; Sidney Berger, advisory editor

George Bernard Shaw and the Socialist Theatre
Tracy C. Davis

Playwrights and Acting: Acting Methodologies for Brecht, Ionesco, and Shephard
James H. McTeague

Israel Horovitz: A Collection of Critical Essays
Leslie Kane, editor

Jung's Advice to the Players: A Jungian Reading of Shakespeare's Problem Plays
Sally F. Porterfield

Where the Words Are Valid: T. S. Eliot's Communities of Drama
Randy Malamud

Greek Tragedy on the American Stage: Ancient Drama in the Commercial Theater, 1882–1994
Karelisa V. Hartigan

"VAST ENCYCLOPEDIA"

The Theatre of Thornton Wilder

PAUL LIFTON

Contributions in Drama and Theatre Studies, Number 61

GREENWOOD PRESS
Westport, Connecticut • London

Library of Congress Cataloging-in-Publication Data

Lifton, Paul.
Vast encyclopedia : the theatre of Thornton Wilder / Paul Lifton.
p. cm.—(Contributions in drama and theatre studies, ISSN 0163–3821 ; no. 61)
Includes bibliographical references and index.
ISBN 0–313–29356–2 (alk. paper)
1. Wilder, Thornton, 1897–1975—Criticism and interpretation.
1. Title. II. Series.
PS3545.I345Z77 1995
812'.52—dc20 95–5675

British Library Cataloguing in Publication Data is available.

Library of Congress Catalog Card Number: 95–5675
ISBN: 0–313–29356–2
ISSN: 0163–3821

First published in 1995

Greenwood Press, 88 Post Road West, Westport, CT 06881
An imprint of Greenwood Publishing Group, Inc.

Printed in the United States of America

The paper used in this book complies with the Permanent Paper Standard issued by the National Information Standards Organization (Z39.48–1984).

10 9 8 7 6 5 4 3 2 1

Copyright Acknowledgments

The author and publisher gratefully acknowledge permission to reprint excerpts from the following copyrighted material:

Brecht on Theatre: The Development of an Aesthetic edited and translated by John Willett. Translation copyright © 1964 and copyright © 1992 renewed by John Willett. Reprinted by permission of Hill and Wang, a division of Farrar, Straus & Giroux, Inc., and of Methuen.

The Alcestiad by Thornton Wilder. Copyright © 1955, 1983 by Grant N. Nickerson, Trustee. Reprinted by permission of HarperCollins Publishers, Inc., and Brandt & Brandt Literary Agents, Inc.

Our Town by Thornton Wilder. Copyright © 1938, 1957 by Thornton Wilder. Copyright © renewed 1985 by Union Trust Company. Reprinted by permission of HarperCollins Publishers, Inc., with approval of Donald Gallup and Brandt & Brandt Literary Agents, Inc.

The Skin of Our Teeth by Thornton Wilder. Copyright © 1942 by Thornton Wilder. Copyright © renewed 1970 by Thornton Wilder. Reprinted by permission of HarperCollins Publishers, Inc., with approval of Donald Gallup and Brandt & Brandt Literary Agents, Inc.

Our Town and *The Skin of Our Teeth* from *Our Town and Other Plays* by Thornton Wilder. Penguin Books, 1962. Copyright © 1938, 1942, 1957 by Thornton Wilder. Reproduced by permission of Penguin Books Ltd.

"American Characteristics" and Other Essays. Ed. Donald Gallup. HarperCollins Publishers. Copyright © 1941, 1969 by Thornton Wilder. Reprinted by permission of Brandt & Brandt Literary Agents, Inc.

The Long Christmas Dinner and Other Plays in One Act by Thornton Wilder. HarperCollins Publishers. Copyright © 1931 by Yale University Press and Coward-McCann, Inc. Copyright © renewed 1959 by Thornton Wilder. Reprinted by permission of Brandt & Brandt Literary Agents, Inc.

The Angel That Troubled the Waters and Other Plays by Thornton Wilder. Copyright © 1928 by Coward-McCann, Inc. Copyright © renewed 1956 by Thornton Wilder. Reprinted by permission of Brandt & Brandt Literary Agents, Inc.

The Journals of Thornton Wilder: 1939–1961. Ed. Donald Gallup. New Haven: Yale University Press. Copyright © 1985. Reprinted by permission of Yale University Press.

Thornton Wilder" by Richard H. Goldstone, from *Writers at Work, First Series* by Malcolm Cowley, Editor. Copyright © 1957, 1958 by *The Paris Review*, renewed © 1985 by Malcolm Cowley, © 1986 by *The Paris Review*. Used by permission of Viking Penguin, a division of Penguin Books USA Inc., and *The Paris Review*.

"Thornton Wilder at 65 Looks Ahead—And Back," by Flora Lewis. Copyright © 1962 by The New York Times Company. Reprinted by permission.

For Joan, with love and gratitude

Contents

Preface

The purpose of this study is to define the aesthetic and philosophical universe of Thornton Wilder's drama, with its complexities and contradictions—and its essential unity—by comparing and contrasting it with a broad spectrum of other dramatic idioms. The movements, styles, and individual playwrights that provide the framework for the analysis were selected for two reasons. Either resemblances between them and Wilder's theatrical aesthetic have been frequently noted in the past and furnish labels commonly applied, rightly or wrongly, to his work; or a link was suggested by some major component or network of components of his theatrical vision (minimalism, pseudoscientific data, and the like). My aim being to construct a comprehensive picture of Wilder's art as a dramatist, I chose an array of analogues that individually illuminate different aspects of that art and collectively allowed me to examine all its characteristic features—from multiple vantage points, wherever possible.

A further aim was to discern the precise relationship in Wilder's plays between style and substance, theme and structure. Hence, a capacity to shed light on both the form and the content of Wilder's drama—or one corner of it—became an important criterion in the selection of movements and authors for comparison. Romanticism, for instance, with which Wilder may be seen to have a close philosophical affinity, was omitted from the discussion because of the marked dissimilarities between the form or style of Wilder's plays and that of romantic drama.

The seeds of the study were contained in a paper I wrote at the University of California. The topic, an examination of naturalistic elements in Thornton Wilder's plays, was suggested by Travis Bogard. For both the original suggestion and his subsequent guidance and encouragement during the research and writing phases, I owe Professor Bogard a profound debt of gratitude. Professors William I. Oliver and William Nestrick also contributed valuable insights and incisive commentary, which helped to keep my vision clear when it was in danger of becoming foggy. Ms. Isabel Wilder also deserves my thanks for her recommendations and advice concerning critical approaches to her brother's plays.

Professors Martin Blank of the College of Staten Island and Donald Haberman of Arizona State University were kind enough to read the manuscript of this volume when it was near completion and offer helpful suggestions and encouragement. Professor David Myers of Moorhead State University examined Chapter 6 and provided valuable critical comment on the overview of existentialist thought contained in it.

Thanks are due as well to two successive deans of the College of Humanities and Social Sciences at North Dakota State University, Margriet Lacy and Interim Dean Robert Littlefield, who were instrumental in providing me with two summer research grants that allowed me to begin the process of transforming my manuscript into the present book. The university also awarded me a travel stipend, which enabled me to conduct research among the Wilder papers in the American Literature Collection at Yale University's Beinecke Rare Book and Manuscript Library. Assistance with minor points connected with that research was rendered by Donald Gallup and Edward Burns, and I am grateful to both men for their time and efforts on my behalf. Finally, I would like to thank my editors, Peter Coveney and Elisabetta Linton, for their patience, expertise, sense of humor, and willingness to guide an uninitiated author through all the swamps and thickets of the manuscript preparation and production process.

Abbreviations

The following abbreviations, used in parenthetical citations in the text, refer to the sources indicated below:

AC—"American Characteristics" and Other Essays. By Thornton Wilder. Ed. Donald Gallup. New York: Harper and Row, 1979.

ATW—The Angel That Troubled the Waters and Other Plays. By Thornton Wilder. New York: Coward-McCann, 1928.

BOT—Brecht on Theatre: The Development of an Aesthetic. Ed. and trans. John Willett. New York: Hill and Wang, 1964.

LCD—The Long Christmas Dinner and Other Plays in One Act. By Thornton Wilder. New York: Coward-McCann, 1931.

SOT—Sartre on Theater. Ed. Michael Contat and Michel Rybalka. Trans. Frank Jellinek. New York: Random House/Pantheon, 1976.

YCAL—Yale Collection of American Literature, The Beinecke Rare Book and Manuscript Library, Yale University, New Haven, Conn.

Chapter 1

Introduction

In a lecture delivered at an international convocation in 1949, and later published in essay form under the title "Goethe and World Literature" (*AC* 137–48), Thornton Wilder identified as one of the most significant characteristics of twentieth-century literature the expanded, multicultural frame of reference apparent in many of its most representative works. He portrayed this feature of modern literature as the partial fulfillment of a prophecy made by Goethe in 1827, to the effect that the literary "wave of the future" would be what the poet termed "world literature."

Wilder defined this "world literature" as "a literature which assumes that the world is an indivisible unit." It grows out of a recognition that "the differences between languages and cultures begin to grow less marked to one who is accustomed to contemplating the unity of the human spirit" (141). In outlining the historical conditions underlying these developments in the literature of the modern era, Wilder noted:

> The mind of modern man has become a hold-all of flying leaves torn from some vast encyclopedia; but these leaves are not merely items of information. Each one is variously vibrant with emotion. . . . World literature will arrive when all this vast body of information is felt as a unity and literature is not only *not* national—it is planetary. (140)

Indications that such a literature is indeed at hand include, for Wilder, T. S. Eliot's juxtaposition in one place of a Sanskrit invocation and a verse from

Gérard de Nerval, James Joyce's use of twenty languages "as a sort of keyboard" in *Finnegans Wake*, and the *Cantos* of Ezra Pound, which "require our familiarity with the civilizations which Frobenius claims to have distinguished in African pre-history, as well as a close knowledge of Chinese history, the Italian Renaissance, and the economic problems of the American Revolution." Moreover, "Such material is not imbedded in these works as allusion, illustration, or as ornament; it is there as *ambiance*, as the 'nation' has been in what Goethe was calling national literature" (141).

Although Wilder's own writings, for the most part, require no such phenomenal erudition on the part of a reader as do the esoteric tours de force just enumerated, his dramatic oeuvre especially may fairly be said to constitute a "hold-all of flying leaves torn from some vast encyclopedia" of philosophical and aesthetic ideas and theatrical practices. The plays—at least the best-known, most characteristic ones—are cast in a heterogeneous "world theatre" idiom comparable in nature and intent to Goethe's "world literature." Wilder noted in his journal in 1954 that "No view of life . . . is real to me save that it presents itself as kaleidoscopic—which does not mean essentially incoherent. (The very children's toys of that name show us always a beautifully ordered though multi-fragmented pattern.)" (*Journals* 328). Far more accessible to the general public than the major works of Joyce, Pound, or Eliot, the plays nonetheless contain features that link them with a variety of aesthetic movements, philosophical systems, and theatrical traditions, both living and extinct, from a broad spectrum of cultures.

In many cases the resemblances may be entirely coincidental, the result of the playwright's having imbibed the waters of the same springs that inspired others, with whose work he was unfamiliar. However, the possibility of a direct influence or "quotation" from another play or body of plays or other works ought never to be immediately discounted, since Wilder was himself something of a "walking encyclopedia," conversant with a prodigious volume of information of all sorts. Tyrone Guthrie wrote of the playwright: "I have never met anyone with so encyclopedic a knowledge of so wide a range of topics. . . . He has been everywhere, has known—and knows—everyone (Guthrie, *Life* 232; qtd. in Goldstein 161). Nor was Guthrie the only one to register this impression of him. His learning could make itself felt almost in spite of himself, as it did once at a party at Moss Hart's home near New Hope, Pennsylvania, where Wilder was appearing in a local production of *The Skin of Our Teeth*. Although he refrained on this occasion from launching, as he sometimes did, into a full-blown discourse, Wilder

> did, however, find that, in responding [to questions from other guests], he inevitably fell into quotations from obscure German poets in their original tongue. [*sic*] Medieval French historians in their language, many quotations from Latin and he may have spoken in English a little too.

Shortly, he looked at his watch and announced that he had a matinee the next day and said he had to leave, and he was gone before midnight. After he departed, George S. Kaufman, who had not said a word so far, spoke up. "You know," he said, with that grimace so characteristic of him, "that's the best educated actor I ever met." (Letter from Franklin Heller to Linda Simon, 17 Oct. 1977, qtd. in Simon 195)

Wilder frequently drew on such extensive resources to expand the aesthetic frame of reference of his plays and novels. For instance, he admitted to one commentator that he had borrowed Mrs. Levi's epigram in *The Matchmaker*, which equates money with manure, from the title of an essay by Francis Bacon and that Emily's farewell to earth in *Our Town* was inspired by a passage in *The Odyssey* (letter from Wilder to John Modic, n.d., qtd. in Modic 60). In addition, the Act I scene in *The Matchmaker* in which Mrs. Levi attempts to convince Horace Vandergelder of "Ernestina Simple's" virtues as a prospective bride is an only slightly modified version of the famous scene between Frosine and Harpagon in Molière's *The Miser*, and the "death-sweat" speech of the Fortuneteller in Act II of *The Skin of Our Teeth* is borrowed in part from *Danton's Death* (*Journals* 180). The playwright also openly acknowledged in a number of cases that whole works were heavily indebted to, and even built upon, the works of other authors. Writing in his journal in 1954, he commented that both *Our Town* and *The Skin of Our Teeth* were

superimposed upon a variety of molds and prior achievements in theatrical art. They derive their air of originality from the facts that: (1) Very few persons knew (or profoundly knew) the great originals; and (2) The variety and disparateness of the models concealed the indebtedness; and (3) The indebtedness was one of admiration and love—which is seldom the case in such borrowings. (326n)

Wilder's penchant for this essentially classical practice of modeling his own works on beloved and admired literary precedents occasioned the second of two major critical tempests that broke upon him in the course of his career (the first being a scathing attack by Marxist critic Mike Gold following the 1930 publication of Wilder's novel *The Woman of Andros*). In December 1942, Joseph Campbell and Henry Morton Robinson, who were working at the time on their "Skeleton Key" to Joyce's *Finnegans Wake*, published an article in *The Saturday Review of Literature* outlining the debt owed to the novel by *The Skin of Our Teeth* (3–4), a debt Wilder himself eventually acknowledged, without comment or excuse, in print (Preface to *Three Plays*, *AC* 110). Although Campbell and Robinson stopped short of accusing the playwright of plagiarism, they did term the play "not an entirely original creation, but an Americanized re-creation, thinly disguised," of the novel by Joyce (Campbell and Robinson 3). They wondered if Wilder were "hoaxing" his audiences and critics. What seemed to disturb them most was his failure to acknowledge the primary source of his inspiration for the play, combined with his apparently resolute determination not to camouflage his borrowings—in fact, to flaunt some of them.

It was this latter consideration that ultimately made the question of plagiarism recede into the background, and the issue was never seriously raised to begin with. It would have been difficult to make such a charge stick, since even Campbell and Robinson noted that "Mr. Wilder goes out of his way to wink at the knowing one or two in the audience, by quoting from and actually naming some of his characters after the main figures of Joyce's masterpiece" (3). Furthermore, Wilder's obsession with *Finnegans Wake* was anything but a secret. He had been lecturing publicly on the work of several years. It would have seemed natural for anyone familiar with the playwright to presume that his scholarly enthusiasm for the novel would eventually find expression in one or another of his own creative endeavors. Thus, although the charge of extensive borrowing was far from unfounded, it was difficult to discern exactly what Campbell and Robinson's objections to Wilder's play were. They were obviously not hostile, in principle, to the concept of a "planetary" literature, since *Finnegans Wake* itself qualifies as a representative or harbinger of such a literature, according to Wilder. Appropriating the "controlling idea" of an entire work by another author is perhaps a more serious offense, it is true, than the sort of piecemeal borrowing (for purposes of reinterpretation) that Joyce practices in *Finnegan*, but Joyce himself could be considered guilty of the former offense in *Ulysses*, to say nothing of the plot borrowings of Shakespeare, Racine, Molière, and countless others. Confusing the issue was the fact that the two critics patently overstated their case, ascribing to Joycean influence several features of *Skin* that were obviously derived from other sources or only coincidentally related to *Finnegan*. For instance, their insistence that the "circular" form of *Skin* was inspired by the similar form of Joyce's novel simply indicates that they were unfamiliar with Wilder's earlier work. The circularity of both is, indeed, one of the coincidental resemblances mentioned earlier. Wilder's novels *The Bridge of San Luis Rey* (1927) and *Heaven's My Destination* (1935), as well as his plays *The Long Christmas Dinner* (1931), *Queens of France* (1931), and *Our Town* (1938), all exhibit cyclical structure to a greater or lesser extent.

However, in bringing to the attention of their readers what they considered to be a case of literary patent infringement, Campbell and Robinson were at the same time pointing out a crucial aspect of Wilder's art: his habit of assimilating and then exploiting for his own purposes features drawn from a wide assortment of literary sources. Robinson himself eventually recognized this habit as a significant element in Wilder's method of working, although he continued to voice his disapproval of such a method. Fifteen years after the original declaration of hostilities, Robinson fired one final salvo on the occasion of the publication of Wilder's first open admission that he had, indeed, drawn heavily on *Finnegan* in composing *Skin*.

Robinson at this time (1957) renewed and expanded his charges of illicit borrowing to include *The Matchmaker* (based on a play by Johann Nestroy) and *The Woman of Andros* (based on Terence's comedy *Andria*). He neglected to mention *The Bridge of San Luis Rey* (portions of which had been inspired by Prosper Mérimée's play *La carosse du Saint-Sacrement*) or *The Trumpet Shall Sound* (modeled on *The Alchemist*), and had he waited another twenty years until *The Alcestiad* appeared in print, or had he attended its world premiere performance at the Edinburgh Festival of 1955, he could have added that play to his list too, since its middle act follows Euripides's *Alcestis* quite closely.

It was Wilder's intention in all this borrowing that Campbell and Robinson originally misconstrued, however. The uncontested fact of the borrowings' abundance does not testify to the author's desire to cash in on the popularity or notoriety of other authors (*Finnegans Wake* could scarcely be called a "popular" novel, then or now) or to dignify and exalt his own more commercially oriented works. Instead, it is attributable to his naturally absorptive, wide-ranging mind, his genuine love for the works and authors from whom he borrowed, and above all, his urge to relate the moment, including his own momentary artistic creations, to all other moments and localities on the planet and, ultimately, to the eternal and universal. Novelist Glenway Wescott, a good friend of the dramatist for many years, wrote of him, "He likes every present expression to hark back to the entirety of beloved accumulated literature, and constantly shows or suggests that every current thought is based on someone else's thinking, every day of our lives is rooted in olden time" (308).

This perception or impulse is reflected in one of the most important thematic threads running through his plays: the problem of the individual's significance in the face of the vast expanses of space and time and the multitude of other individuals that surround him or her. This theme finds perhaps its most direct expression in *Our Town*, but it also appears, implicitly or explicitly, in nearly all his other dramatic works. The question, in fact, informs and unifies his entire dramatic corpus, serving not only as theme but also as structuring device and even generating impulse. He confessed to an interviewer in 1959 (Goldstone, *Writers* 113–14) that it was one of his favorite themes, a fact that is evident from even a cursory examination of the plays themselves.

In the recognition of its central position in his dramatic vision lies one basis for refuting the charges of unoriginality leveled against him by Campbell and Robinson. In essence, the thematic concern, as expressed both in his plays and in his essays, provides a key to understanding the foundations of the playwright's "world theatre" style. The plays' stylistic and philosophical heterogeneity serves to remind their audiences of the artistic and intellectual "immensity" in which the works have their being and which, rather than dwarfing them, nourishes them, just as the life and accomplishments of the human race nourish the individual person. In fact, as Wilder himself asserts in the third act of *The Skin of Our Teeth*, artistic and intellectual traditions and achievements constitute one of the primary means by which individuals may draw sustenance from suprapersonal sources.

His eclecticism is one reason why Wilder's writings, and especially the plays, stubbornly resist categorization. Critic David Castronovo terms Wilder a "protean" writer, "An adapter of styles and assumer of disguises" (1). The plays do not fit neatly in any aesthetic or philosophical pigeonhole because they exhibit similarities with almost the entire breadth of known theatrical styles and modes, both modern and historical, not to mention affinities with, and influences from, countless extratheatrical sources (such as *Finnegans Wake*). Overt borrowings actually constitute only a small portion of the connections between Wilder's plays and the various aesthetic modes and conventions employed by the theatre in modern and former times. The interplay of these diverse aesthetic modes in Wilder's drama not only helps to create the dramatist's unique "world theatre" idiom but also gives his plays a broader, more balanced appeal. Elements of one style or mode frequently counteract the limitations or cancel out or soften the more notable excesses of other styles or modes with which they are mixed.

In borrowing at will from other authors' works, in any case, Wilder is not attempting to establish his credentials as a "serious" artist or to affirm his plays' legitimacy, but is simply endeavoring to set up the appropriate aesthetic mode for his exploration of the relationship between the individual and the vast human and physical universe that surrounds him or her. Just as one play—and even one stylistic detail or dramatic moment—can contain within itself reminiscences and reflections of a range of theatrical styles and aesthetic "languages," so, too, by implication can one individual unite within him- or herself both conscious and unconscious echoes of previous generations and alien races, along with reflections of his or her contemporaries.

Wilder does not imply that it is an easy task to forge or discover such links between the individual and the vast dimensions of the cosmos, nor does he disregard the power of those dimensions to diminish the individual's sense of his or her own significance—their capacity to make anyone's claim to significance appear absurd. On the contrary, in such plays as *Our Town*, he goes to no little pain to summon up those dimensions, to evoke "the eternal silence of infinite spaces" that terrified Pascal. At the same time, however, the playwright's natural response to such terror, his method of confronting and overcoming it, includes the establishment of both stylistic and thematic bonds between his plays and characters and the works of other civilizations, cultures, and epochs. As does Goethe's "world literature," Wilder's "world theatre" presupposes a deep conviction that the "world is an indivisible unit" and its inhabitants more bound by shared needs and attributes than separated by divergent interests, idiosyncrasies, and particular habits of thought.

The problem is more complex than such a statement implies, however. Such fundamental similarities as unite human beings, while enabling the individual to draw strength and confidence from the ties binding him or her to the rest of humanity, nonetheless make it more difficult for individuals to experience and value their uniqueness. Wilder is usually careful, however, to convey to his audiences his own strong sense of the unique and infinite preciousness of each individual's life, and in his most characteristic dramatic pieces, the evocation of cosmic immensity and nameless human multitudes is delicately balanced against the scrupulously faithful—if perhaps, on occasion, gently ironic—depiction of all the individual moments, both transcendent and apparently trivial, that compose the earthly existence of the majority of mortals. Wilder was himself fully aware of this aspect of his dramatic vision, for while working on *The Skin of Our Teeth* in 1940, he commented in his journal: "I bring to it [the play] . . . my characteristic style, which weaves back and forth between the general and the particular" (*Journals* 27). Tyrone Guthrie, in writing of *Our Town*, noted that one of the paradoxes of literature and the theatre is that universality of scope is best achieved by a careful attention to the specifics of place and time (Guthrie 27).

Wilder's attention to specific detail goes beyond what is necessary for the achievement of universal resonance, however. He appears to cherish the momentary and the finite for their own sakes. The contemporary and the immediate in these plays may be largely used as springboards for speculations about the individual's place in the cosmos, but at the same time, the wealth of scientific, geographical, and sociological detail in several of the plays prevents the audience from utterly forgetting the particular in its contemplation of the general.

Similarly, the disparate aesthetic echoes and influences that are perceptible in the plays never obscure completely the traits that stamp these works as unique creations of a single mind. One of those traits may be their philosophical and stylistic heteromorphism itself, but there are also a number of other clues, other trademarks: the figure of the Stage Manager, the subversion and mocking parody of naturalistic and other nineteenth-century staging conventions, the incorporation and compression of large stretches of imagined space and time, and the characterization based on type or stereotype.

Furthermore, Wilder's fundamental concerns as a writer, and even his basic theatrical vision, altered little from his earliest days to his latest. Unlike such writers as Gerhart Hauptmann and Eugene O'Neill, he did not pass through successive phases or "periods" in his professional life. That circumstance is partly due to two related facts. First, the major aesthetic "movements" in the professional New York theatre to which his stylistic experiments seemed most closely related had already run their course by the time his experiments appeared. Second, he himself, as a novelist, lecturer, and part-time educator as well as a playwright, was always somewhat divorced from the hurly-burly of the New York theatre scene. Being "out of synch" with mainstream commercial theatre, he could follow his own idiosyncratic lights without feeling compelled, for economic or other reasons, to jump on or off a particular theatrical bandwagon at a particular time.

His skill and vision expanded and evolved throughout his career, and each of his four major plays represents a radical departure in style and tone, and even emphasis, from the previous ones. However, he frequently resurrected devices he had introduced in earlier plays and reused them—in expanded or otherwise modified form and in different contexts—in later ones. In fact, the seeds of his overall vision, and even many of the specific devices met with in his later plays, are already in evidence in his earliest dramatic writings, the "three-minute," three-character plays in the collection, *The Angel That Troubled the Waters and Other Plays* (1928). Many of these brief playlets had been written and originally published in campus literary magazines while Wilder was still an undergraduate at Oberlin and Yale (1916–1920), and they thus constitute his earliest published works.

Even within this essential unity of vision, however, the various "external" echoes and quotations are usually permitted sufficient autonomy to be readily identifiable, as Campbell and Robinson pointed out. In all Wilder's plays, nearly every "imported" thread woven into the tapestry can be isolated and traced back to its point of origin or matched to a similar thread spun from some outside source, yet the total composition—the total picture— is always recognizably Wilder's. Stylistically as well as thematically, then, the works are suspended between the unique and the universal, the evanescent and the timeless, and there is no ultimate resolution of the tension thus created between these two nodal points in the playwright's work.

He eventually came to perceive this suspension between the individual and the universal, the local and the global, as a fundamental attribute of American culture and consciousness in general. The American present, then as now, drew much of its character from a multitude of foreign and native cultures, pasts, and traditions. The tributary cultures retained a measure of autonomy and recognizability but were all partially transformed and homogenized by, and into, an equally recognizable "American culture." Because of its heterogeneous, global roots and components, that culture might fairly be characterized as a "world culture" analogous in many respects to Goethe's "world literature," but it also had, and has, distinctive traits of its own (such as a fascination with size, speed, and large numbers).

In "Toward an American Language," his first Charles Eliot Norton Lecture, delivered at Harvard in 1950, Wilder described this polarity in

American culture and consciousness, the "here-everywhere" polarity, in the following terms:

> An American can have no such stabilizing relation [as a European] to any one place, nor to any one community, nor to any one moment in time.
>
> Americans are disconnected. They are exposed to all place and all time. . . . They have a relation, but it is to everywhere, to everybody, and to always. (*AC* 14–15)

Elsewhere in the same lecture, he stated, "The American is the first global mind" ("Toward," *Atlantic* 31).

At the same time, however, the American does not deny the significance of particularity; of every individual "one" that goes to make up "everybody"; of every concrete, definite place comprised by "everywhere"; and every moment comprehended within "always." In a 1931 interview with Walter Tritsch, he declared:

> Just think of what it means to every American to believe himself permanently, directly, and responsibly bound to world destiny. The significance that this belief imparts to the simplest dealings and simplest events seems to me the beginning of all achievement. Such a trend precedes all great cultures. (Tritsch 46)

In discussing "The American Loneliness" in another of the Norton Lectures, he observed, "Emily Dickinson . . . solved the problem [of loneliness] in a way which is of importance to every American: by loving the particular while living in the universal" (*AC* 63). The statement could apply just as well to Wilder himself, especially as he is revealed in his plays and essays.

Thus, Wilder's "dramaturgical esperanto" paradoxically seems to augment the purely "American" quality of the pieces. This is the converse of Tyrone Guthrie's observation that universality in a work of art requires careful particularization. In Wilder's art, the playwright's overt attempt to universalize the depicted action can be seen as increasing the plays' purely national, American character, provided one accepts with few reservations Wilder's evaluation of the nature of American culture and consciousness.

Still, Wilder's dramatic vision is unquestionably unique, even among American playwrights. The uniqueness of his style consists, apart from the characteristic elements already mentioned, in three basic components, which appear in varying proportions in nearly all his most typical plays. The elements are realistic detail and dialogue, fantasy or allegory, and theatricalism, or the frank acknowledgement and exploration of the artificiality of the theatrical medium. Each of these three components links the plays with one or more of the major nineteenth- and twentieth-century aesthetic or aesthetic-philosophical movements and/or with the theatrical practices of other cultures, historical or foreign, as well. The most significant movements with which the plays show affinities are symbolism, naturalism, expressionism, futurism, and existentialism; the historical and foreign traditions include classical Greek, medieval, Elizabethan, Renaissance, Spanish, Chinese, and Japanese, as well as American popular or folk entertainments. The relationship of Wilder's theatre to each of these forerunners will be explored in turn in the succeeding chapters.

Chapter 2

"The Void That Contains the Infinite": Symbolist Aspects of Wilder's Theatre

The modern aesthetic-philosophical movement with which Wilder's dramaturgy displays the deepest, most complete, and most striking affinity is French symbolism. The connection is not one that has been fully perceived or explored in any depth to date, either by the playwright himself or by the critics, although some of the latter have touched on it in a very general way while comparing Wilder with Maeterlinck or Proust.[1] The reason for the omission is probably that in this instance, as in others, the resemblance between Wilder's dramaturgy and that practiced or propounded by his predecessors is more the result of general spiritual kinship than of direct—or at least conscious—influence.

At the same time, although it is unlikely that Wilder was intimately acquainted, at least at the time he was writing his major plays, with all the salient features of the symbolist theatre aesthetics developed by Mallarmé, Maeterlinck, Lugné-Poë, and others, he unquestionably was familiar with the methods and most widely known works of some of the movement's leading poets and playwrights—and precursors. His mother, who was his closest confidante and most supportive critic during his youth, had tried her hand at translating some poems by the Belgian symbolist Émile Verhaeren (A. N. Wilder 62), and she knew Maeterlinck's work as well (Harrison 14). Wilder himself, at age 12, was sufficiently familiar with Maeterlinck's style to believe he was imitating it in a letter to his sixth-grade teacher, Miss Ema Juth (qtd. in D. Pollard; wire to T. Colman, 28 Dec. 1952, typescript (ts.), Wilder papers YCAL). Moreover, in 1918 he read Verhaeren's play *The Cloister* "with enthusiasm" and two years later saw it in New York, according to entries in his diary for those years (15 Jan. 1918; list of plays seen, 1919–21, manuscript (ms.), Wilder papers, YCAL).

He developed an enthusiasm early in his career for the poetry and criticism of Paul Valéry (A. N. Wilder 38), and one of his favorite instructors at Princeton (where he was awarded an M.A. in French in 1926) was a man named Louis Cons, who lectured on Baudelaire and Verlaine, among other writers (Simon 42). A reference in Wilder's 1925 theatre review, "The Turn of the Year," shows that at that time, he knew Maeterlinck's *Monna Vanna* ("Turn" 152), and when the Belgian playwright died, Wilder was one of a number of international literary figures who contributed eulogies to a 1949 volume titled *Hommage à Maurice Maeterlinck* (78–79). Wilder's tribute indicates that when he first sought ways to combat the tyranny of the well-made, realistic play, he found the older dramatist's works intriguing and liberating. In a 1965 reply to an inquiring scholar, Wilder's sister Isabel also acknowledged that Maeterlinck (along with William Butler Yeats and others) had influenced her brother's dramatic writing, at least until the *Blue Bird* craze swept the United States in the 1910s (letter to Walter Beaver, 4 Feb. 1965, ts., Wilder papers, YCAL).

A reference in Wilder's 1941 essay, "Some Thoughts on Playwrighting" (*AC* 122), reveals that by that time (between the composition of *Our Town* and *The Skin of Our Teeth*) he had acquired a superficial knowledge of Maeterlinck's influential collection of mystical, inspirational, and theoretical essays, *The Treasure of the Humble*, but the reference contains no indication of the date at which he first became familiar with the volume. On the other hand, lecture notes on tragedy for a course he taught at the University of Chicago beginning in 1930 (before the publication of *The Long Christmas Dinner* and its companion plays) show that he knew then that Maeterlinck favored an essentially static drama (ms., Wilder papers, YCAL), the same point he makes about him in "Some Thoughts." Finally, a 1925 letter to his brother Amos reveals that Wilder at that time was well enough acquainted with the movement in general to refer to it explicitly and comment on the symbolists' admiration for Edgar Allan Poe, which he found perplexing and mildly amusing (8 Feb. 1925, copy in letter bk., ms., Wilder papers, YCAL).

Edmund Wilson correctly identified the Proustian influence in Wilder's first two novels (Wilson 303–5), an influence that can also be detected in several of Wilder's plays, especially *Our Town*. Although, as Anna Balakian points out (159), the concept of a symbolist novel in general involves something of a contradiction in terms, and although Proust in particular deviates from symbolist aesthetics in important respects, his point of departure, as both Balakian (35, 76n) and Samuel Beckett (60) observe, lies within the movement or "on its outskirts" (Beckett 60). The novelist's exploration of the mechanics of human memory rests firmly on the symbolist concept of mystical, suprarational "correspondences," and the famous madeleine, in its capacity to evoke an entire complex of associated impressions, constitutes something of a parallel in the psychological sphere to the multireferential symbol of the symbolist poets, which is itself grounded in the theory of correspondences. Hence, Proust's influence on Wilder's drama can legitimately be considered part of a broader, more specifically symbolist, influence.

All of this is not to suggest that Wilder, even in borrowing ideas from Proust, was consciously attempting to write symbolist plays, as Maeterlinck was at first, or that he would have been at all comfortable seeing himself labeled a "symbolist" playwright. In some unpublished general suggestions for the staging of *The Skin of Our Teeth*, he expressed disagreement with those who recommended using a cyclorama as the backdrop for the play, saying he had "never seen a cyclorama that did not suggest 'beauty' of the poetic drama type" (qtd. in Haberman, *Plays* 69), a type that might be considered to include symbolist drama. He recommended instead that *Skin* be played before "the same brick walls and steam-pipes that were used in *Our Town*" (70).

Indeed, in his plays Wilder sins against symbolist precepts and preferences in a number of significant ways, as will be made clear later in this chapter. Nevertheless, the affinities between him and the symbolists in questions of dramaturgy are both striking and deep. Moreover, questions of influence aside, not only do symbolist theories and techniques constitute one of the central components in Wilder's "world theatre," but the very foundation of the "world theatre" concept may be rooted in certain perceptions or habits of thought that he shares with the symbolists.

As concerns specific affinities between Wilder and the symbolists, among the strongest is a shared philosophical orientation. The aesthetic principles governing both his theatre and theirs are founded on Platonic postulates and convictions, although in certain respects, Wilder's convictions lean more toward traditional, rationalistic Platonism than toward the mystical Neoplatonism of the symbolists. In any case, critic Albert Aurier, writing in the symbolist journal *Le Mercure de France*, asserted that a symbolist work of art ought, in the first place, to be "Ideist, since its unique ideal will be to express the Idea"(Aurier 162, author's translation). The symbolists, however, felt that the Idea, which Plato had considered accessible to human reason, could be apprehended only by nonrational means such as intuition or sudden insight, and that the most effective medium for conveying it was not philosophical discourse but poetry. Wilder, for his part, although perhaps more strongly inclined toward rationalism than toward poetry—or, at least, equally inclined toward both—also propounded unequivocally Platonist views in his essays on the theatrical art. He wrote in his preface to the volume, *Three Plays*: *Our Town*, *The Skin of Our Teeth*, *The Matchmaker*, that "It is through the theater's power to raise the exhibited individual action into the realm of idea and type and universal that it is able to evoke our belief" (*AC* 108). Similarly, in a preface to *Our Town*, originally published in the *New York Times* shortly after the play's opening night, he observed:

> The theater longs to represent the symbols of things, not the things themselves. All the lies it tells [i.e., its foundation in pretense] enhance the one truth that is there—the truth that dictated the story, the myth. . . . When the theater pretends to give the real thing in canvas and wood and metal it loses something of the realer thing which is its true business. (*AC* 102)[2]

Although Wilder may here be thinking of the "truth" in more rationalistic, less mystical terms, the emphasis on the "oneness" of the truth lurking behind the theatre's "lies" actually moves the playwright toward the Neoplatonist, as opposed to classical Platonist, camp in this passage, and the identification of that truth with "myth" tends to counteract the rationalistic tendency evident in other writings of Wilder's.

In addition to Wilder himself, numerous critics have remarked upon the Platonism that informs much of Wilder's imaginative writing, both fictional and dramatic (Burbank 23, 24, 27, 30, 72; Corrigan 170–73; Firebaugh 426–38; Fergusson 544–73; Porter 200–224). In the latter sphere, the playwright's Platonic—and even Neoplatonic—orientation can perhaps most easily be seen in some of the early "three-minute" plays for three characters. Simply in intending these closet playlets for performance in the "theatre of the mind," Wilder was acting in accordance with the preferences of Mallarmé and Maeterlinck, for whom the imagined performance, being in effect an Idea of the play, was ultimately superior to any actual one. At any rate, the most explicitly Platonic of Wilder's brief dramas is the one titled *Centaurs* (*ATW* 83–87). The central thesis put forth in the playlet is that, in the words of the poet Shelley, who appears as a character in it:

> the stuff of which masterpieces is made drifts about the world waiting to be clothed in words. It is a truth that Plato would have understood that the mere language, the words of a masterpiece, are the least of its offerings. (*ATW* 86–87)

According to the play, the *idea* of an unwritten poem by Shelley, "The Death of a Centaur," ultimately took form as Ibsen's *The Master Builder* (itself a favorite play of Mallarmé and other symbolists).

The apparent conceptual gulf between the projected poem and Ibsen's play implies that Wilder here conceives of the Idea more in symbolist or Neoplatonic terms than in classically Platonic ones. Although "Hilde Wangel" in Wilder's play asserts that "both [works, play and poem,] are certainly about centaurs" (86), it is hard to see how she could have arrived by any purely rational process at the conclusion that the character Solness is a sort of centaur. As if to emphasize the symbolist, as opposed to simply

Platonic, bias of Wilder's play, "Ibsen" (another character in it), responding to the line of "Shelley" quoted above, cautions the poet against "revealing all the mysteries" (87) of artistic creation. The invocation of "mystery" just at this point causes the play to incline sharply toward the symbolist camp in this one respect, although, at the same time, it is probable that the entire Neoplatonic foundation of the play has more to do with the real Shelley's own Neoplatonic beliefs than with any symbolist influence or impulses on Wilder's part.

On the other hand, Neoplatonic concepts inform a number of the other "three-minute" playlets as well. One of these is *And the Sea Shall Give Up Its Dead* (*ATW* 99–103), which posits a Neoplatonic conception of the individual. Presenting the playwright's vision of the events following the Final Trumpet, the piece ends with the stripping of their identities from three drowned souls and their simultaneous fusion with the rest of creation in the "blaze of unicity" (103) that follows the world's dissolution. The concept is reminiscent of the Button Moulder in Ibsen's *Peer Gynt*, except that here, as befits Doomsday, *all* individual souls, no matter what they may or may not have accomplished in their lives, are destined to be "melted down" into their primal material, which is even more basic than their Idea or Pure Form. Again, the vision of a fundamental "unicity" at the heart of creation gives this play a distinctly Neoplatonic cast.

In fact, Plotinus, the founder of Neoplatonism, held that the fundamental aim of the soul is to return to its source, of which it is merely an emanation. Thus, although the three souls in Wilder's little play cling desperately to their identities until the very last, the peculiar outcome of Judgment Day presented in the piece—the merging of all individual souls into one—may fairly be said to illustrate a basic tenet of Neoplatonist thought. Wilder apparently continued, moreover, to believe in the eventual extinction of the identity after death, if one can assume that the Stage Manager in *Our Town* is voicing the dramatist's own ruminations when, in attempting to identify the "something eternal about every human being," he poses to the audience the rhetorical question, "what's left when memory's gone, and your identity, Mrs. Smith?" (82).

True, the romantics also believed in the merging of the identity with all of creation following the individual's death, and according to Balakian's analysis of the two movements, Wilder is actually closer to the romantics on this point than he is to the symbolists, since the latter, despite their fascination with death and dissolution, felt that the experience of a mystical union with all creation did not have to wait until the individual's demise (Balakian 19, 25). Nevertheless, the distinction is a relatively narrow one, and since there are strong, direct links between romanticism and symbolism (which was called "neoromanticism" in Germany), Wilder's affinity with one movement can—at least on this theoretical-philosophical plane—be considered an affinity with the other.

One final early playlet informed by Neoplatonic beliefs—and again, equally susceptible of romantic and symbolist interpretations—is the first one in the collection *Nascuntur Poetae (ATW* 19–23), the Platonic elements in which are discussed by Burbank (23). The central character, a child representing the unborn soul of the poet, is told by the Woman in Deep Red, who is preparing him for earthly life, that although others may find some contentment in their lives, for him "there shall be ever beyond the present a lost meaning" (22). This concept of the artist's fate is clearly more romantic than strictly Platonic, yet the belief in a transcendent meaning beyond the present is characteristic of Platonism, too. The fact that it is said to be a "lost" meaning, though, gives the passage a distinctly Neoplatonist (and, consequently, a romantic and, perhaps, a symbolist) aura. It is strongly reminiscent of Wordsworth's ode, "Intimations of Immortality," which may indeed have provided the inspiration for the entire play. At the same time, the particular view of the artist presented in the play—namely, that his or her creativity is a form of "divine madness"—is precisely the same as that set forth in Plato's *Ion*.

The Platonic underpinnings of the major plays are perceptible primarily in the staging rather than in the dialogue, as they are in the "three-minute" plays; and the relationship of those aspects of Wilder's dramaturgy to symbolist theory and practice will be examined later in the chapter. The dramatist's Platonic view of the theatre in general, though, which he plainly enunciated in his essays and journals, provides a clear indication of his intentions in the major plays. In addition, at least one significant Platonic or Neoplatonic element may be seen in the dialogue in *Our Town*. It is contained in perhaps the most famous passage in the play, the Jane Crofut letter referred to at the end of Act I. In the address on the get-well letter sent to Rebecca Gibbs's friend Jane Crofut by her minister, the ever-widening physical contexts of the ailing girl's life are ultimately seen to be encompassed within the "Mind of God" (45), suggesting that the individual's truest essence and, in fact, the essence of the entire physical universe exist as an Idea in the divine consciousness.

Related to, and springing from, Wilder's underlying Platonic or Neoplatonic orientation is a theme central to his dramatic work and also encountered in the writings of Maeterlinck (the symbolist playwright par excellence), the theme that there is infinite, hidden wonder, to which most mortals are blind most of the time, in the smallest of phenomena surrounding each human being. Mallarmé also, according to Haskell Block, conceived of the drama (like the other arts) as a vehicle first and foremost for revealing the "hidden wonder of the universe" (Block 102). Wilder's most explicit statement of this theme may be found in *Our Town*, of course, in Emily's Act III observation, "That's all human beings are! Just blind people" (101), but it also informs *Pullman Car Hiawatha*, *The Happy Journey*, *The Long Christmas Dinner*, and even *The Matchmaker*. A few quotations from Maeterlinck's essay collection, *The Treasure of the Humble*, should suffice to show his kinship with Wilder in this matter—a kinship already noted in passing by Robert W. Corrigan in a 1961 article on the latter playwright (172). First, referring to the "tragical" element in daily life, the Belgian dramatist writes, "Its province is . . . to reveal to us how truly wonderful is the mere act of living, and to throw light upon the existence of the soul, self-contained in the midst of ever-restless immensities" (Maeterlinck 97–98). The entire statement, without modification, could be taken as referring to *Our Town*, *The Happy Journey*, or *Pullman Car Hiawatha*, and especially the first play, with its recurrent references to the temporal, spatial, and populational immensities surrounding each individual life. All three plays could be considered perfect fulfillments of the desires expressed in another passage as well. Speaking of his disappointing experiences in the theatre, Maeterlinck confesses, "I had gone thither hoping that the beauty, the grandeur and the earnestness of my humble day by day existence would, for one instant, be revealed to me, that I would be shown the I know not what presence, power, or God that is ever with me in my room" (104).

In Wilder's plays, it is most often an awareness of, or confrontation with, death that prompts the characters to sense, however dimly or temporarily, the hidden wonder in humble daily existence, and in this respect Wilder is also following, whether consciously or unconsciously, in Maeterlinck's footsteps (although not only in his). In one of his essays, Maeterlinck writes:

> If you knew that you were going to die tonight, or merely that you would have to go away and never return, would you, looking upon men and things for the last time, see them in the same light that you have hitherto seen them? Would you not love as you never yet loved? (180–81)[3]

Emily, in her return to life in Act III of *Our Town*, learns too late the answers to these questions. Unhappily, she finds that she can only "love as [she] has never yet loved" after she has lost her ability to communicate that love and share it. Similarly, Leonora and Genevieve in *The Long Christmas Dinner* make the poignant discovery after the deaths of loved ones that they "never told [them] how wonderful [they] were" (16, 21). Genevieve had thought her mother would "be here forever" (16).

Proust restated the same fundamental thought in an epigrammatic observation that also could serve as an apt summary of the theme of *Our Town*, *Pullman Car Hiawatha*, and *The Long Christmas Dinner*. He wrote, "If there were no such thing as Habit, Life would of necessity appear delicious to all those whom Death would threaten at every moment, that is to say, to all Mankind" (qtd. in Beckett 17). The translation of Proust is by Samuel Beckett, who in *Waiting for Godot* incorporates the converse of the epigram in Vladimir's Act II comment, "habit is a great deadener" (58).

These themes are not the exclusive property of Wilder, Maeterlinck, Proust, and Beckett, however. William Blake, in perceiving the "hidden wonder" embedded in humble, everyday phenomena, found "a World in a Grain of Sand/ And a Heaven in a Wild Flower" ("Auguries of Innocence"), and the Greeks saw the poignancy and absolute value that death confers on the most insignificant aspects of life. If Wilder arrived at these insights through his reading rather than his life experiences, they probably came from Proust or the Greeks rather than from Maeterlinck. Nevertheless, the signal applicability to Wilder's plays of these passages by the Belgian playwright constitutes striking evidence of the spiritual kinship between the two dramatists on this point.

Nor was Maeterlinck the only symbolist playwright to explore these themes, which were so close to Wilder's heart. The decadent aesthete Claudio, the central character in Hugo von Hofmannsthal's *Death and the Fool*, learns to value his life only when he recognizes that he is about to be deprived of it. If any further proof of Wilder's closeness to the symbolists on this point were needed, it could be found in the parallels contained in two final passages—one from *Our Town* and one from Maeterlinck's essays. At the end of *Our Town*, Emily asks the Stage Manager, "Do any human beings ever realize life while they live it?—every, every minute?" (100). He answers in the negative but adds, "The saints and poets, maybe—they do some" (100). In a passage that echoes almost verbatim Emily's query and the Stage Manager's musing reply, Maeterlinck asks: "But cannot we live as though we always loved? It was this that the saints and heroes did; this and nothing more" (178).

In addition to these indications of philosophical and thematic affinities between Wilder and the symbolists, the former's plays contain a number of "symbolist" stylistic devices, albeit usually in modified form. Ironically, Wilder is perhaps least like the symbolists in his use of symbols. His plays are full of them, but they tend to represent only one concept or general category of phenomena instead of being capable of sustaining multiple interpretations, as the symbolists' symbols were meant to be. Later in life, after he had composed all of his major plays, it is true that he asserted in a journal entry,

> a symbol is a lariat; formerly it has been sufficient that the lariat enwrap and bring to its knees a passing fancy, a fragment of a fragment of experience. There is something about the pressure on our minds today that demands that a symbol be a mode of stating the All—only so can it be a growing kinetic action of the mind. All symbols less than that are static metaphors. (*Journals* 215)

Moreover, in another entry of a few days later that carried these same ideas a step further, he described "American Symbol-Making" in terms wholly consonant with (and, in fact, reiterating) orthodox symbolist theory. He wrote:

an American-made symbol . . . at the moment of its appearance in the *Dichter's* mind would be a way of "figuring" to himself the totality of experience. . . .

The picture elements in the symbolic representation are not subject to (*i.e.,* selected by) the conscious rational intelligence, and once present to the American are not so developed, *because* he, having freed himself from tradition, authority, inherited patterns of thinking, is in a position to recognize and trust images and concepts that associationally present themselves to his mind from feeling and intuition. . . .

The American symbol then is cosmological, extra-rational, and non-tendentious. (218)

Setting aside the references to the American mind, this passage sets forth a creed that any avowedly symbolist poet or critic would have wholly supported.

Still, despite Wilder's enunciation in his journals of such unequivocally symbolist views, in the plays themselves it is a very different matter. There the symbols are for the most part just such unambiguous, "static metaphors" as the dramatist here inveighs against. Moreover, they tend, especially in *The Skin of Our Teeth,* to be "public," in contrast to the "private," or obscure, symbols generally employed by the symbolists.

There are a few exceptions, however, especially in the "three-minute" plays. In fact, many of these miniature dramas are cast in a more conventionally symbolist style than any of Wilder's other writings, possibly indicating a symbolist influence on the playwright in the early years of his career.[4] This influence, if that is what it was, perhaps became more diluted or disguised by cross-breeding with other styles and influences as the years passed, although it never entirely disappeared and, indeed, reasserted itself in surprising ways and with renewed vigor in some of his later works.

In any event, in the early playlets perhaps the greatest assortment of symbols (although most of them, it is true, are univalent and unambiguous) may be found in *Nascuntur Poetae* (*ATW* 19–23). The action consists of two conversations involving the central character, a child (who is clearly intended to represent the unborn soul of a poet and nothing else). In the first, he speaks to a woman wearing a chlamys that takes on the colors of the objects around her; the second is between him and her "sister," a woman dressed in deep red. Each of the women prepares him for some aspect of earthly life, with the Woman in Deep Red giving him a golden chain hung with pendants symbolizing the "dark and necessary gifts" (21) attendant upon the artistic life. The woman explains in turn the meaning of each of the pendants, which comprise a staff, a laurel leaf, a tongue of flame, and an unidentified object made of crystal (possibly a ball). The tongue of fire, according to the woman, stands for a "madness" (21) peculiar to poets, which is almost certainly the madness of artistic invention or creativity, the divine "poetic frenzy" discussed in Plato's *Ion.* The pendant representing a leaf of laurel is clearly an indication of fame or success, the pendant in the shape of a staff signifies a life of wandering (whether spiritual or geographical), and the crystal symbolizes the poet's higher-than-normal powers of perception (or perhaps his visionary capacities), which are both a gift and a curse. The chain from which these objects dangle represents the boy's fate.

However, the symbolic meaning of the two "sisters" in the play is much more uncertain, although they are so abstract and so sharply contrasted in both their garments and their gifts that they cannot rightly be considered conventional characters, especially given the allegorical nature of the play as a whole. The color of the second woman's robe has a number of traditional symbolic associations, but there is no indication in the play as to which of these—passion, fidelity, blood, love, shame—one is meant to regard as "correct." The chameleonic nature of the other woman's chlamys also suggests that she represents the power of the senses to reflect or transmit images of reality to the mind, a power that the poet or artist needs in extra measure. The suggestion is reinforced by the Boy's statement that she has "poured on [his] eyes and ears and mouth the divine ointment" (20), but the woman herself denigrates the "tumult of the senses" (20) in her next line, and her costume might symbolize adaptability or mental flexibility as well.

Whatever spiritual agencies, qualities, or influences the women may represent, their ethereal femininity itself lends the play a symbolist aura and links it with the artistic tradition of the symbolist painters Maurice Denis, Gustave Moreau, and Pierre Puvis de Chavannes—and indeed, with the symbolist theatrical tradition as well, since Pelléas in Maeterlinck's *Pelléas and Mélisande* was originally played by an actress (Jasper 98n).

An even vaguer symbolism pervades the collection's title play, *The Angel That Troubled the Waters (ATW* 145–49). The central character is a physician who has come to the biblical pool at Bethesda in order to be eased of his burden of guilt and sin, the nature of which is never specified. The angel whose visitations are responsible for the cures for which the place is famous warns the physician away from the edge of the miraculous pool, however, saying that healing is not for him. His mission in life requires that he continue to bear the burden, which he has hitherto regarded as a hindrance in his life's work, because, as the angel tells him, "The very angels themselves cannot persuade the wretched and blundering children on earth as can one human being broken on the wheels of living" (49). The piece, like *Nascuntur Poetae*, is manifestly a parable, and everything in it—physician, angel, pool, and burden—possesses symbolic weight. However, the range of possible specific meanings for these symbols is literally unlimited, adding to the mystery and vibrancy of the play as a whole.

Conspicuous (and less conspicuous) symbols also enrich the later, better-known, and more stageworthy plays, especially *The Skin of Our Teeth* and several of the one-act plays originally published in the same volume as *The Long Christmas Dinner*. Again, the majority, as befits symbols in works intended for the stage, are clear, unambiguous, and univalent. The setting for *The Long Christmas Dinner* contains two portals that are explicitly said to "denote birth and death" (1). Similarly, the character Genevieve in the play draws the audience's attention to the symbolic nature of the dinner itself when, as a young girl, she vows to sit in the house beside her mother forever, "as though life were one long, happy Christmas dinner" (12).

On the other hand, more pregnant, "symbolist" symbols may also be discerned embedded in the fabric of some of the author's other plays. The archetypal nature of the central characters in *The Skin of Our Teeth,* for instance, gives them, as symbols, a greater resonance and depth than ordinary allegorical symbols, although each of the four—George and Maggie Antrobus, Henry, and Sabina—"stands for" only one specific human type or set of impulses or values. Similarly, on one level "our town" of Grover's Corners functions as a symbol of the human community, a multifaceted, if still unitary, entity, like the "human family" symbolized by the Antrobuses.

However, there is at least one other major symbol in several plays that is more broadly suggestive, although still not ultimately as ambiguous as the more uncompromising symbolists would prefer. That symbol is the journey, the central action of both *Pullman Car Hiawatha* and *The Happy Journey*. It has not gone unnoticed that the physical journeys in Wilder's writings frequently parallel inner voyages of spiritual discovery (Littman 45, 75n; Castronovo 74, 80)—as they do in Strindberg's *To Damascus* plays and countless other works. The climax of *Pullman Car*, the posthumous epiphany of the central character, Harriet, in which she becomes conscious of the music of the spheres and the sounds of the earth, and hence understands "everything now" (68), constitutes a spectacular spiritual discovery, although the fact that it is posthumous inclines the play, on the thematic level, more toward romanticism than toward symbolism in this one respect. In *The Happy Journey,* which depicts in condensed form the Kirby family's automobile journey from Trenton to Camden, New Jersey, the most insignificant events on the trip provide Ma Kirby with an occasion to point out moral truths to her children. In addition, the journey itself brings the family members to a deeper sense of their collective identity, drawing them closer emotionally as well as physically.

The pattern appears not only in these two plays, but also in the "three-minute" playlet *The Flight into Egypt* (*ATW* 137–41), in which a talking donkey carries the Holy Family to safety in Egypt without realizing, until it is almost too late, the nature of the burden she carries. It may also be found in the novels *Heaven's My Destination* and *The Eighth Day* and in the later play *Childhood,* from the projected *Seven Ages of Man* cycle. In all cases, the physical journey accompanies an increase in awareness, whether of the wonders of the universe, both physical and spiritual (as in *Pullman Car*), of the needs and feelings and value of other people, of the interdependence of all human beings, or of the voyager's previously untapped potential. This variation in the specific object or nature of the increased awareness preserves some allusive richness for this pivotal, recurring Wilder symbol.

One particular form of symbolic representation employed in *Pullman Car* and other Wilder plays—personification—also helps to enhance the "symbolist" quality of those plays. One of the more extreme romantic or Neoplatonist beliefs of the symbolists was that objects are endowed with a spiritual dimension, or "soul." Such a belief naturally led to a liberal use of personification in symbolist poetry, one example being contained in Baudelaire's famous "Correspondances," in which the poet depicts life as a passage through "forests of symbols," which regard human beings "with familiar glances" (ll. 3, 4, author's translation). In *Pullman Car*, as the railroad car named in the title speeds through Ohio on its way to Chicago, a series of figures enters and each announces that he or she represents some feature of the landscape—a small town, a field—through which the train is passing. Later in the play, the hours are personified as "beautiful girls dressed like Elihu Vedder's Pleiades" (62), and they recite snatches of philosophy. Then the planets, represented by unspecified persons, put in an appearance and murmur mysterious sounds, the music of the spheres. Each of these "characters" thus stands in a one-to-one relationship with the thing that he or she represents, making the symbolism (if the word even applies) allegorical rather than symbolist.

However, the anthropomorphizing and animation of the countryside and the night sky—indeed, of the entire physical and temporal universe—harks back to the radical personifications of such symbolist poets as Verhaeren and Jean Moréas. In certain of Verhaeren's poems one discovers an almost hallucinatory form of personification.[5] In Wilder's dramatic writings, his experiments with personification can be traced back at least to one of the "three-minute" plays, *Childe Roland to the Dark Tower Came* (*ATW* 75–79). In that play, when the mortally wounded knight, Roland, stumbles up to the Dark Tower seeking admittance and blows his horn, the landscape (a marsh) "collects itself to listen" (75). When he demands that the door to the Tower (which symbolizes death) be opened to him, the landscape "laughs, then falls suddenly silent" (75). Following his next line, it becomes "animated and fully interested in the stranger" (75), and near the end of the play, when Roland shouts for his companions, "The marsh is a little put out by all this strong feeling. It lies quiet" (79).

This use of the pathetic fallacy in lieu of full personification is actually closer to the practices of the symbolist poets than is the type of device employed in *Pullman Car Hiawatha*. However, the playwright's choices in the later play were undoubtedly dictated, in part at least, by the requirements of the stage. In any case, the device in *Pullman Car* is not a purely gratuitous "gimmick" but instead a powerful, effective means of dramatizing Wilder's familiar preoccupation—which he shares with Maeterlinck and other symbolists: the preoccupation with the unseen, unappreciated wonder of the world. Although the remarks of most of the personifications simply lead one to a keener awareness of previously or commonly unnoticed phenomena rather than offering a glimpse of any realm of transcendent Idea behind them, the recitations of the Hours and the murmurings of the Planets begin to hint at the existence of such a realm. In addition, the concentric circles or spheres within which the Pullman car and its occupants move and have their being ultimately do lead to the spiritual sphere, or what the Stage Manager calls "the theological position of Pullman Car Hiawatha" (64).

Given the relative scarcity of polyvalent symbols in Wilder's plays, it is not surprising that there are few symbolist "correspondences" to be found there, either. Nevertheless, several of the plays–particularly *The Skin of Our Teeth* and *Pullman Car Hiawatha*–explore nonrational links between phenomena and ideas or between separate phenomena.

In *Pullman Car*, the correspondences are explicitly drawn but nonetheless enigmatic. To begin with, just before the entrance of the Hours, the Stage Manager characterizes the minutes as "gossips, the hours [as] philosophers, and the years [as] theologians" (62). The passage of time is thus associated with a general increase in wisdom or breadth of vision, but the scene that follows, which involves an association of specific hours of the night with specific thinkers, is also based on, and meant to imply, a nonrational correspondence between the realm of temporal phenomena and that of immortal ideas.

In *Skin*, this same device of the philosopher/hours, which appears reincarnated in the last act with the same hours being given different quotations to speak, is integrated into a larger pattern of legendary and cultural-historical correspondences. The later play, in fact, is wholly constructed out of a seemingly endless web of such correspondences, as *Pullman Car* is not. The universality—the archetypal dimension of the Antrobuses—is established chiefly through the concatenation of these same cultural and mythological parallels. Each of the four central characters is given a variety of more specific identities from the Bible or American popular culture; Sabina, moreover, regularly alternates between her various "roles" (maid, beauty contestant, daughter of the regiment) and her "identity" as "Miss Somerset," the actress supposedly playing the role; and even Moses and Homer and the Muses appear as New York City derelicts or refugees. There is perhaps nothing especially obscure or mysterious about these correspondences, particularly in this post-Frazerian, post-Jungian age, and they may not qualify as strictly symbolist or Baudelairean ones because the basis of the analogy is, in most instances, easily and immediately perceptible. Nonetheless, because the characters are archetypal in origin, the correspondences are founded on alogical, prerational perceptions, and the further, more specific correspondences to which they point can be apprehended most easily by means of intuition or close observation rather than deduction. To this extent, then, they are in harmony with symbolist theory.

In order to establish and reveal such correspondences in their work, and thus indicate the wealth of meanings contained in every one of their symbols, the symbolist poets and dramatists employed a technique that came to be perhaps the most important hallmark of the symbolist style, the suggestion or gradual evocation of their meaning, both connotative and denotative, rather than a bald or direct statement. For example, the "Intruder" in Maeterlinck's well-known play is never explicitly identified as Death—and never actually appears on stage—but his identity and presence are distinctly indicated through the frightened reaction of the swans in the park adjoining the house, the suddenly heard sound of a scythe being sharpened outside the window, and the Grandfather's terrified questions to the others about the unknown being whom he senses sitting among them.

Wilder is generally straightforward, eschewing the vague and nebulous in favor of the direct and unambiguous. There are, in his plays, some notable exceptions to this tendency, however. Again, some of the most striking may be found in the "three-minute" plays, especially *Nascuntur Poetae*. Although much of the latter play's symbolism is no more than "static metaphor" or allegory, the meanings of the symbols themselves are often only indirectly or gradually revealed. For instance, the creative "madness" symbolized by the pendant in the form of a tongue of flame is never explicitly named. The Woman in Deep Red calls it merely "a madness that in a better country has a better name" (21). In reply the Boy pointedly remarks, "These are mysteries. Give them no names" (22). To name an object was, for Mallarmé, "to banish the major part of the enjoyment derived from a poem, since this enjoyment consists in a process of gradual revelation" (qtd. in trans. in Chadwick 2).

The meanings of the other pendants, too, are for the most part suggested rather than stated. The fame or satisfaction symbolized by the laurel leaf is implied in the Woman in Deep Red's reference to "pride and the shining of the eyes" (22) and also in the ordinary symbolic associations of laurel. The crystal pendant symbolizes the gift/curse of heightened perception, but again, the meaning of the symbol is not stated directly but merely suggested in the Woman's discussion of its contradictory or paradoxical qualities—it is "wonderful and terrible" (22)—and its attendant effects.

In the later plays, too, this sort of oblique revelation of meaning may sometimes be encountered, although it seems to be less of a mannerism there than in symbolist writing because the playwright usually provides realistic motivations for its use by the characters. In *Our Town*, for instance, Simon Stimson's "troubles" are never named, perhaps because the other characters already "know the facts about everybody" (8) in the town, especially the alcoholic church organist. Similarly, when before the wedding in Act II, Mrs. Webb expresses her regret that she has never discussed sex with Emily, her Victorian habits of speech prevent her from naming openly—or in euphemistic terms, for that matter—the topic she has failed to broach with her daughter, even though she mentions the omission in a relatively "intimate" aside.

In the less naturalistic third act, the technique is even more liberally used, although each instance of its use may still be justified on realistic, psychological grounds. First, the Stage Manager does not explicitly call the site of the action a cemetery until four paragraphs after he has begun speaking about it. He mentions its beauty and compares it implicitly with more familiar and pretentious final resting places, hinting that one would be just as happy (or happier) to be buried on a windswept New England hillside as in Woodlawn or Brooklyn. Nor does he ever crudely or bluntly state the title of the third act, contenting himself with telling the audience in Act II, "I reckon you can guess what that's [the upcoming act's] about" (47).

Of course, death, like sex, is a subject customarily swathed in euphemism, but it is not the only subject to which the Stage Manager is content merely to allude in his monologue. When faced with the task of explaining how the audience is to regard the dead that they see on stage and how the dead themselves perceive things, he begins by saying that "We all know that *something* is eternal" (81). Again, perhaps out of a spirit of respect for religious diversity, he never explicitly *names* that thing. The speech would almost certainly collapse into banality if he did, but it is nonetheless significant that, in an effort to convey a sense of the immaterial (itself a symbolist aim), the playwright has the Stage Manager fall naturally into nebulous, generalized diction and oblique definition. He undertakes the task of communicating spiritual truth by progressively eliminating incorrect conceptions of it. He observes that the eternal "something" "ain't houses and it ain't names, and it ain't earth, and it ain't even the stars" (81).

Significantly, according to Neoplatonist thinking, one way of beginning to arrive at an understanding of the nature of ultimate Truth or Reality is precisely this *via negativa*, this elimination of qualities or elements clearly *not* attributable to that Reality (Jones 299–300), an approach that, in its indirectness, is related to those employed by Plotinus's symbolist descendants. Wilder may simply wish to avoid belaboring the obvious in this passage, but whatever the reason, the fact remains that apparently, in this matter he shares Mallarmé's distaste for "naming an object" and employs an indisputably Neoplatonist technique for suggesting it instead.

However, the most extended use of the technique of gradual revelation in the play, in which it is made to serve exceedingly pragmatic ends, occurs in the scene following the Stage Manager's opening monologue in the final act. Throughout this scene between Sam Craig and Joe Stoddard, the playwright withholds the identity of the person whose funeral is to be held on this rainy summer day in 1913. One first learns from Sam Craig that it is his cousin who is to be buried, but the cousin's gender is left unspecified. The deceased is said to be "a young person" (83), but Sam's identification of Mrs. Gibbs as his "Aunt Julia" (83) leads one to conclude that it is George or perhaps Rebecca who has died. One finally hears that it is to be a young woman's funeral when Sam asks, "Joe, what did she die of?" (85). Then, at last, her identity is revealed when Mrs. Gibbs explicitly tells Mrs. Soames that it is Emily. This withholding of information is, of course, a standard playwrighting technique for making exposition dramatic, but combined with the other instances of allusion and oblique reference enumerated here, it intimates a deeper mystery, too: the mystery of human life and death and the profound mystery separating the world of the living from that of the dead.

In addition to these features linking Wilder's drama with the symbolist aesthetic in general, several of the plays employ dramaturgical devices and even overall methods or approaches that are perfectly in accord with the symbolists' theatre theories and practices. One fundamental principle in those theories is that since the theatre is, in its essence, a synthesis of diverse constituent arts, all its expressive resources ought ideally to be exploited and fused in performance into an integrated, cohesive artistic unity. This fusion or synthesis is possible, according to symbolist theory, because of—and indeed, it makes manifest the existence of—aesthetic or sensory correspondences comparable to the other kind. As Baudelaire writes in his poem "Correspondances," "Perfumes, colors, and sounds answer to one another" (l. 8, author's translation).

Wilder's plays for the most part do not qualify as quasisymbolist aesthetic syntheses, requiring in performance the continuous and simultaneous fusion of all the subsidiary arts of the theatre, but some of them incorporate a number of those arts at certain points and produce, ultimately, a unified, comprehensive artistic effect. In *The Skin of Our Teeth*, for instance, the playwright at different times introduces slide projections, "strange, veering lights . . . whirling about the stage" (205), a rudimentary sort of dance (the serpentine hop performed by the doomed conveners at the end of Act II), special scenic effects (the leaning and disappearing walls of the Act I set), pantomime (the letter that Mrs. Antrobus hurls into the sea in Act II and the small animal that leaps onto her husband's shoulder at the end of the same act), and song (the popular tunes quietly sung by the refugees at the end of Act I). However, not only are these diverse expressive media for the most part used more conventionally and realistically (or, at any rate, rationalistically) than the symbolists would have preferred, they are rarely combined simultaneously to produce a unified, multifaceted, "total art-work."

On the other hand, although the play as a whole seems very distant stylistically from symbolist dramatic norms, in its conception it is entirely consonant with the ideals and theoretical injunctions of certain influential symbolist critics. First, Mallarmé wished the symbolist drama to relate, not the stories of individual men and women or particular groups of them, but rather, "*la Passion de l'Homme*" (Block 85), the universal story of the human race and its sufferings. A later critic, Albert Mockel, referred to the same ideal as "*l'histoire éternelle de l'Homme*"[6] (qtd. in Block 113). Similarly, Yeats, a second-generation symbolist, wished the actors in his plays to "greaten till they become all humanity" (qtd. in Styan, *Symbolism* 64). Wilder's play might be said to have taken Mockel's statement literally as its starting point. Mallarmé, moreover, admired the vitality of popular melodrama and vaudeville, so *Skin* is not so far from symbolist tastes and biases as it at first seems. In fact, critic Donald Haberman asserts that the most provocative and earthy symbolist drama, Jarry's *Ubu Roi*—and particularly the dramatist's production ideas for the play—directly influenced the development of Wilder's theatrical vision (*Plays* 65–68; Haberman, *Our Town* 20–22). Haberman argues that it was the use of a bare stage in *Our Town*, *The Happy Journey*, and *Pullman Car Hiawatha* and, perhaps, the cartoonlike nature of the main characters in *Skin* that Wilder derived from *Ubu*, but a stronger connection—especially with *Skin*—may be seen in the use of anachronism and scenic incongruity in the famous setting for Jarry's symbolist farce. In his preperformance speech before the curtain to the opening-night audience, Jarry commented, "Just as one good way of setting a play in Eternity is to have revolvers shot off in the year 1000, you will see doors open on fields of snow under blue skies, . . . and palm trees growing at the foot of a bed" (qtd. in Shattuck 206). The Englishman Arthur Symons, an *Ubu* first-nighter, described the scenery as "painted to represent, by a child's convention, indoors and out of doors, and even the torrid, temperate, and arctic zones at once (Symons 373, qtd. in Shattuck 207). Finally, an even closer parallel—in fact, a near-exact precursor of *Skin* in symbolist (or postsymbolist) writing—is critic and poet Édouard Dujardin's "dramatic poem," *Le retour éternel*, in which the central character relives certain key events in the recurring cycle of human history.

In any event, perhaps the most comprehensive instance of artistic synthesis among Wilder's plays is *Pullman Car Hiawatha*. Not only does the playwright here make free use of many different aesthetic "languages," he incorporates into the play fragments of actual works by other authors and artists as well. The only major constituent art of the theatre that is not well represented is dance, although painting and scenic architecture also play a limited role in the work's total effect. It is true that the Hours' slow procession across the stage constitutes a rudimentary dance-like spectacle or the preliminary stages of a "Dance of the Hours"—the suggestion being reinforced by the stage direction at the end of their interlude calling for them to "unwind and return to their dressing rooms" (63)—and the episodes involving the planets virtually cry out for some sort of rotational movement, however minimal, to accompany the heavenly bodies' chorus of hums and beeps. Moreover, Wilder's concern for the visual aspect of the piece causes him to stipulate that the Hours be played by "beautiful girls dressed like Elihu Vedder's Pleiades" (62), thus incorporating into this work, in a "quotation" from another artist's creation, the softly modeled female figure that was a feature of much expressly symbolist painting.

However, it is music that is the most fully utilized of the play's constituent aesthetic "languages." Again, there are quotations—certainly one and possibly two—from specific works. The first is a fragment of a temperance hymn sung by the woman representing Parkersburg, Ohio, and the second, a few lines of Kipling's "The Road to Mandalay"—mistakenly attributed to "Frank W. Service" (60)—which may be sung or may simply be recited by the tramp who has been traveling underneath the Pullman car and asserts his right to appear in the play. More important than these fragmentary snatches of song, however, are three passages in which the personifications of the towns and fields that the car has passed and of the appropriate planets and hours of the night, as well as the human characters connected with the journey, all murmur their individual mottoes or nonverbal sounds, while the Stage Manager adjusts the dynamics and tempo of their murmurings, conducting them "as the director of an orchestra would" (64). The third of these "orchestral" or "choral" sections is, in fact, the climax of the entire piece, Harriet's postmortal epiphany.

Heavily influenced by Wagner in their conception of the theatre as a "composite art work," the symbolists sought to achieve a verbal "musicality" in their writings, both dramatic and lyrical. In performance the same endeavor led to the monotonous chanting or intoning of lines in the early productions of the symbolist Théâtre de l'Oeuvre. However, the movement's adherents disagreed with Wagner in their insistence that poetry—and not music, as he believed—should be the dominant art form in the *Gesamtkunstwerk*. Mallarmé and his followers felt that poetry was sufficient unto itself—that it was, in fact, as much "music" as was music itself.[7] In Wilder's play, the dead Harriet's vision of the "hidden wonder of the universe" is in the *form* of music, the music of the spheres, but in keeping with Mallarmé's preferences, and in opposition to Wagner's, it is a music made up chiefly of words, even though most remain inaudible or incomprehensible in the general murmuring. Since Wilder was a writer and not a composer, perhaps his bias in this matter was a foregone conclusion, but in any case, it is a bias shared by the symbolists.

One final component of the symbolist "total artwork"—pantomime—is not as liberally employed in *Pullman Car* as it is in *Our Town*, *The Happy Journey*, and *The Long Christmas Dinner*, yet the nonrealistic, typically Wilderian staging method of the former play still requires that it be used to an extent. To begin with, since the Pullman car itself is represented by a simple arrangement of chairs suggesting the berths and compartments, the actors must mime opening and closing doors when the script calls for them to perform these actions. At other times they must press invisible call bells to summon the porter or handle imaginary items that fall from the invisible upper berths. Even though pantomime was never incorporated with any frequency into actual symbolist productions, it exerted a strong fascination over such figures as Mallarmé and Lugné-Poë, a hardly surprising circumstance considering these artists' Neoplatonist orientation.

In fact, despite *Pullman Car*'s position as the most complete theatrical synthesis among Wilder's dramas, and despite the obvious affinities between its "musical" passages and symbolist theories, it is *Our Town* and some of the dramatist's other "minimalist" plays, with their deemphasis of concrete phenomena on stage, that are the most recognizably symbolist in style of all the author's dramatic works. The conventional symbolist theatrical style was distinguished not so much by the dramatist's or director's exploitation of all the theatre's expressive resources as by what Haskell Block terms "detheatricalization" (88, 92), the reduction or elimination of such basic elements of theatre and drama as scenery, anecdote, and even dialogue. According to his biographer, Gilbert Harrison, Wilder first conceived of the idea of writing plays requiring a scenery-free stage after he read an account of the staging of André Obey's plays by Michel Saint-Denis at the Théâtre du Vieux Colombier (152); his acquaintance with the minimalist style for which that theatre was famous dates from an even earlier period, since, as several unpublished letters and diary entries attest, he saw numerous productions at the Vieux Colombier in Paris and others by the theatre's "Compagnie des Quinze" (directed by its founder, Jacques Copeau) in New York in 1917–1918 or 1918–1919.[8] He even wrote jocularly in a diary entry for 9 February 1918, "all my plays are written for the Vieux Colombier" (diary 1918–1928, ms., Wilder papers, YCAL). However, Copeau's famous *tréteau nu* itself has its roots in the symbolist aesthetic. The French director was strongly influenced by the ideas of both Adolphe Appia and Edward Craig (Rudlin 2, 26, 37–39, 55–59; Styan, *Symbolism* 91), and his reverence for the dramatic text is more than a little reminiscent of the attitude of Mallarmé and his disciples. In addition, though, Mallarmé was himself fascinated by the expressive potential of the utterly bare stage (Styan, *Symbolism* 92; Robichez 44), and Lugné-Poë agreed with him that the best setting for a symbolist play was one that boasted "Pas de décor, ou peu" (Block 106). In 1891, critic Pierre Quillard wrote:

> The word creates the decor along with the rest. . . . The decor ought to be a simple ornamental fiction that completes the illusion by analogies of colors and lines with the drama. Most of the time a backdrop and some movable draperies will be sufficient. (qtd. in Robichez 188, author's translation)

The trellises in *Our Town* and the portals in *The Long Christmas Dinner* are neither more nor less than "simple ornamental fictions," although the portals do not so much "complete the illusion by analogies" as destroy the theatrical illusion to call attention to deeper truths. Yeats, finally, wrote after a performance in Lady Cunard's London drawing room of his play *At the Hawk's Well*,

> My blunder has been that I did not discover in my youth that my theatre must be the ancient theatre that can be made by unrolling a carpet or marking out a place with a stick. . . . It has been a great gain to get rid of scenery, to substitute for a crude landscape painted upon canvas three performers who, sitting before the wall or a patterned screen, describe landscape or event. (qtd. in Styan, *Symbolism* 68–69)

Wilder's previously quoted comment, "When the theatre pretends to give the real thing in canvas and wood and metal it loses something of the realer thing which is its true business," might have been appended to this paragraph by Yeats.

The deemphasis of material reality on the stage has its foundation, of course, in Neoplatonist principles, since the absence or reduction of visible phenomena on stage leaves the spectator nothing to contemplate but the Ideas of those and all phenomena. Moreover, Mallarmé, in a famous phrase, spoke of the Idea in terms of absence. He noted that his task as a poet, if he is describing a flower, is to evoke *"l'absente de tous bouquet,"* the "absent one from all bouquets," the universal flower corresponding to none on earth (Mallarmé 213, qtd. in Chadwick 3–4). The phrase is, on one level, a superbly apt description of Mrs. Gibbs's heliotrope.

Both Wilder and the symbolists, furthermore, conceived of the material impoverishment of the stage as serving another, more practical purpose besides the Platonic one. That purpose was to impel the spectator toward a more active involvement in the performance. Mallarmé addressed his projected dramatic poem *Igitur* "to the Intelligence of the reader which stages things itself" (Mallarmé, *Selected* 91). Earlier, Baudelaire had gone further, observing that in all the arts—music, painting, and imaginative writing—"there is always a lacuna completed by the auditor's imagination" (Baudelaire, "Richard Wagner," 1210–11, author's translation). Wilder, too, actively sought by means of his minimalist techniques to involve the spectator's imagination actively in the cocreation of the dramatic reality. In the preface to *Our Town* he justifies his decision to require that the play be staged without scenery, "The spectator through lending his imagination to the action restages it inside his own head" (*AC* 101). Moreover, in a journal entry from 1948 concerning his projected play, *The Emporium*, he notes, "Foremost [among the advantages of a bare stage for this play] is the already proven suggestibility of the imagined scene" (*Journals* 43). The bare stage, then, for both Wilder and the symbolists, inherently promotes suggestion rather than direct statement in the visual sphere, thus paralleling the symbolist poets' efforts in the same direction in the verbal sphere.

Along with a reduction of decor and other physical phenomena on stage, the symbolists advocated and practiced in their plays a reduction or elimination of dramatic incident or intrigue, and even, at moments, of dialogue.

The element of "anecdote" in Wilder's plays, and especially *Our Town*, *The Happy Journey*, *Infancy*, and *Pullman Car Hiawatha*, is negligible, and although in one essay the playwright argues against Maeterlinck and asserts that drama as a representation before an audience necessarily involves forward movement (*AC* 122), many of his own plays exhibit only cyclical movement at best. Moreover, the patiently expectant attitude of the dead in Act III of *Our Town* resembles the somewhat tenser, more fearful expectancy of the waiting characters in Maeterlinck's *The Intruder* and *The Blind*.

The temporary abandonment of dialogue in suspenseful, enigmatic silences, which help to underscore the atmosphere of anticipation, adds a further Maeterlinckian tinge to the same act of Wilder's play. Two of the most noteworthy of these silences occur after Emily first settles down in her chair/grave and after she returns from her attempt to relive her twelfth birthday, but the Stage Manager's opening monologue also contains numerous vacant pauses. Mysterious, unfathomable silences similar to those in *The Intruder*, *The Blind*, *Interior*, and *Pelléas and Mélisande* are even more abundant in the first act of the play as well. After remarking that the morning star "always gets wonderful bright the minute before it has to go" (6), the Stage Manager "stares at it for a moment, then goes upstage" (6). At the end of his description of the town's layout, he again pauses for a moment before commenting, "Nice town, y'know what I mean?" (7). When, later that night, the ladies return from choir practice and notice the moonlight falling all about them, they become "silent a moment, gazing up at the moon" (38). When Dr. and Mrs. Gibbs stroll through their garden a few minutes later, they, too, fall silent for a short time as they smell the heliotrope in the moonlight. In fact, the playwright's beloved and admired mentor, Charles Wager, was most deeply moved by the silences when he read the play (letter from Wager to Wilder, qtd. in Harrison 180), and Wilder himself, as early as 1922, had noted in his journal, with reference to a play he was working on at the time, "I believe my best efforts will lie in the poignant effects gained by silent suffered action" (entry for 28 Sept. 1922, ms., Wilder papers, YCAL).[9]

Maeterlinck described the inexplicable, cosmic silence that he regarded as "the source of the undercurrents of our life" (11–12), an enveloping presence in everyday existence, in the following terms (replete with personification): "Let one of us but knock, with trembling fingers, at the door of the abyss, it is always by the same attentive silence that this door will be opened" (11–12).

Silences are, of course, as typical of Chekhov's style as they are of Maeterlinck's, and it may therefore be as valid to characterize Wilder's play as "Chekhovian" in this respect as it is to term it "Maeterlinckian." The somewhat random quality of the action in Act I of *Our Town* strengthens even further the resemblance to Chekhov, whom Wilder admired and whose life and work he investigated in the 1910s and '20s. However,

Chekhov, for all his lampooning of the symbolist style in Konstantin's play in *The Seagull*, was certainly not immune himself to symbolist influence. One has only to think of his heavy reliance on such central and richly suggestive symbols as the seagull itself and the cherry orchard in his final play, to say nothing of the oft-noted "static" quality of his drama. Thus, describing Wilder's play as both "Chekhovian" and "Maeterlinckian" may not, in the final analysis, entail any fundamental inconsistency.

In symbolist aesthetics, in any event, mysterious silences were not only the temporal counterpart of the bare stage, a manifestation of the "void which contains the infinite" (a favorite conception of Mallarmé's), they were also a component in the verbal "musicality" aspired to by symbolist playwrights (and poets). The most noteworthy example of such musicality in Wilder's plays is the series of "orchestral" passages in *Pullman Car Hiawatha*. However, other features of Wilder's style (apart from the silences) move the dialogue in his other plays in the direction of spoken "music" as well. The most obvious of these features is verbal repetition, the same device one meets in the early plays of Maeterlinck, especially *Princess Maleine*, *The Blind*, and *The Intruder*.

The use of repetitive language already characterizes Wilder's "three-minute" plays, the earliest of the playwright's dramatic efforts. Furthermore, as Rex Burbank points out in his study of Wilder, repeated phrases and cadences remain characteristic of the dialogue in the later plays as well (29). In the major works, the repetitions strengthen the conversational colloquialism of the characters' speech, whereas in the earlier playlets, they unfortunately give the lines a stilted, self-consciously "poetic" quality, although for that very reason the device is more apparent and its musicality more obvious in the playlets. The following excerpts should suffice to show the extent to which Wilder relies on repetition in the language of the playlets:

THE WOMAN IN THE CHLAMYS: Be not so eager for life. Too soon you will be shaken by breath; too soon and too long you will be tossed in the tumult of the senses. (*Nascuntur Poetae*, *ATW* 20)

THE BOY: Take back the chain. Take back your gifts. Take back life. For at its end what can there be that is worth such pain?

THE WOMAN IN DEEP RED (Slowly drawing back into the shadow of the wood): Farewell, child of the muses, playfellow in the bird-haunted groves. The life of man awaits you, . . . You are to give it a voice. Among the bewildered and stammering thousands you are to give it a voice and to mark its meaning. Farewell, child of the muses, playfellow in the bird-haunted. . . . (*Nascuntur Poetae*, *ATW* 22–23)

Come, long-expected love. Come, long-expected love. Let the sacred finger and the sacred breath stir up the pool. Here on the lowest step I wait with festering limbs, with my heart in pain. Free me, long-expected love, from this old burden. Since I cannot stay, since I must return into the city, come now, renewal, come, release. (*The Angel That Troubled the Waters, ATW 145–46)*

The greatest number of repeated phrases to be found in any of Wilder's plays, though, is contained in *The Long Christmas Dinner*, which depicts ninety successive Christmas dinners in the Bayard household, condensed and spliced together so as to appear to be a single meal. The play, in keeping with its theme that "it'll all be the same in a hundred years" (which is, itself, stated twice by different characters) (6, 24), is virtually built on redundancy. Each new generation of Bayards unconsciously (or consciously) reiterates the same observations and expresses the same sentiments as were expressed by the preceding ones. Each year at dinner on December 25, for example, someone comments, "Every least twig is wrapped around with ice," adding with unconscious irony, "You almost never see that" (3, 13). Similarly repeated thoughts are met with at every turn in the piece.

Repetition is also built into the structure of *Our Town*. Many phrases—and even whole conversations—are repeated word-for-word during the play. Some of these are the result of the dramatist's focus on the cyclical nature of town life. Others stem from his decision to show simultaneously two nearly identical households on stage. Thus, in Act II Howie Newsome has to deliver to both Mrs. Gibbs and Mrs. Webb his wife's message that the two of them hope George and Emily will "be very happy" and that they "Know they *will*" (50). Other characters repeat news or queries to each new person they meet, just to make conversation. For instance, Doc Gibbs, at the start of Act I, holds nearly identical conversations dealing with the weather and the morning's events with the paperboy and the milkman, and Constable Warren does the same with the milkman and Editor Webb in Act III. Even strong, simple rhythmic patterns are repeated in the dialogue, a particularly striking and memorable instance being the passage wherein Editor Webb informs the audience:

Politically, we're eighty-six per cent Republicans; six per cent Democrats; four per cent Socialists; rest, indifferent.

Religiously, we're eighty-five per cent Protestants; twelve per cent Catholics; rest, indifferent. (23)

Such strongly rhythmic passages render the play's dialogue "poetic," if not exactly "musical," but of course Mallarmé would not have recognized such a distinction as valid.

All these "symbolist" features of Wilder's plays do not, again, necessarily make him a certifiable "symbolist playwright." His dramatic work exhibits too encyclopedic or kaleidoscopic a style to allow any one label to be unhesitatingly applied to any one of his plays. However, even this aspect of his theatre has precedents in symbolist theory, if not in symbolist practice. Yeats consciously sought to achieve a playwrighting style "that remembers many masters, that it may escape contemporary suggestion" (qtd. in Styan, *Symbolism* 64). Wilder's adoption and refinement of such a style allowed him to do one thing of which Mallarmé could only dream—namely, create a drama that is both popular and, to a high degree at least, symbolist.

NOTES

1. The resemblance to Maeterlinck is noted in Corrigan (172). Proust's influence on Wilder was first identified in Wilson; most subsequent commentators refer to it also, especially Burbank (35, 41), and Goldstone in *Thornton Wilder: An Intimate Portrait* (7, 51, 85–86). Burbank also mentions Maeterlinck briefly as a kindred (antinaturalistic) spirit to Wilder but goes into no further details.

2. A similar thought is recorded in a 1940 entry in Wilder's journal, where he writes of his "favorite principle that the characters on the stage tend to figure as generalizations, that the stage burns and longs to express a timeless individualized Symbol. The accumulation of fictions—fiction as time, as place, as character—is forever tending to reveal its true truth: man, woman, time, place" (*Journals*, 24).

3. The character of the Old Man in the dramatist's short play *Interior* echoes these sentiments also in the course of his discussion with the Stranger.

4. A letter from the dramatist's sister Isabel to "Miss Salvo" (18 July 1973, ms., Wilder papers, YCAL) suggests that the three-minute playlets could conceivably be characterized as symbolist works.

5. See, for example, "The Mill" and "The Factories"; see also Henri de Regnier's "Town of France," and "A Young Girl Speaks," by Jean Moréas. The symbolist fondness for personification is noted in Cornell (71).

6. Balakian (9–11) stresses the cosmopolitan, international character of the movement—its "non-temporal, non-sectarian, non-geographic, and non-national" focus—even while it was centered in France.

7. According to a possibly apocryphal story, Mallarmé's dismayed response on learning that Claude Debussy had composed a "Prélude" to "L'après-midi d'un Faune" was, "I believed I had put it into music myself."

8. For example, diary entries for 7, 9, and 10 June, 1921, and 9 Feb. 1918, ms., Wilder papers, YCAL.

9. In the same entry, however, Wilder identifies dramatic silences with an earlier, nonsymbolist theatrical style, noting that "'Les silences d'Aeschyle' were famous before Bernard [the author of a 1918 article in *Le Mercure de France* that Jules Romains had given him to read and that had prompted his meditations on the subject]."

Chapter 3

"The Smallest Events . . . the Largest Dimensions": Naturalistic Aspects of Wilder's Theatre

In Wilder's "characteristic style" which "weaves back and forth between the general and the particular" (*Journals* 27), the symbolist or quasisymbolist elements strengthen the plays' inclination toward the former pole. His focus on the latter, on the other hand, is one major factor—although by no means the only one—linking his theatre with that of another important nineteenth-century aesthetic movement, naturalism. Philosophically, his agreement with the views of Zola and his followers is limited. Dramaturgically, he was forever in revolt against the cornerstone of naturalistic theatre aesthetics, the "photographic" reproduction on stage of ordinary, everyday "reality." Nevertheless, his dramatic vision exhibits, in addition to his appreciation of particular—even microscopic—detail, such naturalistic features as a pretense of objectivity in his attitude toward his characters; a fascination with extended spatial and temporal scope; a relatively faithful, accurate manner of rendering characters' speech and behavior; and a disdain of "well-made" intrigue. In thematic concerns and philosophical orientation, too, his works provide incontrovertible evidence of his genuine—if partial—acceptance of the naturalistic position. The naturalistic elements in the plays help to tone down or counterbalance the symbolist dimensions, making them more accessible to the greater number. However, that is not their sole raison d'être.

Of course, all serious thought and art in the post-Darwinian age has been forced to take account, in one way or another, of the cosmological and religious implications inherent in *The Origin of Species.* The naturalistic writers' reaction was at first to embrace science as offering the potential for improving humanity's lot through a kind of controlled evolution—both biological and social. Ultimately, however, the scientific, mechanistic view of human existence came to be seen as necessarily tragic, with little hope discernible for the future betterment of humankind. The human and natural environments, defined in terms of forces, could not be predicted or controlled to any meaningful extent, and hence there was no guarantee that either social or biological evolution could be made to serve the best interests of the human race.

The solution of the New Humanist critics Paul Elmer More and Irving Babbitt, who influenced Wilder both directly and indirectly in his early years, was a return to traditional morality, subjugation of humanity's "lower" desires, and ultimately, the revival of Christianity. In essence, they called for a resurrection of the values of the past, as embodied in the great works of art and literature of former ages. Such a reactionary position was ultimately as unsatisfactory as the rigidly pessimistic position of the later naturalists.

Rather than simply reacting reflexively against the challenge of naturalism, as More and Babbitt did, Wilder attempted to meet the force of its arguments with cogent, practical rebuttals and alternatives. As Rex Burbank remarks in his study of Wilder, "he . . . accepted responsibility for affirming traditional moral and religious values by confronting rather than evading the most compelling claims of philosophical naturalism against them" (32). That confrontation eventually led the playwright (and the novelist) beyond a simple affirmation of traditional values to an enthusiastic adoption of the existentialist philosophy of Kierkegaard and others. However, even in such early works as *The Bridge of San Luis Rey* and *The Cabala*, Wilder evinces a willingness to question the comforting assurances of traditional Christian dogma and to recognize the ineluctability of the natural drives that determine much human behavior.

Wilder's attempt to confront and transcend naturalistic dogma was perhaps not wholly conscious on his part, but there can be little doubt of his familiarity with the general thrust of naturalistic philosophy and aesthetics. He makes no reference to Zola in any of his published writings—with the exception of a brief comment in a 1951 entry in his journal (*Journals* 88–89)—nor to Joseph Conrad,[1] Stephen Crane, Jack London, or Frank Norris. He never speaks of "literary naturalism" per se. However, he was well acquainted with a number of important naturalistic novels, and during the years when his dramatic vision was gestating, he saw such naturalistic stage works as Maxim Gorki's *The Lower Depths* (translated as "*Night Lodging*"), O'Neill's *Beyond the Horizon*, and Tolstoy's *The Power of Darkness* (List of plays seen, 1910s and 1920s, ms., Wilder papers, YCAL; diary, 1918–1927, ms., Wilder papers, YCAL).

In fact, the playwright's first acquaintance with the naturalistic movement seems to have been made still earlier. When he and his siblings were attending high school in Berkeley, California, their mother often took them to the theatre in nearby Oakland. There, Wilder was first introduced not only to melodrama of the traveling stock company variety, which he was later to lampoon affectionately in *The Skin of Our Teeth* and *The Matchmaker*, but also apparently to at least one of the works of Thomas Hardy. His older brother, Amos, in 1980 recalled vividly a stage adaptation of *Tess of the D'Urbervilles* that he (and, the context implies, Thornton as well) had witnessed in Oakland as a teenager (A. N. Wilder 53). Wilder himself makes frequent reference to the Hardy novel in his literary and theatrical essays, indicating a persistent attraction to it, or memory of it, in later life.[2] Moreover, while still a youth, the future playwright also read *The Return of the Native* several times, as well as certain novels of Conrad (Harrison 30, 43). While on an excursion in England in 1928 with a group of his students from the Lawrenceville School (where he taught French), he even delivered an impromptu lecture on Hardy to his charges (113).

In addition, according to the critics Haberman (*Plays* 12) and Goldstone (*Portrait* 118), Wilder developed an adolescent enthusiasm for the bizarre, crudely written *Plays Natural and Supernatural* of Theodore Dreiser. Some of Dreiser's plays are anything but naturalistic in style; they are brief and often wildly fantastic, mingling spirits, spectres, and living characters, and, like Wilder's "three-minute" playlets (some of which show evidence of Dreiser's influence), they were never intended for performance—indeed, are mostly impossible to perform. The ideas contained in them, though, are largely naturalistic, despite being occasionally tinged by homespun spiritualism or theosophy. For example, Dreiser's play *The Blue Sphere*, in its depiction of a number of converging lines of action, might be termed an expressionistic variation, transposed into the dramatic mode, on the theme of Hardy's poem about the sinking of the *Titanic*, "The Convergence of the Twain."

However, the chief influence on Wilder seems to have been exerted by the non- or antinaturalistic externals of Dreiser's plays—their "liberated" form, incorporation of both human and nonhuman characters, freedom of movement in time and space, and, occasionally, cosmic vision. *The Blue Sphere* might have made the strongest impression on Wilder in these respects. The combination in Dreiser's play of a shadowy female spirit and an "exceptional" child may have furnished Wilder with some of the inspiration for *Nascuntur Poetae*, but the resemblance in other respects is slight. In *The Blue Sphere*, the child is deformed and mentally deficient—a monstrosity, in fact—and the female shadow, rather than preparing him for life, tempts him, by offering him a mysterious blue sphere with which to play, to his merciful death under the wheels of the Fast Mail, in the fatal convergence already mentioned.

The train is itself a "character" in the play, although it is not personified but merely given "lines" consisting of the sounds it makes in its approach toward the town. Since Wilder is known to have admired these plays of Dreiser's, the idea of combining personification with a railroad journey in *Pullman Car Hiawatha* may have come to him from this source.

Goldstone even goes so far as to suggest that *The Blue Sphere* exerted an influence on Wilder in the composition of *Our Town* (*Portrait* 118–19). The settings for both plays simultaneously depict interior and exterior locales in and around two adjacent houses in small towns, and both also later expand to incorporate other locations within their respective towns. At times Dreiser even portrays several lines of action occurring simultaneously in different locations (the front yard and the kitchen, the kitchen and the railroad tracks), as Wilder does in Acts I and III of *Our Town*.

However, one must take care not to stretch credibility beyond the breaking point by implying that much of Wilder's dramatic vision, naturalistic or nonnaturalistic, has its roots in *The Blue Sphere*. On the other hand, the play would necessarily have introduced him to at least one major concern of the naturalists, the problem of disadvantageous mutations or abnormalities and their relationship to an organism's success or failure in the battle for survival.

Wilder's acquaintance with the naturalistic style and method, as opposed to naturalistic themes and motifs, broadened during his adult years. His critical overview, "The Turn of the Year" (1925), includes appreciative mention of Sidney Howard's *They Knew What They Wanted* and Eugene O'Neill's *Desire Under the Elms* (143), two "regional" plays that were not only deeply informed by naturalistic thought but also composed in an unwaveringly naturalistic style. Moreover, in a letter to his mother he reported that as a result of the publication of this article, when he attended a rehearsal at Princeton of a play being directed by a friend, he was regarded by the student actors "as a sort of visiting Antoine" (16 Apr. 1925, copy in letter bk., ms., Wilder papers, YCAL). In the Preface to *Three Plays*, Wilder again speaks of his admiration for *Desire Under the Elms* (*AC* 104), and entries in his travel diary published under the title, "Playgoing Nights," show that he and his sister Isabel saw two of Gerhart Hauptmann's naturalistic plays, *The Beaver Skin Coat* and *The Weavers*, in Germany in 1928 (413–15).

Probably the clearest testimony of Wilder's familiarity with at least the theatre style and dramaturgical aesthetics of the naturalists, however, is simply his lifelong campaign against them. In addition, his writings contain positive evidence that he was thoroughly acquainted with the definitive qualities of the aesthetic against which his campaign was directed. For instance, a passage from the Preface of *Our Town* (cited in Chapter 2) challenges the absurdity of pretending to give an audience the "real thing in canvas and wood and metal" (*AC* 102). Thus, although he commonly makes the box set his primary target in his assault on realistic convention, he is really opposing a much more comprehensive, far-reaching set of theatrical conventions. The box set was not a feature unique to the naturalistic stage, being a mainstay of romantic and Scribean staging methods as well. Wilder was campaigning against scenic realism in general, the faithful reproduction on stage of what he, quoting William James, once referred to as "abject truth" (101), the reality of particular, everyday phenomena. This sort of realism, of course, constituted the heart and soul of conventional naturalistic staging.

Ironically, it was in a similar reaction against the stale, shopworn conventions of mid-nineteenth–century staging and playwrighting—the bombastic acting and exaggerated diction and gesture, the standardized settings, and the mechanical "well-made" plots—that the naturalists formulated their basic aesthetic program for the theatre. The "slice of life" was their answer to the hackneyed formulas of the *pièce bien faite*, and the detailed naturalistic settings and unstudied naturalistic acting style were meant to supplant their artificial, conventionalized counterparts in the "mainstream" theatre of the day.

Here, then, is one area of agreement between Wilder and the naturalists, although Wilder's feelings toward the well-made play and nineteenth-century staging methods were always ambivalent, and his fondness for intrigue, if not for anecdote, is apparent in *The Matchmaker*. It matters little that naturalism itself eventually came to be perceived (and not only by Wilder) as a set of stale conventions. Such a development is an inevitable stage in the life of any artistic movement.

It is not even the immediate *aims* of naturalistic dramaturgy to which Wilder objected so much as its *methods*. It is for failing to elicit his *belief* in their plays that he, in the Preface to *Three Plays*, upbraids the realistic playwrights of the early 1920s (and that period's producers of classic plays as well) (*AC* 104). Such belief is also, of course, one of the implicit and explicit goals of the naturalists.

Even though Wilder's theatre, then, like that of Brecht and Pirandello, calls attention to itself as theatre—and thus as artifice—his intention is not, like Brecht's, to force his audiences to regard the dramatic action with skepticism or detachment, nor does he wish, like Pirandello, to call into question the very idea of verifiable, hard-and-fast truth. Rather, his various reminders to the audience that they are watching a play are, in a sense, efforts to gain the spectators' trust, to assure them that there is no intent to deceive on the part of the performers or the dramatist, so that he can then legitimately solicit a more profound belief in the psychological and spiritual truths he is attempting to convey.

Of course, the truth he is most concerned with depicting is a generalized, transcendent one, as opposed to the literal, journalistic, particular truth of the naturalists. Whereas their "scientific" orientation made them strict empiricists and uncompromising materialists, his Neoplatonic bias made him seek truth *behind* or *beyond* phenomena. Nevertheless, Wilder also recognizes the validity of the naturalists' sort of truth, the particular or "abject." If he writes in the Preface to *Three Plays* that the theatre is primarily "the vehicle of the generalized [occasion]" (*AC* 108), in contrast to the novel, which is the vehicle of the "unique" one, he writes elsewhere in the same essay:

> The theatre is admirably fitted to tell both truths [the particular and the universal]. It has one foot planted firmly in the particular, since each actor before us (even when he wears a mask!) is indubitably a living, breathing "one"; yet it tends and strains to exhibit a general truth since its relation to a specific "realistic" truth is confused and undermined by the fact that it is an accumulation of untruths, pretenses and fiction. (107–8)

He also acknowledges that "Every action which has ever taken place—every thought, every emotion—has taken place only once, at one moment in time and place" (107).[3] Moreover, in his Preface to *Our Town*, which was originally published as a preopening commentary on the play in the *New York Times*, he writes, "I wished to record a village's life on the stage, with realism and with generality" (101). The naturalistic note evident here in the reference to "realism" is augmented by the playwright's choice of the word "record" to describe his aims, a choice that suggests a quasinaturalistic pretense of journalistic objectivity—an intention of presenting on the stage an unembellished, unedited "slice of life."

In keeping with his partial sympathy with the aims of the naturalists, Wilder occasionally introduces one or another of their favorite themes or motifs—usually in modified form or with changed emphasis—into his own writings, both plays and novels. In many instances, these themes are incorporated simply for the sake of argument, as part of his attempt to uphold traditional, humanistic values by, as Burbank puts it, "confronting rather than evading the most compelling claims of philosophical naturalism against them" (32). Indeed, Wilder on several occasions explicitly repudiated the doctrine that forms the cornerstone of that same philosophical naturalism: determinism. Three years after a blistering attack by Marxist critic Michael Gold, which was prompted by what Gold considered the elitist, escapist character of Wilder's early novels and playlets, Wilder was quoted as making the following oblique reply:

> These radical critics are, in my opinion, wrong in their claim that man is solely the product of the economic order under which he lives. . . . If my characters are not starved, if they have a little something for their stomachs, then they will be much the same in any environment. (*Honolulu Advertiser*, Nov. 5, 1933, qtd. in Simon 87)

In addition, in the *Paris Review* interview, he is quoted as saying in regard to his fiction-writing techniques:

> The problem of . . . imaginative narration . . . lies in the effort to employ the past tense in such a way that it does not rob those events of their character of having occurred in freedom. A great deal of writing and talking about the past is unacceptable. It freezes the historical in a determinism. (Goldstone, *Writers* 105)

All the same, Wilder does acknowledge the existence and power of a limited, benevolent form of determinism at work in human affairs, and Burbank even observes that there are deterministic elements of a more tragic sort in both *The Cabala*, Wilder's first novel, and *The Bridge of San Luis Rey* (44–45). In *Our Town*, though, nature's "pushing and contriving" (71), according to the Stage Manager, is responsible for George and Emily's wedding (as well as most others). This expression of faith in nature's benevolence is reinforced by a later comment in the same speech, in which he remarks that although "We all know nature's interested in quantity," he believes "she's interested in quality, too" (71), that belief being one reason why he is "in the ministry" (71).

Such a remark might be seen as a simplified restatement of the Shavian concept of "creative evolution" (or of Charles Darwin and Herbert Spencer's opinion that evolution leads to ever-improved species), and Wilder might have taken the notion from George Bernard Shaw, whom he met in 1928 (Simon 65). However, it is much more likely that it came to him originally through Goethe. In "Goethe and World Literature," one of the ideas he explores at greatest length is the German master's theory of the *ewig Wirkende*, the perpetually achieving force at work in the universe, which Wilder characterizes in his essay as "God-in-Nature," a force that "wishes us to develop into ever more excellent states" (*AC* 146) despite the fact that it may not treat us as we would wish it to. While we are waiting to connect ourselves with this force in such a manner as to derive maximum benefit from it, we need merely to work, for "We are nature—and productivity and fertility are the first law of nature" (147). Even though in *Our Town* the Stage Manager's progression from his optimistic view of nature and determinism to a belief in God is decidedly unnaturalistic, the passage as a whole is sufficient to demonstrate Wilder's recognition, however qualified, of the role played by deterministic forces in the biological and emotional life of the human species.

There is also a flicker of deterministic philosophy of a more pessimistic or cynical variety in Act III of Wilder's play. The dead Simon Stimson tells Emily bitterly: "That's what it was to be alive. To move about in a cloud of ignorance; to go up and down trampling on the feelings of those . . . about you. . . . To be always at the mercy of one self-centered passion, or another" (101). Mrs. Gibbs refutes Stimson's assessment immediately, but she only says that it "ain't the whole truth" (101). Stimson is obviously not voicing

Wilder's own beliefs here, nor is he stating the point of the play as a whole. However, the truth of his assertion that people are blind, self-centered, and ignorant has already been realized by Emily during her painful return to life.

Moreover, the monistic cosmology portraying human beings as wholly consubstantial with nature, which underlies the naturalists' deterministic conception of human life, can also be seen in the final passage from "Goethe and World Literature" quoted here, and even in the Stage Manager's characterization of nature as the "pushing and contriving" force attempting, through George and Emily, to "make a perfect human being" (71). Even more significantly, that same cosmology finds direct expression in at least one of Wilder's other plays, *The Skin of Our Teeth*. The "convention" of the second act is partly a playwright's device to get all the necessary animals assembled, without recourse to divine intervention, for a reenactment of Noah's flood. However, the overall unity of the human and natural realms is underscored in a comic manner by the announcer's repeated references to Mrs. Antrobus as a "gracious and charming mammal" (165) and by her husband's salutation, at the beginning of his speech to his Order: "Fellow-mammals, fellow vertebrates, fellow-humans" (163). Shortly afterwards, also, he admits, "a few months before my birth I hesitated between . . . uh . . . between pinfeathers and gill-breathing,—and so did many of us here—but for the last million years I have been viviparous, hairy, and diaphragmatic" (164). The effect is comic, and the comedy itself reveals Wilder's dualistic, platonist bias, since Antrobus must be more than a brute beast in order to comment as he does on his animal nature or take pride in it. Even more important, his remarks give the impression that his biological makeup was a matter of free choice, an impression that is incompatible with naturalistic—or scientific—thought. Nonetheless, the sense given by the entire act is of a deep bond of kinship uniting humans and animals.

This impression is strengthened by the presence in the first act of the prehistoric animals, the dinosaur and mammoth. They are pets in the Antrobus household, but they also partake of the joy of the humans when paterfamilias George returns. In addition, the fact that all life forms are subject to the same natural forces is symbolically conveyed at the end of the act. As the wall of ice draws nearer to Excelsior, New Jersey, the animals must pass outside to their deaths in order to make room for the human beings, who are destined to survive the Ice Age. Although not even remotely realistic (nor intended to be so) as a depiction of the actual process involved in the extinction of the dinosaurs and early mammals, the incident nonetheless constitutes a cogent, effective symbolic representation of evolution through competition between species for the limited amount of the physical resources—space, heat, and food—necessary for survival.

Again, however, a recognition that human beings are a part of nature does not immediately qualify one for inclusion in the ranks of the naturalists. Evolutionary theory was scarcely a subject of heated controversy, even in 1942—at least among aware, well-educated writers who were not religious fundamentalists or reactionaries. The New Humanists, too, acknowledged that people belonged at least in part to the natural order (Burbank 30). Wilder expressed surprise to the young Henry Luce, whom he first met when both were students at the China Inland Mission School in Chefoo, China, upon learning from Luce that Darwin's theories were still questioned in China among the children of English missionaries. Even at this time (1910), those theories, as Wilder told Luce, were accepted without objection in the United States, where young Thornton had previously attended school (Harrison 23).

At the same time, however, the scientific data supporting a monistic point of view in Act II of *The Skin of Our Teeth* is not included simply to amuse the audience or impress them with the playwright's erudition. Besides conveying a sense of the interrelatedness of all species, an interrelatedness that assumes even greater significance at the end of the act, when the deluge forces representatives of all species to band together in order to survive, Antrobus's allusion to his own prenatal history, during which he underwent all the traumas of evolution in his own person, helps to expand still further his already multidimensional character. Not only is he Adam, Noah, and man in general, he also bears within him the traces of earlier life forms. Darwin regarded the imitation of evolution by the human embryo as evidence of the validity of his theories. Wilder uses it as a basis for a partial answer to the problem of individual significance, since it indicates that every human being not only is a distillation of influences from a myriad of historical and prehistorical human epochs but also contains physical or behavioral vestiges of even earlier, prehuman ages.

A different and less explicitly (but no less firmly) monistic perspective can be seen in the harmony between certain characters in other plays by Wilder, especially *Our Town*, and their environment. These characters all seem to draw strength from that harmony, even though their oneness with their surroundings actually helps to prevent them from attaining a full realization of the wonder inherent in their everyday lives. In depicting this harmony between habitat and inhabitant, Wilder is treating one facet of the naturalistic concern of adaptation, a concern ordinarily manifested in naturalistic works in the depiction of a conflict between the individual and an unfamiliar or hostile environment.

In *Our Town*, the harmonious relationship between the majority of the townspeople and their geographical surroundings is presented more as an implicit, underlying "given" than as a subject for exhaustive scrutiny. However, the intimate bond between the citizens of Grover's Corners and their native region is explicitly presented both in general terms and through specific examples in the play. Goldstone even goes so far as to assert that the subject of the entire play is belonging (*Portrait* 140), although such an assertion entails distortion of Wilder's theme and intention. All the same, the Stage Manager indicates in his opening monologue the continuity in the genetic composition of the town's population, noting that the earliest tombstones in the cemetery bear the "same names as are around here now" (7). Such continuity is clear evidence of successful adaptation. Editor Webb, too, observes in the first act that despite the town's limitations, "our young people here seem to like it well enough. Ninety per cent of 'em graduating from high school settle down right here to live—even when they've been away to college" (24). The statistic simply confirms "scientifically" the impression given in the play of a powerful attachment to their home soil on the part of numerous individual characters.

The dramatist balances the picture by including two characters, Rebecca Gibbs and Sam Craig, who exemplify the 10 percent who move away, but the other 90 percent are ably represented not only by George and Emily, but by their parents and, especially, by the Stage Manager himself. The Stage Manager, in his capacity as town "tour guide" for the audience, and especially in his references in his first monologue to "our mountain" (6) and the other glories of the local landscape, conveys perhaps the strongest sense of "belonging" of any of the play's characters. However, Editor Webb, too, comments on the pleasure he and the other townsfolk take in the birds, the seasons, and "the sun comin' up over the mountain in the morning" (25).

This depiction of a deep bond uniting the townsfolk of Grover's Corners with their native soil seems at first glance to be wholly inconsistent with Wilder's declaration, in his 1950 Charles Eliot Norton Lecture at Harvard, that "Americans are disconnected", that "Place and time are, for them, negative until they act upon them, until they bring them into being"; and that "This unrelatedness to place goes so deep that, in an Old World sense, America can have no shrines" ("Toward," *AC* 15). However, despite the obvious existentialist note struck in the first two passages, he did not alter his fundamental beliefs in the years between the composition of *Our Town* (1938) and his delivery of the Norton Lecture.

The solution to the apparent inconsistency lies in a consideration of the ideas of Gertrude Stein, whose influence on Wilder, and specifically on *Our Town*, has been recognized (and even grossly exaggerated) by nearly all critics of Wilder's work and by Wilder himself (*AC* 14; Goldstone, *Portrait* 127).[4] In his introduction to her *Geographical History of America*, the playwright summarizes in the following terms Stein's crucial distinction between Human Nature and Human Mind, her conceptions most relevant to the present discussion:

> Human Nature clings to identity, its insistence on itself as personality, and to do this it must employ memory and the sense of an audience. By memory it is reassured of its existence through consciousness of itself in time-succession. By an audience it is reassured of itself through its effect on another.... The Human Mind, however, has no identity; every moment "it knows what it knows when it knows it." It gazes at

pure existing. It is deflected by no consideration of an audience, for when it is aware of an audience it has ceased to "know." (*AC* 187–88)

Both Wilder and Stein perceive in certain features of the American national character the attributes of Human Mind. Those features, according to Stein, are the result of the geographical situation in which the majority of the American people live. Wilder describes the relationship as follows:

The valley-born and the hill-bounded tended to exhibit a localization in their thinking, an insistence on identity with all the resultant traits that dwell in Human Nature; flat lands or countries surrounded by the long, straight lines of the sea were conducive toward developing the power of abstraction. Flat lands are an invitation to wander, as well as a release from local assertion. Consequently, a country like the United States, bounded by two oceans and with vast portions so flat that the state boundaries must be drawn by "imaginary lines," without dependence on geographical features, promises to produce a civilization in which the Human Mind may not only appear in its occasional [literary] masterpiece, [as is ordinarily the case,] but may in many of its aspects be distributed throughout the people. (*AC* 192)

The American "unrelatedness to place" perceived by Wilder is thus an attribute of Human Mind, infused into the national temperament somewhat paradoxically through the influence of the national geography. Unrelatedness to place is obviously not the same thing as unrelatedness to geography. It is simply "a release from local assertion." The denizens of Grover's Corners, inhabiting a hilly, enclosed terrain, are for the most part still subject to "local assertion." At the same time, however, despite Wilder and Stein's belief that minds are "formed by the physical character of the environment in which they live," that "Everyone is as their land and water and sky are" (qtd. in *AC* 211), an environmental determinism does not lie at the heart of the two writers' conception of the relationship between the individual and geography. That fact is made clear in Wilder's Norton Lecture, in which he comments that the first European settlers who populated this country, although originally inhabitants of an enclosed, localizing terrain, did not derive their sense of identity or their qualities of mind from their relation to their environment (*AC* 10).

Thus, the monistic perspective in *Our Town* that depicts the town's inhabitants as (for the most part) at one with their environment is only a partial perspective. Its truth is limited and incomplete. As more than one commentator has observed, *Our Town* is "about human nature" without being of it (e.g., Burbank 97). It is a picture of Human Nature, as expressed in the lives of the "valley-born and hill-bounded" citizens of Grover's Corners, painted from the vantage point of Human Mind. Emily's sudden realization of the earth's wondrousness is nothing but a shift in consciousness to the perspective of Human Mind, although at the same time she remains attached to the old Human Nature associations of home, family, and familiar objects. Thus, the naturalistic elements and themes in the play, while genuine and true, are merely one level of truth in the playwright's total vision in this work. Stein's ideas apparently helped Wilder to "[confront] rather than [evade] the most compelling claims of philosophical naturalism" by providing him with the means to use naturalistic assumptions and methods to transcend the rigid, mechanistic determinism of the traditional naturalistic point of view. Stein enabled Wilder to discover a quasinaturalistic justification for his inherently unnaturalistic Neoplatonism.

However, Wilder's acceptance of a limited naturalistic perspective on the topic of "belonging" does not end with his portrayal of a harmonious relationship between individuals and their environment, whether "hill-bounded" or boundless. He also presents a number of characters in several plays who are in direct conflict with their environment or, at the very least, poorly adapted to it. This latter type of character is usually more central in traditional naturalistic works (for example, Conrad's *Heart of Darkness*, Zola's *Thérèse Raquin*, O'Neill's *Beyond the Horizon* and *Desire Under the Elms*), largely because conflict of any type adds interest to a story. In Wilder's plays, although the conflict between a character and his or her environment is ordinarily removed to the fringes of the action (except in *The Skin of Our Teeth*), it always remains in plain sight.

In *Our Town*, for instance, Simon Stimson is indirectly described as not cut out for "small-town life" (40). He is a typical naturalistic misfit, the sensitive, artistic person who is overly refined (although Wilder does not imply that he is overly *evolved*) for his surroundings, the sort of personality Thomas Hardy explored in the characters of Jude Fawley and Eustacia Vye. A Wilder character in a similar situation, although not a sensitive, creative type, is the younger Roderick, who makes a brief appearance in *The Long Christmas Dinner* and for whom, ironically, "Time passes so slowly [in the town where he was raised] that it stands still" (23). Like Stimson, Roderick has to drink in order to tolerate the dull, stifling life in the town. His restive nature carries him far away from the bosom of his family, and when last heard from, he is "selling aluminum in China" (24).

Another character in the same play is also at odds with her environment, or at least painfully sensitive to it, although in her case the environment is less an adversary in itself than a convenient scapegoat and symbol of time's relentless passage. The maiden aunt, Genevieve, who has spent twenty-five years grieving for her mother, remarks with dismay late in the play that the Bayard house is now surrounded by factories and that the omnipresent soot requires them to "change the window curtains every week" (25). Although she may see the encroaching factories only as reminders of time (which she has sought to deny), they are real enough in their own right as well. When one recalls the earlier assertion by the "first" "Mother Bayard" that she could remember when there were Indians on the very ground where the house now stands, the factories also begin to mark the irresistible interplay of large social and economic forces that can irrevocably alter the environment and require that individuals adapt themselves, leave, or die.

A much more obviously hostile—even overtly threatening—environment is the setting for the most naturalistic of the "three-minute" plays, *The Angel on the Ship* (*ATW* 59–63). One feature of the playlet that gives it a naturalistic tinge is the fact that the characters are all members of the lower classes and are uneducated and inarticulate, an unusual circumstance in Wilder's writings. Their situation is also quintessentially naturalistic. They are adrift on the ocean, helpless, and facing death by starvation and dehydration. They might be lifted from the pages of Conrad or London, and their plight resembles that of the three characters in one of O'Neill's early one-act plays, *Thirst*. Their reversion in their extremity to a form of pagan idolatry, which involves their praying for rescue to the figurehead of the ship, illustrates the common naturalistic theme of cultural or psychological retrogression in response to natural or social pressure. The naturalism of the piece is tempered, however, by the implication that their prayers for rescue have been answered at the end and that the "Great Gawd Lily" (60) is, after all, only another face of the one true God, who always answers when His children call. There is, on the other hand, no hard evidence in this play that the rescue of the stranded party is not pure coincidence, and the action depicted is undeniably the final phase of a particularly intense and progressively more desperate quasinaturalistic struggle for survival.

The concept of living as struggle also appears in *The Skin of Our Teeth*. Sabina enunciates the orthodox naturalistic position on this theme in comic, colloquial terms when, in Act III, she tells her employer and admirer:

> You're a very nice man, Mr. Antrobus, but you'd have got on better in the world if you'd realized that dog-eat-dog was the rule in the beginning and always will be. And most of all now. (*In Tears*) Oh, the world's an awful place, and you know it is. I used to think something could be done about it; but I know better now. (245–46)

Of course, one could scarcely regard Sabina, who has difficulty even understanding what the play means, as an exponent here of Wilder's own point of view. Moreover, four years earlier, the playwright had, in the person of Mrs. Gibbs, effectively answered this naturalistic view of interpersonal relations as it was voiced by Simon Stimson in the last act of *Our Town*.

However, Mr. Antrobus himself, Wilder's Everyman, concedes in so many words in Act III that "living is struggle. I know," he says, "that every good and excellent thing in the world stands moment by moment on the razor edge of danger and must be fought for—whether it's a field, or a home, or a country" (247–48). The struggle to which Antrobus refers seems, it is true, to be something other than a simple naturalistic struggle for survival. Rather, it appears to be a struggle to preserve humanity's ideals or the practical achievements of civilization. It seems necessary simply to prevent the race from relapsing into barbarism and poverty. At the same time, the "good and excellent" objects of the struggle are all territorial in nature, the implication being that the struggle itself, if not purely biological, still has its roots in basic biological urges.

A more obvious divergence from, or repudiation of, naturalistic thought on this topic can be seen in the dramatic scheme of the play as a whole. The work's subject seems to be humanity's struggle for survival and recurring attainment of its goal "by the skin of our teeth," but one dramaturgical weakness is the playwright's failure to dramatize the struggle itself. Act I treats what might ordinarily be subject matter for a typical naturalistic play: the struggle between a handful of people and a menacing, unpredictable natural environment. The wall of ice moving down from the north is sweeping churches, post offices, and city halls—in short, all human institutions—before it as it advances. However, the survival of the small band of humans appears to depend, not on their superior adaptive capacity or intelligence, as manifested in a direct confrontation with the forces threatening them, or even on a fatal convergence of several chains of incidents and accidents, but rather on a conscious decision on the part of "Everyman," Antrobus. The end of the act shows, instead of an actual struggle to survive against overwhelming odds, a struggle to rekindle the *will* to survive, the successful outcome of which will itself automatically assure the race's survival. Thus, survival is presented more as a matter of "existential choice" than as a natural, inevitable consequence of biological or intellectual superiority or even chance.

The structural rhythms of the rest of the act, too, support the notion that despair rather than nature is humanity's chief enemy in its struggle to survive. Early on in the act, Sabina is overwhelmed by a consideration of the hostile forces (natural and social) arrayed against the family. She concludes, "It's easier being dead" and then "flings her arms on the table and buries her head in them" (118). Mrs. Antrobus, too, temporarily loses heart when she sees the mark of Cain on Henry's forehead. The women overcome their despair with the aid of distractions (the interruption of the telegraph boy, the arrival of Antrobus), rather than through a conscious decision, but the recurring pattern of a temptation to fall into despondency, followed by its conquest or by liberation from fear and hopelessness, adds emphasis to the final scene of the act when, in order to regain the will to live, Antrobus must conquer his despair at the news that his son, Henry, has apparently murdered the boy next door.

Moreover, choice is clearly responsible for the family's survival in the other two acts as well. Humanity's adversary in Acts II and III is not nature or society, but rather its own moral and psychological character, an opponent that is presumably more subject to control by the individual will. However, the difficulty of resisting psychological impulses is illustrated by the assault in Act III by the actor playing Henry on his colleague playing

Antrobus. Thus, the decision to continue the struggle is never presented as easy. However, in the flood at the end of Act II, the survival of the world's animal species is ultimately due neither to protracted struggle nor direct divine intervention, but rather to Antrobus's decision to stop pursuing Sabina and face up to his responsibility to "Save the [human] Family" (167). In Act III, too, he must rediscover the will to persevere in order to preserve his family and the civilization it has built.

Although in this play Wilder is treating subject matter that is central to many naturalistic novels and plays, his emphasis on, and apparent faith in, the power of the human will leads him away from the traditional naturalistic position on this point. One can see him beginning to propose an existentialist answer to one of naturalism's fundamental challenges.

Heredity, the other major influence on human destiny besides environment (according to the naturalists), is not as obvious a concern of Wilder's in his plays as is environment itself. In some of the novels (e.g., *The Cabala* and *The Eighth Day*), he gives it greater consideration. However, its influence can also be felt to a limited degree in some of the plays, chiefly, *The Long Christmas Dinner* and *Our Town*. In the former, the survival of spoken expressions, insights, and behavior patterns from one generation of Bayards to the next suggests the presence of hereditary influences, but the suggestion is ambiguous since speech and behavior patterns are learned, not passed on genetically. In fact, Wilder has outsiders who marry into the Bayard clan, such as Leonora Banning, use some of the same characteristic phrases (many of which are clichés in any case) as do direct descendants.

In *Our Town*, on the other hand, the playwright clearly intends his audience to be aware of heredity as a factor—if not a determining factor—in human behavior and personality. The topic is first broached explicitly by Professor Willard, who reports, while providing anthropological and demographic data on the town, that there are "possible traces" (22) of Cotahatchee Indian blood in three families. One is never told what effect, if any, the Indian blood has on the behavior of the members of those families; in fact, it is nowhere implied that the Cotahatchee genes affect more than the carriers' physical appearance.

However, there are other references in the play, both direct and indirect, to genetic determinism. Before the wedding in Act II, the Stage Manager reminds the audience of the force of heredity in human affairs by admonishing them not to forget "the other witnesses at this wedding" (71): the ancestors of the betrothed pair, "Millions of them" (71). Considering that the dead are described in the final act as being gradually "weaned away" (81) from earth over the years, the only likely way that the myriad ancestors of George and Emily could be considered present at the wedding is in the couple's genetic composition. Even more expressly deterministic is the Stage Manager's assertion implying that this particular wedding has actually been brought about through the good offices of these two particular sets of genes, which are the legacy of all those ancestral millions seeking to ensure their survival and perfection. Paraphrasing "one of them European fellas," the Stage Manager avers that "every child born into the world is nature's attempt to make a perfect human being" (71). Such a statement savors more of Goethe than of Darwin or Mendel, but it can also be seen as a reasonably valid poetic description of the basic impulse involved in sexual selection.

Moreover, other kinds of genetic influence are explored, or at least suggested, in the play. For instance, the Gibbs children, George and Rebecca, appear to have inherited (or absorbed) their parents' opposing propensities in one respect. Mrs. Gibbs, whose desire to travel is revealed in the "bean-stringing" scene in Act I, apparently passes her restlessness on to her daughter (whether genetically or by example), since Rebecca, unlike the majority of Grover's Corners natives, moves away when she grows up. Similarly, George, in his attachment to his native soil and his indifference to the charms of new places and new people, seemingly takes after his father, who is afraid it might "make him discontented with Grover's Corners to go traipsin' about Europe" (20). The contrast between the two siblings may be gender-related, since Myrtle Webb, too, reports having had difficulty getting her husband to take her to see the Atlantic ocean, but gender-related tendencies are even more unequivocal evidence of genetic determinism than are familial peculiarities.

The overpowering sense of fatality or inevitability apparent in much naturalistic writing (a corollary of the naturalistic doctrine of determinism) is largely absent from Wilder's plays. However, there are a few exceptions. One of these is the one-act play, *Queens of France*, in which a shady lawyer in nineteenth-century New Orleans swindles—or attempts to swindle—several bored, unfulfilled women by convincing each that she is the long-lost heir to the French throne and saying that he needs funds for the conclusive research that he must undertake to validate her claim. As soon as the nature of the lawyer's game becomes clear to the audience (that is, as soon as he addresses his second visitor as "Your Royal Highness"), it is evident that a final break with each of his victims is, at some point, inevitable. Since the forces leading to that rupture are entirely under the control of the lawyer, M. Cahusac, and not vast, impersonal natural or social processes, the "mechanism" at work in the piece is not truly deterministic or inescapable. At the same time, the suggestion in the play that the relationship between the lawyer and his clients is a symbiotic one—satisfying both his needs and theirs—hints at a deeper sort of determinism, that of interconnected motivations, which makes the overall course of the relationship all but inevitable.

The Long Christmas Dinner is another one-act play by Wilder in which the outcome appears inevitable from the start. However, the inevitability is simply that of human mortality, which is a universally recognized existential fact and not a theme unique to the naturalists. The destined end of each individual in the play is accomplished through the agency, it is true, of a vast, uncaring, irresistible force—time—but the naturalists were not the only (or even the first) writers to recognize its complete sway over all creation. The impression of inevitability is reinforced by the recurring phrases uttered by successive generations, and indeed by the cyclical form of the entire play, which depicts the broad outlines of human life in terms of the natural cycle of birth, maturation, decline, and death. However, there is nothing inevitable about the direction taken by the life of each individual character, with the possible exceptions of the maiden aunt, Genevieve, and her nephew, the younger Roderick. The dark portal symbolizing death constitutes a visual reminder of the omnipresent fact of human mortality, but the hall door upstage center, through which several characters exit as they leave the house forever, implies that human beings can exercise some free choice in their lives and thereby escape, if not death itself, then at least a particular death in a particular environment.

On the other hand, the cyclical form of several of Wilder's other plays gives their outcomes, as well, an appearance of ineluctability. As in *The Long Christmas Dinner*, however, within the lives of individual characters there is normally no such inevitability. Except perhaps for George and Emily's wedding, the specific course of action taken by Wilder's characters at any given time does not appear fated, although their lives follow in general outline the same pattern as the lives of all mortals. The daily cycle of life in Grover's Corners may vary little over the years, but the predictable recurrence of the milkman's and paperboy's rounds does not determine such things as the circumstances of Emily's death, nor is the survival of the human family in *The Skin of Our Teeth* guaranteed by the same forces that create the cyclical shape of that play. Rather, the cyclical shape is itself dependent on the family's survival from act to act, and that survival is, again, largely an act of will.

Like the numerous naturalistic themes and motifs, the cosmological core of naturalistic philosophy—a conviction that God is either nonexistent, absent, unconcerned about humanity, or unknowable—is also perceptible, to a limited degree, in Wilder's plays. A self-confessed "believer," at least in his youth (Simon 35), he never claims in his writings that the universe is entirely comprehensible to human beings. Instead, he adopts a position midway between that of the majority of the naturalists and that of the unquestioning devout. His attitude is ultimately no more skeptical than that of such religious thinkers as Tertullian, Pascal, and Kierkegaard.

On the other hand, although Rebecca Gibbs in *Our Town* mentions the Mind of God as the culmination of the ever-widening frames of reference in the address on the letter written to Jane Crofut by her minister, the nature and attitude of that Mind itself remain inscrutable, and the same mystery may be perceived in Wilder's other plays and novels. For instance, in *The*

Bridge of San Luis Rey, where this very problem is central, the author purposely leaves unanswered the question of whether the collapse of the bridge was "accident" or "intention." In *Our Town*, the bare stage—the framework within which the action occurs—can be regarded as symbolic of the naturalists' view of the human condition, a vast, impersonal void or unanswered question in which the characters play out their pedestrian personal dramas. Although Wilder's bare stage has more in common stylistically with the theatre of the symbolists than with that of the naturalists, philosophically or symbolically it might be considered a link with either movement, the two being not so far apart *au fond* as perhaps at first appears. At least one critic has observed that Maeterlinck's characters are just as helpless—just as powerless to alter their destinies—as the characters in naturalistic dramas (Clancy 161). Moreover, the symbolist-inspired set designs of Craig and Appia all tend to dwarf the individual actor, and Kenneth Macgowan actually censured Craig for his contemptuous attitude toward the actor, saying that such an attitude was worthy of the naturalists (Macgowan and Jones 19). However, whereas the naturalists would perceive no spiritual presence within the cosmic void represented by the bare stage in Wilder's plays, Wilder himself, along with Mallarmé, attempts to present the void in such a manner as to make it reveal the infinitely significant, if not wholly comprehensible, Idea that lurks in its depths.

The Mind of God is also perceptible—and not only in the pervasive biblical references—in *The Skin of Our Teeth*, even though a strict, literalistic interpretation of the action might hold that in that play, it is humanity that must save itself.[5] There is, it is true, no direct divine intervention to preserve the human race in any of the three acts. Even the boat that saves the Antrobuses and Sabina from the deluge in the second act is tied up at the pier only by chance (and the playwright's contrivance). The presence in Atlantic City of two of every kind of animal is also a fortunate coincidence, it seems—if not a believable natural occurrence—although there are definite implications (as there are in *The Bridge of San Luis Rey*) of a purpose other than the requirements of the author's craft behind these "chance" events. More significantly, though, when it is a question of destroying the unregenerate specimens of humanity gathered in Atlantic City, the voice of God is intelligible enough and His hand is easily discernible. The gypsy, Esmeralda, sets forth, in no uncertain terms, the Almighty's grievances against sinful humankind, and the weather indicator, the four black discs that announce the end of the world, is obviously a vehicle for registering direct dispatches from on high.

In *The Alcestiad*, the universe is presented as even more incomprehensible than it is in the earlier plays. The divine, in the person of Apollo, appears on stage, but he is portrayed as limited, by the conditions of human existence and the weakness of human consciousness, in his ability to communicate with mortals. The primary inspiration for the play lies in existentialist thought (this aspect will therefore be treated more fully in Chapter 6), but the ultimate incomprehensibility of the universe constitutes one significant point of agreement between the naturalists and the existentialists, a point that can be readily located within Wilder's play. For instance, in a despairing moment in Act I, Wilder's Alcestis remarks, "we are indeed miserable. Not only because we have no aid, but because we are cheated with the hope that we might have aid" (30). Her great fear is that she will die knowing nothing "of why we live and why we die" (15). A clear statement of the same concern may be found in Hardy's poem "Nature's Questioning," which contains the line, "We wonder, ever wonder, why we find us here" (12).

The similarity between Wilder's outlook and that of the naturalists goes beyond the thematic and philosophical elements in the plays to include one facet of his fundamental attitude toward playwrighting. When, in the mid-1930s, he temporarily renounced writing novels in favor of composing plays, he gave as one reason the increased objectivity required of an author by the dramatic form (Parmenter 10). In the *Paris Review* interview, he defined a dramatist as "one who believes that the pure event, an action involving human beings, is more arresting than any comment that can be made upon it" (Goldstone, *Writers* 108). Moreover, he was reported in a 1938 interview to have maintained that "drama was superior to fiction because it was freer from the 'editorial presence'" (Parmenter 10). He conceded that the Stage Manager in *Our Town*, along with the similar figures in *Pullman Car Hiawatha* and *The Happy Journey*, was a "hang-over from a novelist technique." By way of excusing such a device, he stated that perhaps, in an age of heterodoxy like the present one, "a commentator is useful for delivering signposts" (10). Actually, of course, the interruptions of the laconic, meditative Stage Manger in *Our Town*, like those of his counterpart and of Lily-Sabina in *The Skin of Our Teeth*, serve to distance the audience from the main action of the play. The greater the distance, the greater the objectivity, that is necessary to reduce the danger that the one play will lapse into sentimentality and the other into preaching. Wilder admitted in the *Paris Review* interview that there was a strong didactic tendency in his work (Goldstone, *Writers* 111), making it perhaps more important for him than for other writers to give an impression of objectivity. Whatever the reason, though, his goal of an objective, undistorted presentation of his material makes him a kindred spirit to the naturalists, with their pretense of "scientific" neutrality. Although Zola, in his well-known definition of a work of art as "a corner of creation, as seen through a temperament" ("Proudhon" 24, author's translation), acknowledges the integral role played by the artist's subjective vision in the creation of art, he also writes in his theoretical essay, "The Experimental Novel," that "the personal feeling of the artist is always subject to the higher law of truth and nature" (*Novel* 51).

In keeping with his interest in conveying an impression of objectivity, Wilder takes pains in at least one play, *Our Town*, to establish the work's "documentary" credibility. The Stage Manager, who perceives the play to be a valid anthropological document, proposes in Act I that a copy be sealed into the cornerstone of the Cartwrights' new bank building. Moreover, Wilder's own pose as a mere recorder of anthropological data is bolstered by his inclusion in the play of a wealth of scientific detail about his fictional New Hampshire microcosm. Professor Willard delivers all the town's vital statistics as well as its geographical and human history, and Editor Webb presents its religious and political profiles.

Wilder often treats such scientific or pseudoscientific data in his plays with irony or humor, as at the beginning of Act II of *The Skin of Our Teeth*, where Antrobus reports his "decision" to be "viviparous, hairy, and diaphragmatic" (164). Similarly jocular is the "Field's" disclosure in *Pullman Car Hiawatha* that it contains "51 gophers, 206 field mice, 6 snakes and millions of bugs, insects, ants, and spiders. All in their winter sleep" (59). In *Our Town*, the relative importance of scientific data in general is wryly called into question by the Stage Manager's vaguely condescending treatment of Professor Willard. He finds it necessary to remind the Professor that time is limited, and he ultimately must interrupt him to prevent him from exceeding his allotted time.

Of course, Wilder's attitude toward all such "abject truths" was always partly ironic and playful. Even in cases involving the apparently straightforward presentation of plausible "scientific" facts, one must be wary of giving credence too naïvely or automatically. For instance, the carefully and precisely stated geographical coordinates of Grover's Corners place the town approximately 100 yards off the beach at Rockport on Cape Ann, Massachusetts, in the middle of Sandy Bay (Littman 137, n44), and not in New Hampshire "just across the Massachusetts line" (5) at all. Other inconsistencies in the play also undermine its correspondence to external reality. For example, Mrs. Webb and Mrs. Gibbs (and later Emily) are shown unseasonably stringing (imaginary) beans in May, and Editor Webb, whose newspaper is explicitly described as a biweekly, is seen returning home late at night, reportedly "after putting his newspaper to bed" (42) on a day that began with its early morning delivery by Joe Crowell, Jr. If the playwright was unaware of these inaccuracies, improbabilities, and inconsistencies (he must have selected the town's latitude and longitude in full knowledge of what he was doing), he doubtlessly would have been untroubled by them since, for him, the theatre was "an accumulation of untruths" (*AC* 108), and to pretend otherwise was childish.

At the same time, the scientific detail in *Our Town*, *Pullman Car*, and *The Skin of Our Teeth* performs a function essential to the playwright's overall design and is not included simply to enable him to ridicule or parody the naturalistic style. The Professor's geological data helps to expand *Our*

Town's temporal frame of reference and place Grover's Corners in a context of vast dimensions of space and time, dimensions also evoked by the dead man in Act III, who announces that it takes millions of years for the light from a given star to reach the earth. These particular scientific details thus help effect Wilder's stated plan to make "as preposterous as possible" the claim that the smallest events in our daily life possess "a value above all price" (*AC* 109). At the same time, they demonstrate that the present moment and immediate place contain "the largest dimensions of time and place" within them, and that the individual consciousness is capable of making direct contact with the distant past merely by gazing at a star or climbing "A shelf of Devonian basalt . . . with vestiges of Mesozoic shale" (21).

In addition to their thematic and methodological or teleological similarities to naturalistic works, Wilder's plays often display somewhat surprising structural and stylistic resemblances to them as well. The number and degree of these resemblances is all the more surprising considering Wilder's explicit repudiation, in both his theoretical essays and his best-known, most characteristic plays, of the central principle of naturalistic theatre aesthetics: realism. His objections to real or realistic objects on stage have already been mentioned. Going into greater detail, in "Some Thoughts on Playwrighting," he writes:

> The stage is fundamental pretense and it thrives on the acceptance of that fact and in the multiplication of additional pretenses. When it tries to assert that the personages in the action "really are," really inhabit such-and-such rooms, really suffer such-and-such emotions, it loses rather than gains credibility. . . .
>
> If Juliet is represented as a girl "very like Juliet" . . . moving about in a "real" house with marble staircases, rugs, lamps, and furniture, the impression is irresistibly conveyed that these events happened to this one girl, in one place, at one moment in time. When the play is staged as Shakespeare intended it, the bareness of the stage releases the events from the particular and the experience of Juliet partakes of that of all girls in love, in every time, place, and language. (*AC* 123–24)

In contrast, one might cite the admiring reaction of one critic to a naturalistic production at André Antoine's Théâtre Libre: "It is singular, but it seems that there is no stage, and that the raised curtain of the Théâtre-Libre discloses people in their houses going about their affairs unconsciously and without knowing that they are watched" (qtd. in Waxman 97).

The actor in Wilder's plays, on the other hand, must frequently break the naturalistic "fourth-wall" convention. In fact, in each of the author's full-length dramatic works, there is at least one occasion when a character is required to address the audience directly. In *Our Town*, not only does the Stage Manager, like his counterpart in *Pullman Car Hiawatha*, supply background information and food for thought with his running commentary on the action, but Professor Willard and Editor Webb also speak directly to the assembled spectators at one point. Sabina/"Miss Somerset," Esmeralda, and the Stage Manager in *The Skin of Our Teeth* do likewise, and Dolly Levi, Malachi Stack, and Horace Vandergelder and his clerks (in *The Matchmaker*), as well as the Watchman (in *The Alcestiad*), follow suit. In addition, there are, of course, a dizzying array of other anti-illusionistic or theatricalist features in all the playwright's most typical works for the stage.

Despite his disparagement of, and departures from, realistic norms and conventions, however, Wilder wrote several early plays in the very style he was later to attack. Even two of the "three-minute" playlets, *Fanny Otcott* and *The Angel on the Ship*, qualify as conventionally realistic dramatic works. Both are readily stageable as written, and neither contains any overtly supernatural, surrealistic, or fantastic incidents or heightened, "poetic" dialogue, although the language sounds a trifle stilted at times. *Fanny Otcott* (*ATW* 33–40) is set in a corner of the garden in Wales where a retired Irish actress of the Restoration and Augustan ages is reliving her erstwhile triumphs with the aid of a scrapbook, and *The Angel on the Ship* transpires entirely on "the fore-deck of the NANCY BRAY lying disabled in mid ocean" (59). *The Trumpet Shall Sound* is also technically a realistic play, although its allegorical overtones carry it beyond "pure" or photographic realism. There are numerous improbabilities of character and incident, too, such as the dispensation granted by the New York City Police Department to one man, the owner of the Washington Square mansion where the play is set, which allows him to sit in judgment over his tenants—who have, in fact, moved in and been misbehaving in his absence. However, there is nothing physically impossible in the play's action and nothing stylized, abstract, distorted, or anti-illusionistic in the manner of its presentation.

At least two of the one-act plays published in the same volume as *The Long Christmas Dinner*—*Queens of France* and *Love and How to Cure It*—are also unswervingly realistic. In fact, the former play is strongly reminiscent of Henri Becque's play *Les corbeaux*, which also depicts the machinations of an unscrupulous attorney. Although Becque himself refused to be classified as a naturalist, his plays (primarily *Les corbeaux* and *La Parisienne*) are commonly considered the most successful French embodiments of the movement's dramaturgical ideas. *Love and How to Cure It*, which is set on an empty stage in a darkened London music hall in 1895, portrays the attempts of two seasoned vaudevilleans, a man and a woman, to convince a young university student to give up his anguished courtship of the woman's niece, a beautiful and remote young dancer who is completely indifferent to the boy and is irritated by the violence of his passion.

In addition to the entirely realistic mode of these plays, one can perceive important realistic elements in a number of those plays that otherwise deviate radically from basic illusionistic conventions. Perhaps the most obvious and widespread of these elements are the characters themselves—recognizable, ordinary individuals who express themselves in commonplace, colloquial language. The characters in *The Long Christmas Dinner*, *The Happy Journey*, *Our Town*, and the majority in *Pullman Car Hiawatha*, as well as the late play *Childhood*, all fit this description. They are, on one level, typical and generalized, and none would qualify as an unforgettable human being, but they are distinguished from one another in simple but effective ways. The distinguishing traits even determine the course of the action to a degree. For instance, in *Our Town* the fact that Mrs. Webb is "a thin, serious, crisp woman" (8), reserved and somewhat repressed, adds significantly to Emily's frustration and to the tension and pathos of the scene as a whole when she attempts to relive her twelfth birthday and tries to bridge the emotional gulf separating her from her mother. Conversely, the "plump, pleasant" Julia Gibbs (8), with her soothing personality, makes an ideal spiritual guide for Emily in her transition to the unfamiliar world of the dead.

One reason why Wilder's characters on the whole seem more generalized than those of Zola and his followers, besides Wilder's obvious orientation toward the universal and typical, is simply that they are more ordinary. As a number of commentators have observed (e.g., Carter 56–57), Zola deliberately sought to portray exceptional characters in extreme situations, presumably in order to make his literary "experiments" as definitive as possible. Frank Norris wrote of his predecessor and master:

> We, the bourgeois, the commonplace, the ordinary, have no part nor lot in the *Rougon-Macquart*; [Zola's series of novels about French Second Empire society]. . . . To be noted of M. Zola we must leave the rank and file, either to run to the forefront of the marching world, or fall by the roadway; we must separate ourselves; . . . become individual, unique. (71–72)

Norris's own *McTeague*, Dreiser's play *The Hand of the Potter*, and numerous other works show that Norris' remarks apply just as well to himself and his fellows as to Zola.

Nevertheless, although Wilder's characters tend to be excruciatingly commonplace, he renders their conversations with a sensitivity to subtle individual differences of cadence and vocabulary. Zola—who insisted that naturalistic dialogue should be "the language as it is spoken every day" and should preserve "the particular turn of mind of each talker" (*Novel* 154)—would have fully approved of such sensitivity. Wilder had an especially good ear for regional speech patterns and those indicative of social class. The spare, dry, ironic New England dialect spoken by his New Hampshire townsfolk still sounds natural, unaffected, and convincing. Similarly, the Kirby family in *The Happy Journey* converse in a fluid, believable lower-middle-class idiom.

Moreover, in Wilder's plays, individual characters within a single region or class employ language differently from each other, whether because of age, gender, or personality. For example, in *Our Town*, the calm, measured, reassuring cadences and relatively flexible and precise diction and grammar of Editor Webb may be contrasted with the abrupt, energetic fusillades and faulty English of Constable Warren; the ironic, drawling phrases of Simon Stimson; and the genial, buoyant, or deferential accents and elliptical syntax of Howie Newsome. The sharp, economical utterances of Myrtle Webb stand in distinct contrast to the breathless, chirpy, repetitive loquacity of Mrs. Soames. Even George and Emily distinguish themselves from one another by their use of language—his being more innocent, wide-eyed, provincial, and colloquial and hers, more reserved and elevated. For example, she addresses and refers to her parents as "Papa" and "Mama," whereas he is content with the plainer, homelier (and more conventionally masculine) "Pa" and "Ma." In *The Happy Journey*, too, the laconic, deliberate, meditative speech rhythms of Elmer, the Kirby paterfamilias, provide a strong counterpoint to the spontaneous, expansive manner characteristic of his wife.

These simple distinguishing habits of speech do not by themselves necessarily constitute evidence of naturalistic propensities on Wilder's part. Any competent playwright will exploit the inherent capacity of spoken language to define the speaker's character. However, such individualizing linguistic touches, combined with the faithfully (and accurately) transcribed regional and class-related dialects, create in these plays a spoken language that is in complete conformity with Zola's requirements regarding dramatic dialogue.

The French novelist's concern with establishing and conveying a sense of the environment of the story in fiction translated itself into agitation for scrupulously realistic, usable, three-dimensional scenery in the theatre. Zola felt that settings performed a function similar to that of descriptive passages in a novel (*Novel* 152). Wilder, at first glance, seems to stand directly opposed to such an aesthetic agenda, having eliminated scenery completely in *Our Town* and a number of the one-acts and called for stylized or obviously artificial or symbolic settings in *The Skin of Our Teeth*, *The Matchmaker*, and *The Long Christmas Dinner*. However, he takes pains to establish the particular—and often, very real—physical environment of the action in *Our Town*, *The Happy Journey*, and *Pullman Car Hiawatha*, at least. His use of abundant scientific and documentary data performs roughly the same function in *Pullman Car* and *Our Town* as do the detailed illusionistic settings in more conventional, realistic plays. The data allows Wilder to reverse the equation that Zola perceived between scenery on the stage and description in the novel. While eliminating realistic settings for these plays, Wilder includes precise descriptions of the physical environment, which accomplish practically the same purpose at the same time that they support or illustrate his principal themes.

Careful, "scientific" description of the physical environment is especially evident in *Pullman Car Hiawatha*. In that play, the Stage Manager mentions the exact date and time periodically and the audience is told the precise animal population of the Field by the person representing it, as well as the human populations of Grover's Corners (Ohio) and Parkersburg, by the persons representing them. A mechanic also gives a thorough, specific account of the weather conditions surrounding, not only the railroad car, but also the entire northeast corner of the nation. The meteorological, biological, and demographic data may all be spurious, but it is plausible and helps to ground the play's action (fantastic and allegorical as much of it is) in a concrete place and time. It does not, however, serve a profoundly naturalistic purpose, since to all appearances this precisely described or imagined environment does not directly, or even indirectly, affect events on board the train. The primary purpose of the "scientific" details—and of the play as a whole—is the Maeterlinckian or symbolist goal of leading audiences to a keener awareness of the richness and variety of the world encompassing their prosaic daily activities. This symbolist or nonnaturalist function of the environmental data Wilder provides is especially clear in *The Happy Journey*, where the Kirby family's delighted awareness of the geography through which they pass seems to strengthen the ties binding them to each other and their home state, but the environment itself is nowhere portrayed—implicitly or explicitly—as either having made them who they are or exerting a major influence on their actions or their moods during the journey.

Another formal or stylistic feature imparting a naturalistic flavor to many of Wilder's plays is their panoramic spatial or temporal scope—which is, however, always compressed, and often drastically so. This scope is another of the peculiarly (although not exclusively) "American" qualities of Wilder's naturalism. Vast spatial or temporal scope is not in itself an attribute unique to naturalistic writing, of course. It may be encountered in *Little Dorrit*, *Moby Dick*, Shakespeare's "Wars of the Roses" history cycle, and even in the single play *Pericles*. However, Zola himself never claimed to have invented naturalism and naturalistic techniques, and panoramic scope is definitely one of the distinguishing characteristics of much naturalistic literature, from Zola's Rougon-Macquart series of novels (which fill twenty volumes, cover several generations, and portray a total cross-section of Second Empire society) to Frank Norris's uncompleted wheat trilogy (of which the initial volume is *The Octopus*), Theodore Dreiser's trilogy focusing on the millionaire Charles T. Yerkes, and Eugene O'Neill's dramatic trilogies such as *Mourning Becomes Electra*.

The practical problem of audience attention span, which O'Neill tended to address by means of a direct, frontal assault, would seem to militate against the composition of conventionally naturalistic plays of expanded spatial and temporal scope, and in truth, there have been few. Wilder solved the problem by means of the nonnaturalistic technique of telescoping. The time-lapse photography technique of *The Long Christmas Dinner* is one example of such condensation. Time and (imagined) space are both compressed in *Pullman Car Hiawatha*, in which the train containing the car travels from a point outside New York City to the station in Chicago in approximately twenty-five real minutes and the vastness of the heavens is shrunk to the dimensions of a runway at the back of the stage. *The Happy Journey*, which also lasts approximately thirty minutes in performance, compresses time and space in depicting the Kirbys' automobile trip from Newark to Camden, New Jersey, which begins in the afternoon and ends after sundown.

Extended temporal scope—in a condensed form—is also evident in *Our Town*, *The Skin of Our Teeth*, and *The Alcestiad*. The first play might almost be called a trilogy in brief, since an entire human life cycle is shown or implied in it. In the first act, the routine of an ordinary day begins with the birth of twins. The second act treats "Love and Marriage," and the third begins with a funeral. The only epoch of human life that is missing is old age. Additionally, the first act itself compresses an entire day into thirty or forty stage minutes. The role of the tombstones and the geographical and astronomical data in expanding the play's spatial and temporal scope has already been discussed. *The Skin of Our Teeth* telescopes several thousand years of human existence into three short acts, although the actual compression of time occurs only between the acts, historical epochs are seen as synchronous rather than successive, and the events depicted are, in any case, mostly legendary or archetypal, so that human history is presented symbolically rather than literally. *The Alcestiad*, like the first act of *Our Town*, compresses the events of an entire day into the continuous action of each of its three acts and follows its protagonist from youth through old age.

The naturalistic method of expanding the human or social scope, along with the spatial or temporal scope, of their works—which involved the creation of a "broad canvas" or multifocal composition without a single, dominant protagonist (as, for example, in Hauptmann's *The Weavers* and Gorki's *The Lower Depths*)—may also be met with, in modified form, in some of Wilder's plays. Perhaps the most obvious example is *The Long Christmas Dinner*. The play presents no comprehensive social vision, dealing as it does with a single upper-middle-class family (and their invisible servants), but its basic underlying premise makes the absence of a distinct protagonist inevitable. The passing generations make it impossible for any one character to remain on stage throughout the piece, although clearly some characters are more important than others.

A multifocal compositional technique can also be seen in *Pullman Car Hiawatha*. In fact, the social vision in this play is much broader than that in *The Long Christmas Dinner*. Although Harriet is clearly the central character in *Pullman Car*, the focus is less on the poignancy and pathos of her death and the process whereby she arrives at her epiphany than on the content of that epiphany—the nature of the vision vouchsafed her. It is such an all-encompassing vision that its presentation necessarily entails the careful incorporation into the play of a wealth of subordinate characters. In fact, it is only after the play is nearly half over that one can begin to sense who its protagonist is—or even that it has one. Wilder's (and Harriet's) vision in this play is not limited, of course, to the merely human, but even on that plane the breadth, if not the depth, of the playwright's portrait of society rivals that of Zola's portrait in his Rougon-Macquart novels. The only element missing from *Pullman Car* is the highest stratum, whose members would be unlikely to travel by Pullman car, anyway. For the rest, the play provides an audience with glimpses of the social order from the lowest classes (the Tramp) to the professional ones (the Doctor and the Engineers), with nearly everything, urban and rural, in between. There is even an appearance by a former member of a peculiarly American social class, the ghost of an immigrant workman. Harriet's story is also prevented from dominating the play's action by the dramatist's inclusion of a kind of alter ego for her in the person of the Insane Woman, who is nearly as important a character as Harriet.

Although *Our Town*, with its action centering primarily on the affairs of two families belonging to the professional class, might seem at first glance to lack the social scope of a play like *Pullman Car*, it is one of Wilder's most complete portraits of an entire society. Not all social strata are fully represented on stage, but they are present in the visible characters' references to them. Although Banker Cartwright and the Polish mother, Mrs. Goruslawski (along with the drunken man who nearly froze to death on Emily's twelfth birthday), have no influence on the course of the play's action, they hover around its periphery, representing the two extreme ends of the social scale in Grover's Corners. In between these extremes lie the milkman, constable, church organist, doctor, journalist, housewives, sexton, and college professor, not to mention the stage manager-druggist-minister, all of whom appear on stage along with members of other assorted professions and their wives and children. Moreover, the frequent universalizing devices, such as the Stage Manager's observation in Act I that "All 2,642 [inhabitants] have had their dinners and all the dishes have been washed" (26), help, obviously, to extend subtly the play's social scope while maintaining a necessary primary focus on the two "average" families of Dr. Gibbs and Editor Webb.

In *The Skin of Our Teeth*, the dramatist concentrates almost exclusively on four characters, but he uses other devices to expand the social scope of the play. The refugees in Act I and the black chair-guides in Act II represent the lowest social stratum, although the former are in reality legendary or mythological personages. The next lowest stratum, that of the skilled blue-collar workers, is represented by the theatre personnel who assume the roles of the Hours in Act III. The upper echelons of society are suggested in Act II when Antrobus himself achieves the acme of power and prestige, the honorary presidency of the human race. The most obvious device used by the playwright to bring the multitudes into his story, however, is the generalized, archetypal nature of the four main characters, a patently *anti*naturalistic device.

If the extended spatial, temporal, and social scope of Wilder's most typical plays is achieved with the help of dramaturgical methods having little in common with those of the naturalists, though, several of his dramatic works, or portions thereof, exemplify another and more typical naturalistic dramatic form, the "slice of life." The resemblance of these plays to the slice of life form is due to a combination of two factors: the realistic dialogue and incidents in them and the dramatist's disregard for linear, "well-made" plots or intrigue. This latter characteristic is also a symbolist aspect of Wilder's drama (see Chapter 2). The two "pureist" examples of the slice of life form among Wilder's plays are *Queens of France* and *The Happy Journey*, although both have perhaps a more obviously patterned structure than the usual or ideal naturalistic slice of life. The former is built on repetition—like *The Long Christmas Dinner*, *Our Town*, and *The Skin of Our Teeth*—and the latter, with its withheld revelation of the purpose of the journey (the oldest Kirby daughter's need for emotional support following a stillbirth), seems, on the whole, relatively "well-made." However, each play depicts no more than a series of relatively discrete moments in the lives of the characters, and the action of both is clearly presented as no more than a fragment of a larger action, an episode in an ongoing story.

The first act of *Our Town* is also nothing more at bottom than a slice of New Hampshire village life. Its title alone, "Daily Life," is sufficient evidence of its closeness to the naturalistic form. If one removes the more obvious nonrealistic devices—direct address, simultaneous scenes in different locations, interruptions by "audience members"—one is left with a collection of vignettes of daily life, beginning with breakfast and the early-morning milk and newspaper deliveries, proceeding through the housewives' morning chores and the children's return from school, and concluding with the evening's activities. In the course of this series of loosely related scenes or miniature slices of life, certain unifying themes or threads are introduced and amplified and even resolved—such as Mrs. Gibbs's attempt to induce her husband to take her to Europe, George's neglect of his chores, Emily's intelligence, and George's mental slowness. However, there is no "well-made" plot structure linking all these vignettes; they do not build steadily to a strong climactic incident, nor is there, at the end of the act, an unsolved mystery or suspended line of action or conflict intended to provide a springboard into the next act.

This structure involving an assortment of loosely related vignettes, along with the prosaic—even trivial—subject matter and frequent pauses enumerated in the previous chapter, gives the act as a whole a distinctly Chekhovian air. Chekhov, like Maeterlinck, found significance in the apparently trivial and ordinary. In fact, if the similarity between Chekhov's plays and *Our Town* (and, to a lesser degree, *The Long Christmas Dinner*) can be construed as evidence of a naturalistic tendency on Wilder's part, it can also be argued that it is largely the result of symbolist tendencies on the part of both playwrights. At the same time, although Wilder's theme in *Our Town* may be the Maeterlinckian (and, to a lesser extent, Chekhovian) belief that the humble events of daily existence possess a splendor or meaning unperceived by the majority of mortals, that theme is conveyed in dialogue, at least, that is wholly naturalistic (if not exactly Chekhovian) and not at all self-consciously "poetic" or Maeterlinckian.

Another attribute of many naturalistic writers, from Zola himself through London and Dreiser—namely, a highly developed social conscience and reforming zeal—seems largely absent in Wilder. In a review of Wilder's early novel *The Woman of Andros*, Marxist critic and novelist Michael Gold accused the author of willfully and irresponsibly refusing, in this novel and his earlier writings, to concern himself with pressing American social and economic issues of the day. Wilder's fondness for exotic foreign and historical settings in his novels and playlets, coupled with his penchant for exploring abstract philosophical and theological questions, struck Gold as epitomizing the worst sort of Olympian, even effeminate, escapism, which he deemed an utterly inappropriate response to the harsh realities of Depression-era America. "Where are the modern streets of New York, Chicago, and New Orleans in these little novels?" asked Gold.

> Where are the cotton mills, and the murder of Ella May and her songs? Where are the child slaves of the beet fields? Where are the stockbroker suicides, the labor racketeers or passion and death of the coalminers? . . . Wilder takes refuge in the rootless cosmopolitanism which marks every *emigré* trying to flee the problems of his community. (Gold 237)

Although Wilder could never be called a social crusader in his writings, a dollop of generalized, noncontroversial social commentary is served up in many of his later plays and novels.[6] Such commentary is not, indeed, entirely absent from the author's first three novels, *The Cabala*, *The Bridge of San Luis Rey*, and *The Woman of Andros*. At any rate, members of the working classes (and even the unemployed) are sympathetically and sensitively portrayed in *Pullman Car Hiawatha*, *Love and How to Cure It*, *Our Town*, *The Skin of Our Teeth*, and especially, *The Happy Journey*, which remained Wilder's favorite among his own plays. The folly and tragic waste of war are suggested in an least three plays. In *The Long Christmas Dinner*, one Bayard father is an unthinking, complacent apologist for war, considering it a sort of safety valve for releasing social pressures that have accumulated within nations, until his own son is killed in World War I. The incident serves to expose the weaknesses in the mechanistic and fundamentally naturalistic view of war expressed by the older man. In *Our Town*, the Stage

Manager, while relating the life story of the paperboy, Joe Crowell, Jr., remarks that after a brilliant scholastic career, he was killed in France during the war, and "All that education [went] for nothing" (10). On the other hand, in Act III of the same play he implicitly eulogizes the town's Civil War dead as having laid down their lives for a good cause. Similarly, Ma Kirby in *The Happy Journey* recalls with patriotic pride that one of her sons "gave his life for his country" (107). Moreover, despite the horrors of war evoked in the last act of *The Skin of Our Teeth*, Antrobus implies at one point that something positive, a vision of a better life, can come out of an armed conflict.

Other, more unequivocal social comment may be discerned in *The Long Christmas Dinner* and *Pullman Car Hiawatha*. In the former play, Genevieve's outburst against the soot that clings to the curtains in the Bayard house may be primarily directed against the memories that haunt the place, but her complaints also underscore the mushrooming industrial pollution of the early twentieth century, some of it no doubt caused by the family's own factory. In *Pullman Car*, the tramp traveling underneath the car on December 21, 1930, asserts his right to recognition and a hearing, to "be in this play" (59). The playwright thus reminds his audience of the realities of the Depression and solicits sympathy for its victims. The audience is reminded, also, by the appearances of the German workman's ghost and the watchman in the tower farther up the line of society's dependence on the countless anonymous workers, living and dead, who keep the wheels of daily life rolling.

Besides these rather conventional and, in some cases, somewhat oblique instances of social comment, there is at least one direct response to Gold's attack in Wilder's plays. In Act I of *Our Town*, when Gold's fictional double, a Belligerent Man in the back of the auditorium, asks if anyone in Grover's Corners is aware of social inequality, Editor Webb wryly answers: "Oh, yes, everybody is—somethin' terrible. Seems like they spend most of their time talking about who's rich and who's poor" (25). When asked why no one does anything about it, Mr. Webb replies:

> Well, I dunno. . . . I guess we're all hunting like everybody else for a way the diligent and sensible can rise to the top and the lazy and quarrelsome can sink to the bottom. But it ain't easy to find. Meanwhile, we do all we can to help those that can't help themselves and those that can we leave alone. (25)

This pronouncement may be seen as Wilder's way of sidestepping the issue, and his criticisms of war in *The Long Christmas Dinner*, *Our Town*, and *The Skin of Our Teeth* may seem a trifle hypocritical in light of the more militaristic or patriotic sentiments expressed elsewhere in these and other plays and in light of Wilder's own two enlistments in the army in 1918 and 1942 (Simon 32, 164). No doubt part of him agreed, if only in a very limited sense, with Sabina in *The Skin of Our Teeth* that "Everybody's at their best in wartime" (227). In a 1962 interview, in remarks that sound as if they could have been made by Spencer, he acknowledged the natural, biological basis for war, saying:

> War is in all of us and is a very natural phenomenon indeed. . . . During the millions of years that certain mammals developed into man, the aggressive instinct was of the greatest importance. Civilization—the art and practice of living equably in the community—is merely a few thousand years old. What are we to do with all that fine belligerence within us which helped us so long, all that adrenalin and visceral turbulence? (Lewis 28)

However, Sabina's status as a disruptive and destructive force in *Skin* has been firmly established by the time she speaks the line quoted here, and Wilder's enlistment in the army during World War II, when he was forty-five years old, was motivated by a genuine—and quite understandable—conviction that the Axis was too great a menace to civilization to be allowed to go unopposed.

Ultimately, Wilder's temperament and outlook, while not complacent, were geared more toward an acceptance of life, people, and society than toward crusading for radical social (or any other) change. The courtesan, Chrysis, in *The Woman of Andros*, voices what might be his own point of view regarding the problem of evil in the world and in society (and obviously was one of the things that irritated Gold about the novel), when she remarks:

> I have known the worst that the world can do to me, and . . . nevertheless I praise the world and all living. All that is, is well. Remember some day, remember me as one who loved all things and accepted from the gods all things, the bright and the dark. And do you likewise. (107)

In one final area of apparent disagreement between Wilder and the naturalists, the distance between him and them turns out, on closer examination, to be not so great as at first appeared. The naturalistic view of the individual seems at first glance diametrically opposed to that of Wilder. However, it is actually nearly as ambivalent as his, although for somewhat different reasons. On the one hand, the individual must dwindle into utter insignificance in the interplay of vast natural or social forces that was the naturalistic writer's supposed primary interest. This is indeed the typical naturalistic point of view regarding the individual, and one of the clearest, most succinct statements of it may be found in Jack London's *The Sea Wolf*. When, in that novel a novice sailor is caught up on one of the masts of his ship and, in mortal terror, attempts to descend to the deck without losing his life, he elicits the following comments to the narrator from the ship's captain (the title character, "Wolf" Larsen), who serves as the voice of philosophical naturalism in the work:

> Why, if there is anything in supply and demand, life is the cheapest thing in the world. There is only so much water, so much earth, so much air; but the life that is demanding to be born is limitless. Nature is a spendthrift. Look at the fish and their millions of eggs. For that matter, look at you and me. In our loins are the possibilities of millions of lives. . . . Life? Bah! It has no value. . . . Nature spills it out with a lavish hand. Where there is room for one life she sows a thousand lives, and it's life eats life till the strongest and most piggish life is left. (68)

Wilder attempts to refute this point of view by absorbing and transcending it in *Our Town*. As he writes in the Preface to *Three Plays*, he makes the individual's claim to significance "as preposterous as possible" by setting "the village against the largest dimensions of time and place" (*AC* 109). In addition, in the *Paris Review* interview he is quoted as saying, "I see myself making an effort to find the dignity in the trivial of our daily life, against those preposterous stretches which seem to rob it of any such dignity; and the validity of each individual's emotion" (Goldstone, *Writers* 114).

The recurring words in *Our Town* (and in *The Skin of Our Teeth* as well) are "thousands" and "millions," as they are in the passage by London just cited. The naturalistic conception of the individual as dwarfed by nature and the rest of humanity apparently provided a spur to Wilder's creativity and helped him establish a spatial, temporal, and human context for his plays.

Within that context, however, he sought to go beyond the naturalists' cynicism and assert the individual's absolute significance. Although he maintains in the Preface to *Three Plays* that "Each individual's assertion to an absolute reality can only be inner, very inner" (*AC* 109), he continually affirms the value of the individual human life in other, subtler ways as well, even, as has been shown, drawing strength for his attempts from the very immensity that seems to negate them. In *Our Town*, for instance, the Stage Manager remarks at the end of the play that the earth seems to be the only planet in the universe that sustains life. Thus, although, as the dead man reminds his listeners, it takes millions of years for the light from a star to reach the earth, the playwright implies that the light was traveling all that time toward a destination of unique and remarkable value.

Actually, the seeds of an "inner, very inner" assertion of the absolute value of the individual are contained in another passage in *The Sea Wolf* that immediately follows the one just quoted. After the sailor has found a way to safety, Larsen observes to the narrator:

> Do you know the only value life has is what life puts upon itself? And it is of course overestimated, since it is of necessity prejudiced in its favor. . . . There is plenty more life demanding to be born. Had he [the sailor] fallen . . . there would have been no loss to the world. He was worth nothing to the world. The supply is too large. To himself only was he of value, and to show how fictitious even this value was, being dead he is unconscious that he has lost himself. (69)

The germs of an existentialist view of the individual are perceptible in this passage, and it is perhaps this very problem of the individual's significance in an immeasurable cosmos that led Wilder eventually to embrace existentialist thought since it offered a possible answer to the naturalistic position, an answer similar to the one he had previously formulated on his own.

However, the naturalists' own doctrines and methods implicitly endowed the individual with significance in a more direct way. For instance, Zola advocated individualized dramatic speech that would capture "the particular turn of mind of each talker" (*Novel* 154). The naturalists' focus on details and the reproduction of reality logically led them to pay careful attention to all the singular traits that make each human being different from every other. In naturalistic theory, the individual might be no more than a product of the interplay of hereditary and environmental forces, but given the infinite number of possible combinations of those forces and their relative strength or weakness in combination, in naturalistic practice, the writer inevitably had to consider each person as a special case, a unique illustration of the operation of a unique combination of determining forces or influences.

Thus, to the limited extent that his characters are individualized, Wilder exhibits naturalistic tendencies as a playwright, just as he exhibits symbolist tendencies to the extent that the characters are generalized or universal types. Moreover, to the extent that he places them in a minutely realized physical environment, (whether depicted or merely described) and avoids elaborate intrigue and well-made plots in several of his plays, attempting instead to convince his audience that they are witnessing an artless, if incomplete, transcription of external reality, and to the extent that he seeks to incorporate vast reaches of time and space and vast multitudes of human beings into his plays, he exhibits naturalistic (although not exclusively naturalistic) propensities. Despite his explicit rejection of orthodox naturalistic philosophy and the naturalistic theatrical style, then (which was, in fact, only a partial rejection), Wilder apparently found much to stimulate his dramatic imagination in the practices and programs of the movement. Furthermore, by his deliberate juxtaposition of the trivial and everyday with the naturalistic expanses of space and time that dwarf the individual, Wilder applied a sort of touchstone to the Maeterlinckian theme that the commonplace possesses transcendent value. His assertion of the significance of the apparently trivial and the dignity of the individual's emotion is thus more authoritative and more cogent than Maeterlinck's. Wilder ultimately upholds Maeterlinck's fundamental claim, but he does not deny the difficulty of doing so. As Burbank observes, he gives the "compelling claims of philosophical naturalism" (32) their due while at the same time attempting to challenge them, and his argument against them is thereby strengthened and raised above the level of a simple, reflexive reaction.

Naturalism itself, with its ambivalent view of the individual, furnished him with much of the ammunition he needed for his argument.

NOTES

1. Nonetheless, in a 1927 letter to his Lawrenceville friend Winifred Bronson, he discusses Conrad's death and mentions *Nostromo* with apparent admiration (letter of Sept. 2, 1927, in Bronson family papers at the Bancroft Library, University of California, Berkeley). Moreover, early diary entries show him to have read *Under Western Eyes* with interest and to have seen in the theatre a dramatization of Conrad's novel *Victory* (diary, 1919, ms.; list of plays seen, ms., Wilder papers, YCAL).

2. For example, in "George Bernard Shaw," 93; "Some Thoughts on Playwrighting," 124; and "Joyce and the Modern Novel," 174.

3. Compare also "Joyce and the Modern Novel," 174.

4. Critics include Burbank (82–87); Goldstein (98–100); Haberman, *Plays* (37–38, 55–56, 88, 90, 95–102); Sawyer (27). Sawyer is guilty of the greatest exaggeration of Stein's influence.

5. Goldstein (123) propounds just such an interpretation.

6. He even came to wonder, after becoming acquainted with the works of Herbert Marcuse in the 1960s, if he were not himself something of a "crypto-Marxian" (qtd. in Harrison 351).

Chapter 4

The Style but Not the Substance: Expressionist and Brechtian Features of Wilder's Theatre

If it is classified at all by a critic, Wilder's dramaturgy is most likely to be designated "expressionistic," and there is a certain limited validity to the label.[1] However, the numerous and pronounced differences between Wilder's plays and those of the expressionists—both German and American—render the designation even less satisfactory than "symbolist" or "naturalistic" when one is seeking to characterize the whole body of the playwright's work, or even the whole of a single play. Wilder's dramaturgical technique does venture unmistakably into expressionist territory, especially in *Pullman Car Hiawatha* and *The Skin of Our Teeth*, and certain central motifs of expressionist drama materialize, too, in *Skin*, *Pullman Car*, and *The Alcestiad*. However, Wilder's primary impulses as a playwright differ distinctly from those motivating the expressionists, and his plays ultimately concern other things than theirs do and make different points. The same relationship also exists between his theatre and that of Bertolt Brecht, a dramatist whose vision developed out of expressionism and to whose dramatic technique Wilder's is also frequently likened.[2]

One feature of expressionism itself (although not of Brechtian theatre) that made it easier for Wilder to imitate some of its techniques and incorporate some of its characteristic motifs into his plays while at the same time remaining uninfected by its fundamental spirit was the movement's philosophical incoherence or heterogeneity. It is difficult to speak of expressionist "doctrine" in clear and consistent terms. The movement was essentially a somewhat anarchic rebellion against the prevailing styles and ruling powers of the day—a social as well as artistic revolt, but one without a well-defined program or cogent alternative vision to propose. Its adherents included writers who later became Nazis, Communists and socialists, religious mystics, liberal pacifists, and Zionists, and in each case, the "conversion" involved no radical break with basic expressionist impulses or values.

This situation is partly due to the fact that the movement arose without the aid of a "fountainhead" figure comparable to Zola or Mallarmé. The term *expressionism* appeared first in the arena of art criticism and was then applied by literary critics to describe phenomena already perceptible in German literature and theatre in 1911–1912.

The movement's loose, contradictory nature was also a function, however, of the one common denominator in all expressionist art: subjectivism. Expressionism may, in fact, be defined as the attempt to render and convey subjective and, especially, subconscious—experience directly in concrete artistic terms, although such a general definition could also fit surrealism and there are significant, if subtle, differences separating the two movements. At the same time, subjectivism was never the sole defining feature of expressionist art; the movement had a complex, multidimensional character that was sufficiently coherent and distinct to qualify it as a full-fledged aesthetic mode or system. The movement is sufficiently distinct and multifaceted, in fact, to make it a relatively easy matter to determine precisely wherein Wilder's theatre is and is not "expressionist." In fact, ironically, it is simply the chief defining trait of expressionism, the aim of directly depicting the subjective and subconscious life, that is most conspicuously absent from Wilder's dramatic universe.

There is no doubt that at the time he was writing his own plays, Wilder was familiar with the theatrical manifestations of expressionism, but it is difficult to ascertain the precise extent of his acquaintance with them or determine whether it was with the German or the American branch of the movement that he was more familiar. As far as the German branch is concerned, according to Haberman (*Plays* 70), when Wilder was in Rome in 1920–1921, a German there lent him some expressionist plays to read by Georg Kaiser, Fritz von Unruh, Oskar Kokoschka, Walter Hasenclever, and Carl Sternheim. Years later, Wilder said that he did not remember them and that, in any case, his German was not good enough at that time to permit him to get much out of them (70). However, other sources convey a different picture. In a 1951 letter, Wilder wrote, "Way back in 1920 and 1921 I read all the Kokoschka plays I could find; I collected them in Rome through a bookstore" (letter to H. M. Wingler, 3 Apr. 1951, qtd. in Valgemae, 114). In a 1964 letter to scholar Mardi Valgemae, Isabel Wilder describes her brother in 1920–1921 as aware of the movement and important expressionist productions—through reading newspapers in many languages, talking with people, and muddling through with the German—and indicates that he "understood more than he knew" about the phenomenon (letter of 8 June 1964, ts. copy, Wilder papers, YCAL). Furthermore, journal entries from 1922 show him undertaking at that time to read all Sternheim's protoexpressionist plays about the Maske family, *Scenes from Heroic Bourgeois Life*, although he indicates that he had to abandon the project after finishing *Die Hose* (which he found vulgar) because Sternheim's unusual German was too difficult for him (journal 1922, ms., Wilder papers, YCAL). A letter from 1923 reveals that by then, he knew and admired Strindberg's *A Dream Play* and *The Ghost Sonata* and had eagerly sought out information about Max Reinhardt's planned production of the former play (to B. Pemberton, 20 May 1923, copy in letter bk., ms., Wilder papers, YCAL), and he later wrote that his acquaintance with Strindberg's chamber plays dated from 1920–1921 (dictated letter to Sr. A. Gertrude, n.d., ts., Wilder papers, YCAL).

Wilder's acquaintance with German expressionism proper might have been strengthened on his 1928 trip to Germany, during which he and his sister Isabel at one point saw fifty-two plays in sixty-three days. By 1928, however, the movement had effectively spent itself in Germany. Some expressionist plays might have been revived during the Wilders' visit, but there is no record in the diary entries (published as "Playgoing Nights") of their having attended any such revivals. Nonetheless, several references in other entries indicate a sufficient familiarity on Wilder's part with the expressionist style in general to permit him to apply the label to a number of plays or productions, either in part or in toto ("Playgoing" 413, 418). Moreover, one of the entries contains the playwright's comments on a production of Frank Wedekind's *Lulu*, a program consisting of *Erdgeist* (*Earth Spirit*) and *Der Buchse von Pandora* (*Pandora's Box*) (419). Wilder found the play "revolting" but admired the production as wholly appropriate and properly intense. Wedekind, along with Sternheim and Strindberg, is generally regarded as a protoexpressionist (Ritchie 23–24; Sokel 22, 57–63; Garten 103).

Further acquaintance with German expressionism could have come, at second hand, through Wilder's friendship with Max Reinhardt, whom he met briefly in New York in 1923 at a performance by the Moscow Art Theatre (letter to Isabella Wilder, 15 May 1923, copy in letter bk., ms., Wilder papers, YCAL) and then came to know more fully in 1931 in Salzburg, Reinhardt's home city (Simon 92). Wilder had admired Reinhardt at least since his early youth, when he had memorized the casts and other personnel for all of the great *régisseur*'s productions, none of which he actually saw (Harrison 67). He did manage to attend a festival of Reinhardt productions in New York in 1927–1928 (Simon 55), and Reinhardt was to direct, in 1939, the first (disastrous) production of *The Matchmaker*, in its original incarnation as *The Merchant of Yonkers*. The renowned director, who had staged or produced such expressionist plays as Sorge's *The Beggar* (the first identifiably expressionist German play), Goering's *Naval Encounter*, and Kaiser's famous *From Morn to Midnight*, could easily, in the course of casual discussion, have helped to familiarize Wilder with the movement with which he, Reinhardt, had been so intimately connected.

In any case, there is incontrovertible evidence in an "Author's Note on the Staging of [*The Skin of Our Teeth*]" (qtd. in Haberman, *Plays* 69–70) that by the time Wilder wrote the note, he knew enough about the German movement to be able to recognize some of the ways in which his own Joycean fantasia resembled it. He acknowledges in the note that *Skin* resembles "German expressionism," along with musical comedy turns, comic strips, and "dream plays" (69). However, the playwright does not elaborate on any of the specific ways in which his play is, as he perceives it, expressionistic, so it is difficult to judge which of its expressionistic aspects he was aware of while he was writing the play and which, if any, were the result of coincidence.

As regards American expressionistic drama, Wilder could hardly have escaped exposure to such plays as *The Adding Machine* (1923), *The Hairy Ape* (1922), *Beggar on Horseback* (1924), *The Great God Brown* (1926), and *Machinal* (1928), given his regular attendance at the theatre in New York during those years; and notations on a list of Theatre Guild productions in one of the playwright's diaries suggest that he saw the 1922 Guild production of *From Morn to Midnight* (diary, 1918–1927, ms., Wilder papers, YCAL). In addition, in his 1925 *Theatre Arts* article, "The Turn of the Year," he mentions with admiration the American expressionist play *Processional*, by John Howard Lawson (152–53).

As is the case with other American expressionist playwrights—such as George S. Kaufman and Marc Connelly, and even Eugene O'Neill—Wilder's debt to the movement lies more in the area of style or technique than in that of theme or overall vision, although here, too, there are striking resemblances between his work and that of the expressionists. His interest and belief in a truth that lies beneath the surface of the external, sensory world, for instance, links him as much with the expressionists as it does with the symbolists (and, in fact, there were close connections between the two movements themselves). However, Wilder tends to conceive of that profounder truth in mystical, supraconscious "symbolist" terms, rather than in subjectivist, emotional, or subconscious "expressionist" ones.

For the sake of clarity, then, it will be useful to spell out the thematic and philosophical—and even temperamental—differences separating Wilder and the expressionists in order to appreciate better the extent and significance of the few noteworthy areas of agreement between them. The expressionist rebellion against the established social order manifested itself in four basic ways: virulent opposition to mechanized industrial production, with its accompanying regimentation and dehumanization of the individual worker; contempt for the bourgeoisie, which profited from such mechanization; ardent pacifism or a commitment to total nonviolence; and an Oedipal antagonism toward the older generation (especially fathers) as the most conspicuous representatives of entrenched authority. Wilder, for his part, was always inclined more to accept "all things, the bright and the dark," than to foment revolution, unless in the matter of theatre aesthetics. He takes no stand in his plays against mechanization or industrialization, unless one chooses to view *Our Town* as primarily a nostalgic, sentimental paean to an uncomplicated rural past. In that case, however, his response is more in the nature of a symbolist/romantic (or neoromantic) retreat from the horrors and complexities of modern life than a direct, expressionistic confrontation of them. Not even in *The Long Christmas Dinner*, with its reference to the sinister, gradually encroaching factories, is there an extended exploration of the dehumanizing, demoralizing effects of modern assembly-line mechanization.

Similarly, Wilder's tendency toward acceptance of the world, in combination with his apparent acceptance of his own thoroughly middle-class background, prevents him from attacking bourgeois values and mores in his plays. His regard for the American middle class may have been fostered partly through his association with Gertrude Stein, who also professed esteem for its ethos. In any case, not only are the vast majority of Wilder's major dramatic characters—in *Our Town*, *The Long Christmas Dinner*, *Childhood*, *Infancy*, and even *The Happy Journey* and *Pullman Car Hiawatha*—sympathetically portrayed members of the bourgeoisie (whether upper, lower, or middle), but his Everyman, George Antrobus, is a New Jersey commuter and head of a thoroughly, typically bourgeois household, complete with maid.

The one exception to this general tendency might be *The Matchmaker*, in which the tyrannical, narrow-minded, materialistic "merchant of Yonkers," Horace Vandergelder, is ridiculed by the playwright and duped and robbed by the other characters; the Puritan work ethic is called into question when Vandergelder's two clerks and, later, his millineress-fiancée and her assistant all decide on their own initiative to take a holiday; and the prudent bourgeois attitude toward money is undermined in the assertion by the title character, Mrs. Dolly Levi, that "Money . . . is like manure," of no value unless it is liberally "spread about encouraging young things to grow" (396). However, all these subversive, antibourgeois sentiments and acts in the play owe more to conventional farce structure (to say nothing of Wilder's source, the play by Nestroy) than they do to any deep-seated "expressionistic" hostility on the playwright's part to the middle class mentality.

The expressionists' rejection of bourgeois values involved a rejection also, on the part of some writers, of at least one article of traditional bourgeois religious faith, the doctrine of original sin. These writers asserted flatly that "Man is good."[3] Wilder's treatment of the character of Henry in the last act of *Skin* reveals his disagreement with this point of view. He includes explicit instructions that Henry, in his confrontation with Antrobus, be played "not as a misunderstood or misguided young man, but as a representation of strong unreconciled evil" (235). At the conclusion of the play, as Mr. Tremayne, Antrobus's dresser, begins to recite the opening verse of Genesis, "HENRY appears at the edge of the scene, brooding and unreconciled, but present" (249), an inescapable member of the human family. Sabina, too, although a more attractive character than Henry, is fundamentally sinful and just as impossible to get rid of as he. Although Wilder's depiction of evil may strike some as unconvincing or bland, he does not appear to possess the expressionists' idealistic faith in human goodness.

Wilder's position is somewhat closer to the expressionists' on the subject of pacifism. However, despite his obvious distaste for war, which is evident in *Our Town*, *The Long Christmas Dinner*, and especially *The Skin of Our Teeth*, his tendency to regard it as a necessary—and inborn—evil (examined in depth in Chapter 2) sets him apart from the true, and even ardent, pacifists among the expressionist writers.

One motif that is prevalent in expressionist plays does appear in relatively unadulterated form in *The Skin of Our Teeth*. That motif is the conflict between generations, and particularly between father and son. In the conflict between Henry and George Antrobus in Act III, Wilder is carrying on the tradition of dramatized Oedipal fantasies that was begun by such expressionist plays as Hasenclever's *The Son* (which ends with a scene in which the title character is about to shoot his tyrannical father when the old man dies of a heart attack) and Arnolt Bronnen's *Parricide* (which culminates in a literal enactment by the teenage protagonist of his Oedipal desires regarding both his parents). In Wilder's play Henry's murderous hatred of his father is given full, explicit expression—possibly even too simplistic or bald expression. He admits that in the war, he was really seeking to kill his father and that the "others [he] killed were just substitutes" (227).

However, despite the obvious resemblance between this passage and similar Oedipal confrontations in numerous expressionist plays—a resemblance that is almost certainly due to Wilder's interest in the theories of Freud, whom he sought out and met in 1927, rather than to his interest in expressionism—there is one major difference separating Wilder from the expressionists on this topic: a difference of perspective. In all the expressionist plays with Oedipal motifs, the intergenerational conflict is presented from the son's point of view, or at least with greater sympathy for his position.[4] Wilder, on the other hand, presents the son, with his Oedipal impulses, as unambiguously evil. He does not imply, certainly, that those impulses are themselves evil or unnatural, and indeed, he tries to present a balanced picture by having the actor playing Antrobus admit that the actor playing Henry would not be in danger of losing self-control and strangling him if there were not something overbearing or patronizing about his own personality or behavior. Nevertheless, the playwright's sympathies are entirely with the father in this case. "Sabina" even refutes the Henry-actor's story of his unhappy childhood and tyrannical father, implying that it is a complete fabrication used as a rationalization for his outbreaks of uncontrollable violence.

On the other hand, the playwright does seem to side with the son in *Infancy* (1960), the first one-act play in the uncompleted *Seven Ages of Man* cycle. The bulk of the play is composed of the dialogue of two infants, played by grown men in bonnets, who lie in their adjacent baby carriages in Central Park one afternoon. Moe Boker, one of the infants, reveals at one point his blinding hatred for his father, who frequently addresses him jocularly as "stupid" (15), and the boy expresses his fervent desire to "do something so that he won't *be* any more. He'll be away—away where people can walk on him" (15). Although the perspective in this play (in which the Oedipal conflict is, in any event, only briefly presented) is closer to that in expressionist drama, the comic context and the baby's utter impotence to act on his desires allow the spectator to assume a detached and condescending attitude toward the son, which an expressionist play would scarcely permit.

An intergenerational conflict also appears in *Childhood* (1960), the second play in the cycle. The favorite game of the three children in the play, who are all members of a single family, is pretending that their parents have died. However, the conflict is not expressly Oedipal (two of the children are girls), and the fact that it finds an outlet in harmless fantasy (harmless except that it tends to give one of the girls nightmares) removes it even further from the conventional motif as it appears in expressionist drama.

The expressionists' attack on mechanization, the middle class, war, and fathers was balanced by an idealistic vision of a Utopian future to be brought about through the regeneration of society. This regeneration, as envisioned in such expressionist plays as Kaiser's *Gas I* and *The Burghers of Calais*, was to be accomplished by a "New Man," a qualitatively different type of human being, who was to be healed of the psychological fragmentation induced by modern technology and made spiritually whole and sound in a manner and to a degree never before known. This new human being, in turn, would be produced through the radical spiritual transfiguration, or *wandlung*, of the individual. Such transfigurations are frequently depicted, therefore, in expressionist plays, some noteworthy examples being found in *From Morn to Midnight*, Ernst Toller's *Masse-Mensch*, and of course, his first play, *Die Wandlung*, the work that popularized both the motif and the term.

With respect to this common expressionist thematic motif, the relationship between Wilder's drama and that of the expressionists is somewhat more complex and problematical. Expressionist writers did not fail to recognize—or evoke—the Christian overtones inherent in the notion of spiritual rebirth, and Wilder's religious orientation therefore causes somewhat similar motifs or concepts to appear in his plays on occasion. However, his fascination with eternal verities and recurring cycles prevents him from heralding the advent of a new Golden Age peopled by a new, qualitatively different type of human being. The "New Man" is, in fact, noticeably absent from virtually all expressly expressionist American plays.

A concept related to that of the New Man that does emerge in Wilder's plays is that of individual perfection or perfectibility, although the concept is usually treated with a certain amount of playful irony such as would not be found in an unqualifiedly expressionist play. Mention was made in Chapter 3 of the Stage Manager's borrowed observation in *Our Town* that "every child born into the world is nature's attempt to make a perfect human being" (71). In the soda fountain scene in the same act, during George and Emily's discussion of the flaws in their respective characters or constitutions, each confesses to the other that he or she feels members of the opposite sex are, or ought to be, perfect. The adolescent naïveté of these confessions places the entire discussion in a rather humorous light, making it obvious that although perfection may be an ideal toward which nature strives, it is not a possibility genuinely within the individual's grasp. In a 1940 journal entry, the playwright acknowledges the infantile character of the desire for perfection—a desire he recognizes in himself and others, and which he identifies as an essentially religious impulse (*Journals* 5–6).

This same ambivalent, ironic/indulgent attitude toward the human drive for perfection—especially as it is manifested in the expectation that others be perfect—also pervades *The Skin of Our Teeth*. In Act I, for instance, Mrs. Antrobus tries to shame her daughter, whom she has caught wearing rouge, by reminding her that her father "couldn't live if he didn't think you were perfect (132). At the same time, it is Gladys's proud revelation that she was "perfect" (157) in her poem recitation in school that enables Antrobus to overcome his momentary despair and continue the struggle to survive in the face of the advancing ice. In Act II, Mrs. Antrobus points out to her husband that their marriage came about, not because they were perfect in themselves or perfect for each other, but because they made one another a promise that made up for their numerous imperfections. This more balanced, objective assessment helps to place in the proper ironic light the earlier, more idealistic sentiments expressed by and to Gladys. However, idealism reasserts itself at the beginning of Act III, when Sabina enters with the news that, the war being over, Mr. Antrobus now expects his dependents all "to settle down and be perfect" (212). There is clearly more than a touch of sardonic flippancy in her choice of words, but at the same time, Antrobus's idealism is evident in the specific plans he has for all the women, which, as Sabina reveals to Mrs. Antrobus and Gladys, include their learning algebra and history.

Wilder's conception here has more in common with the rationalistic, Enlightenment belief in human perfectibility and progress, however, than with the expressionists' utopian vision of an imminent millennium of peace, prosperity, and universal brotherhood to be brought about through a spiritual transformation of the individual or a sort of "quantum leap" of the entire human race to a new plateau of existence. "Perfection," in fact—especially perfection of the individual, in the sense of flawless knowledge or behavior—plays a very small or nonexistent part in the expressionists' Utopia. Moreover, the fact that such "perfection," for Wilder, is to be achieved via study (and the study of history, at that) rather than through a radical break from tradition or a total spiritual conversion is evidence of the gulf separating him from the expressionists—at least, the German expressionists—on this point. His "eternal," archetypal characters are by their very nature incapable of a decisive, qualitative *wandlung*, a fact underscored by the ending of the play, in which Sabina repeats the lines with which she opened the first act and then informs the audience in an aside, "We have to go on for ages and ages yet" (250).

Perhaps it was partly the different historical situation in which Wilder wrote his play that made it impossible for him to believe in and herald the dawn of a new Golden Age. With humanity in 1942 plunged once more into global conflict, it must have seemed unlikely that a permanent elimination of war and exploitation and the establishment of worldwide social harmony could truly be effected in modern times.

At the same time, characters in other plays by Wilder do experience conversions or transfigurations of various sorts. Alcestis in *The Alcestiad* is one such character. However, the play itself is not conspicuously expressionistic, either in style or in its use of the motif. Alcestis's experiences of regeneration or conversion are much more explicitly identified with Christian rebirth or resurrection than they would be in most expressionist plays, although again, the expressionists did not hesitate to underscore the Christian overtones of the *wandlungen* that they dramatized. A more important distinction between this play and expressionism is the fact that Alcestis's "transfiguring" experiences, or epiphanies, do not alter her character in any radical way. She grows in knowledge and wisdom following each of them, but she embraces no idealistic social vision as a result and, in fact, seems instead to withdraw from the world as she grows old.

Pullman Car Hiawatha depicts the transfiguration of the central character, Harriet, but this event occurs after and as a result of her death, so it cannot possibly lead to a complete regeneration of society, except insofar as an audience watching the play takes her message to heart and looks at the world with new awareness and appreciation. However, as in *The Alcestiad*, the playwright does not appear to have any ulterior social purpose in picturing his heroine's transformation. Nonetheless, Harriet's is the most complete and "expressionist" *wandlung* depicted in all Wilder's plays.

When the archangels first attempt to take her with them, she is overcome with shame and a sense of unworthiness. She wants to remain dead in her old, familiar surroundings. Eventually, however, she begins to change her mind. After the angels have convinced her that her sins have been atoned for by Christ and that they really want her to come, she muses, "what wonderful things must be beginning now" (67). As they start leading her down the aisle of the car, she blurts out, "Let's take the whole train . . . let's all go" (67). Just before she ascends to Heaven, she apologizes for talking so much, saying: "I never used to talk like this. I was so homely I never used to have the courage to talk. Until Philip came. I see now. I see now. I understand everything now" (68). Thus, she metamorphoses posthumously from a timid, self-effacing invalid (except, perhaps, with her husband) into an impulsive, outgoing, voluble soul. Death itself is naturally a type of *wandlung*, but it need not be portrayed as entailing an alteration of personality such as one sees in Harriet. It is not so portrayed in the case of Simon Stimson in Act III of *Our Town*, for instance. The ecstatic nature of Harriet's transfiguration, along with the sudden and radical character of the personality change that is depicted, place it squarely and incontrovertibly in the expressionist tradition.

Hast Thou Considered My Servant Job? (*ATW* 129–33) also contains an apparent *conversio*, but it is only briefly sketched, without elaboration or development. If there is anything ecstatic about it, it lies outside the action depicted and must be inferred from the final lines of the piece. The playlet is based on an inversion of the situation and dialogue presented at the beginning of the Book of Job. In Wilder's playlet, Satan, in conversation with Christ, points with pride to his "servant Judas, . . . an evil and a faithless man, one that feareth [him] and turneth away from God" (129). Christ challenges Satan to allow him a free hand in trying to win Judas to his cause, and Satan agrees. After his thirty-three years on earth, which pass in a brief stage direction, Christ returns to Satan, who believes he has won the contest for his "servant's" loyalty. When Judas himself appears, however, with the rope marks still on his neck, he repudiates the Prince of Darkness, muttering softly and with lowered eyes, "Accursed be thou from eternity to eternity" (133), after which he and the Son of Man ascend together to paradise. Judas's radical conversion, his rejection of Satan prompted by his remorse, is symbolically represented in the play by an event described in the stage directions. Before Judas himself appears,

> the thirty pieces of silver are cast upward from the revolted hand of Judas. They hurtle through the skies, flinging their enormous shadows across the stars and continue falling forever through the vast funnel of space. (132)

The stage direction is itself heavily expressionistic, making use, as it does, of exaggeration and intensification in order to give concrete form to a subjectively perceived meaning in the coins themselves and to an inner action, the revolt that their upward flight symbolizes. The playlet is, altogether, one of the most expressionistic of Wilder's dramatic works, but even here the playwright stops short of dramatizing or even describing Judas's *wandlung*; and the dialogue between Satan and Christ, which constitutes the bulk of the work, is classically elegant, restrained, artful—even studied—rather than elliptically emotional, lyrically subjective, or coldly mechanical, as in the typical expressionist play.

Just as Wilder's plays occasionally resemble those of the expressionists in theme and motif, so do they, at certain points, resemble them in form. However, as is the case with the themes and motifs, the structural resemblances are usually imperfect or approximate.

First, the radical subjectivism of the more extreme expressionists is alien to Wilder's vision. In this respect, his expressionism, such as it is, is characteristically American. None of his plays can rightly be classified as expressionistic monodrama, where the action seems to be occurring entirely within the mind of the protagonist or author. The characters in all the plays seem to have an objective, autonomous existence. However, in some plays a few passages might be regarded as "monodramatic," and other plays contain sections resembling, if only slightly, miniature or fragmentary expressionist "dream plays."

The most obvious and indisputable instance of monodrama in Wilder's works occurs in *The Skin of Our Teeth*. At the conclusion of Act III, Antrobus recalls how, during the war, he would try to remember (perhaps while standing all night on a hill) passages from his favorite books. He also relates that he would give names to the hours of the night, with nine o'clock being "Spinoza." As he begins to recite the passage from Spinoza that he associated with nine o'clock, the back wall of the set disappears and the captain of the ushers, bearing a Roman numeral IX, crosses the stage, reciting the passage in full. He is followed by other members of the theatre's staff, who represent the later hours and recite the thoughts of other philosophers, ending with the opening verse of Genesis. Thus, the scene is patently intended as an objective, literal representation of Antrobus's conceit regarding the hours of the night, the sort of externalization one finds in many expressionist plays. Interestingly, the passage's monodramatic quality may be due only to an effort by the playwright to clarify the import of the "Hour-philosophers" device and integrate it more fully into the action than is done in *Pullman Car Hiawatha*. The device's meaning is clearer in *Skin* than it is in *Pullman Car*, where it is first utilized, not only because Sabina and the stand-ins discuss possible interpretations with the Stage Manager before rehearsing their parts, but also because Wilder (as he does *not* do in the earlier play) clearly outlines here the origins of the conception in Antrobus's imagination and then introduces the device as the direct representation of the character's mental image. In any case, the expressionist character of the passage is diminished by the fact that what is being depicted is an image from Antrobus's conscious, and not his subconscious, mind.

In contrast, in *Pullman Car Hiawatha* it is nowhere implied that the "vision" in which the Hour-philosophers appear—the parade of representatives of all that surrounds the train—is a projection from Harriet's conscious or subconscious mind after her death. Although the fantastic, allegorical section of the play does not begin until after she has died, she seems as oblivious as the sleeping passengers to the wonders passing before the audience's eyes. The stage directions state that her "face has been toward the wall" (66) throughout the procession of local representatives and allegorical figures, and she does not turn back until the archangels reach her bedside. It might be argued that since she is (apparently) facing upstage, she could indeed be observing the figures as they pass by on the walkway called for by the playwright, which he stipulates should be placed against the rear wall of the theatre. However, the entrancing vision seemingly has no effect on her, if she has indeed seen it, since she is still bound to earthly life—particularly her own home and daily routine—when the angels first speak to her. She first seems to perceive the planets, hours, towns, and workmen during her "musical" epiphany, after she has ascended part of the way to Heaven and can look back on earth, and thus can "understand everything now." The entire pageant, given the context of the rest of the play, is presented as "revealed" to Harriet from without rather than generated by her from within her own consciousness.

There is one slight suggestion of expressionist monodrama in *Pullman Car* in the depiction of the Insane Woman in the third compartment as a kind of alter ego to Harriet. Her mental illness parallels Harriet's physical illness, and she is the only other passenger besides Harriet to perceive and speak to the archangels. She grieves at one point because she is not beautiful, anticipating Harriet's later remark that she herself was so homely that she could never summon the courage to talk to anyone. The Insane Woman's dissimilarity to Harriet is also significant, as is natural for an alter ego. First, she wishes to go with the angels, whereas Harriet at first wishes to remain. Second, she has contempt for the other passengers because they "have never suffered" (66) and are therefore "like children" and without "logic" (66), whereas Harriet sees so many appealing faces among them that she wants to "take the whole train" with her to her new abode. However, despite the strong parallels and sharp contrasts between the two characters, the Insane Woman is too fully drawn and too important dramatically to qualify as a mere dream projection of Harriet's own psyche. She is even given a name, "Mrs. Churchill," as one indication of the difference between her and the typically nameless subsidiary characters in an expressionist monodrama.

One critic (Fulton 411) has gone so far as to propose that *Our Town* could be regarded as a monodrama, with the action occurring entirely within the mind of the Stage Manager. Although such a reading appears at first glance to be a ludicrously facile distortion of the play, the Stage Manager's omniscience provides just enough grounds to make it sound plausible. However, if the play might be considered a monodrama, it can by no stretch of the imagination be regarded as an expressionist one. The characters plainly enjoy an independent existence, and if the action is occurring within the Stage Manager's mind, it is action *remembered* or *recorded*, and not the externalization of subjective, heightened perceptions and events issuing from the subconscious level of the psyche. One misses in the play precisely the distortion and exaggeration that characterize expressionist monodrama—and, indeed, expressionist art in general—and betray its subjectivist foundation.

Some portions of individual plays by Wilder do exhibit limited affinities with the related expressionist dramatic form, the dream play. In certain passages in *Pullman Car* and one passage in *Our Town*, the characters' subconscious impulses and thoughts are presented directly to the audience, as they are in dream plays, but in these instances Wilder employs a decidedly unexpressionistic technique. Wilder's characters in these passages simply utter fragments of their respective streams of consciousness (or subconsciousness). As Walter H. Sokel points out (41–44), this method, like that in O'Neill's *Strange Interlude* and *The Great God Brown*, which could conceivably have served Wilder as models for his passages, is closer to naturalism than to expressionism. In any case, in *Pullman Car*, as the archangels pass by the berths on their way to Harriet, the sleeping passengers mutter excerpts from their running subconscious monologues. Although, taken out of context as they are, the excerpts sound mysterious and elliptical, they actually convey mundane, prosaic thoughts—for example, "Some people are slower than others, that's all" (65); and, "I can teach sewing" (65). In each case, not only is the insight one that the character's conscious mind is fully capable of attaining on its own, but it is reported by the character as if he or she were talking in his or her sleep, which is a perfectly normal, natural phenomenon. The dramatist makes no attempt to render in visual terms the content of the various characters' dreams, as an expressionist playwright would have done. The device is merely a variation of that used in the earlier passage in the play when, taking their cue from the Stage Manager, who tells the audience he wants them to hear the passengers (and the porter) think, the same characters utter their conscious thoughts aloud in a manner reminiscent of the Joycean stream-of-consciousness technique.

In *Our Town*, the playwright simply lets the characters speak their subconscious thoughts aloud, as if under hypnosis, rather than presenting them to an audience "expressionistically" in symbolic or dream-like images. Before the wedding in Act II, both George and Emily have separate, sudden attacks of terror. The Stage Manager implies beforehand that these moments ought not to be taken as having literally occurred as depicted. They are essentially subconscious or semiconscious internal conflicts that are given utterance by the characters themselves. George's moment of turmoil is clearly meant to be perceived as subconscious since, after confiding to his mother his fear of growing old and his desire just "to be a fella" (74), he "comes to himself and looks over the scene" (74), telling Mrs. Gibbs, who has expressed consternation at his behavior: "Cheer up, Ma. I'm getting married" (74). Emily, on the other hand, appears to be fully conscious of her thoughts—and her surroundings—as she speaks. She calls her father to her as she comes to the head of the aisle, pleading with him to take her away somewhere where they can live together. He calms her fears and calls George over to take her hands and reassure her as well. Although these incidents may not have occurred "in reality" at George and Emily's wedding, they are presented in a wholly naturalistic manner in the play. Not only does Wilder have the young couple *report* their feelings and thoughts rather than dramatizing them directly in dream-like images and actions, but he lets the parents hear the sentiments voiced by the pair and react to them as they would in reality—with alarm, surprise, and concern.

In one of the "three-minute" plays, *Mozart and the Gray Steward* (*ATW* 117–25), there does occur a brief dream, which is fully dramatized and even stageable. However, the episode does not, of itself, permit the play to qualify as a truly Strindbergian or expressionistic dream play. It is strongly implied in the play that the dream is, in fact, a message to the dying Mozart from an external spiritual agency, and not a creation or projection of his own psyche. Taking the form of a conversation between the composer and the Gray Steward, who has just brought him the Count von Walsegg's commission for a Requiem Mass and who now reveals himself to be none other than Death, this dream has more in common with the dreams depicted in such plays as Goethe's *Egmont* and Shakespeare's *Richard III* than with such expressionist dramas as Toller's *Masse-Mensch* or *Die Wandlung*, Ivan Goll's *Methusalem*, or even Connelly and Kaufman's *Beggar on Horseback*. In fact, the infrequency with which actual dreams occur in Wilder's dramatic works is one indication of the distance separating him from the true expressionists.

In at least a portion of the late play *Childhood* (1960), on the other hand, the playwright produces something resembling a dream play, although again it is not an especially "expressionistic" one. The section in question is explicitly termed a dream, but it is actually a waking fantasy. The play begins realistically, with the children of an unnamed, average, middle-class family trying to determine what game to play and eventually settling on a perennial favorite, in which they make believe that they have recently been orphaned. However, before they are able to begin, their father returns home from work and they scatter. Their mother tells her husband of the children's morbid obsession with death and their fondness for imagining themselves parentless. After his wife goes back inside to finish preparing dinner, the father wishes out loud that he could, just once, be an invisible witness at his children's games. As the "game, which is a dream" (79) begins, the children return, but their father does not see them and moves into the house, calling their names. After an imaginary funeral, which is attended by the mother, who wears a long veil, the children decide to set out on an imaginary journey, but they are joined by their father and mother, who assume the roles of bus driver and passenger, respectively. The children guardedly, and with some curiosity, accept the adults as guides and companions on this make-believe world tour. The journey itself occupies the rest of the play and, in typical Wilderian style, it is conjured up through dialogue alone, while the characters remain stationary on low chairs arranged to suggest a vehicle. The family thus travels to distant, imaginary lands, passes through dire perils, and eventually finds its way home again. After the three children take leave of their adult companions, the game ends and the action shifts from the dream mode back into that of ordinary reality, with the realistic action recommencing at approximately the point where it left off.

The dramatist never really resolves the question of whose "dream" the game (comprising the funeral service and journey) is. The father has expressed a wish to participate unseen in his children's games, but it is unlikely that the entire dream transpires in his imagination since he does not appear at the make-believe "funeral service" held for him and his wife; moreover, the dream quality of the entire game is indicated by the playwright's device of having the children run on stage, invisible to their father, as he strolls off into the house, calling them. None of the other characters appears to be the controlling force behind the dream-game, either. It seems to have none, in fact. Even the playwright remains a relatively neutral—in fact, nearly impalpable—presence.

Indeed, it is this authorial "objectivity" that ultimately is responsible for the gulf separating the play, despite its incorporation of an actual dream sequence, from expressionist practices and impulses. The expressionist "dream play" was modeled on the Strindbergian prototype, and the Swedish master's definition of the genre he invented provides a cogent indication of the extent to which the dream passage in Wilder's play diverges from expressionist concepts. In his "Author's Note" on *A Dream Play*, Strindberg describes his aims and methods in the following terms:

> the Author has sought to reproduce the disconnected but apparently logical form of a dream. Anything can happen; everything is possible and probable. Time and space do not exist; on a slight groundwork of reality, imagination spins and weaves new patterns made up of memories, experiences, unfettered fancies, absurdities, and improvisations.
>
> The characters are split, double, and multiply; they evaporate, crystallise, scatter and converge. But a single consciousness holds sway over them all—that of the

dreamer. For him there are no secrets, no incongruities, no scruples, and no law. He neither condemns nor acquits, but only relates. (193)

Very little, if any, of all this is perceptible in Wilder's "dream play." The action of the game is fluid and logical and not at all disconnected; except for the nonrealistic transitional passages, the dream is an unswervingly realistic depiction of a typical children's game. True, it involves fantasy and improvisation, but the dream is presented as it would appear to the average observer's waking consciousness, with both the adult participants and their children behaving precisely as they would if the game were really taking place as depicted. Time and space are not abolished except in the characters' imaginations, and the characters at no time "split, double, . . . evaporate, . . . [or] converge," except in their assumption of fictional roles in the game, a feature owing much more to Pirandello than to Strindberg. Wilder's authorial objectivity or neutrality seems at first to resemble the dreamer's attitude described in the last two sentences of Strindberg's note, but the subjective freedom and moral impartiality to which the latter playwright is referring are very different from the sort of naturalistic "invisibility" practiced by Wilder in this play. The emphasis placed in Strindberg's note on the paramount role played in a dream play by the dreamer's consciousness inherently implies the active *involvement* and *presence* of the dramatist in such a work.

On the other hand, one particular "dream play" technique, the compression and even reversal of time, is liberally used by Wilder in many of his plays. One of the ways in which Strindberg abolishes time in *A Dream Play* is by requiring one character, an officer, to experience an accelerated aging process in the course of a few brief scenes, during each of which he is shown holding a bouquet of flowers while awaiting the arrival of his beloved. He is the only character in these scenes to age so rapidly, but the entire device is, of course, strikingly reminiscent of the technique employed by Wilder in *The Long Christmas Dinner*. However, Wilder's treatment of time in his plays differs subtly but significantly from Strindberg's treatment of it in *A Dream Play*, as well as from the treatment one encounters in actual dreams. For Wilder, time generally does exist and make its presence felt. Its inexorable advance gives poignancy to *The Long Christmas Dinner*, and even in *Pullman Car Hiawatha* and *The Happy Journey*, where it is condensed, it flows continuously in a single direction. Strindberg's officer regains his youth in his final appearance in *A Dream Play*. Even in *Our Town*, where the playwright and/or Stage Manager freely reverse time or "fast-forward" it, one of Emily's chief complaints when she relives her twelfth birthday is that "It goes so fast" (100). Furthermore, this particular device of compressing or accelerating time is not a common feature in expressionist drama proper. It is more frequently met with in futurist theatre pieces and will therefore be examined more fully in the next chapter.

Apart from the passage at the end of *The Skin of Our Teeth*, then, there is no clear-cut instance in Wilder's plays of an expressionistic monodrama or even a true expressionistic dream play. Rarely does the principle of subjectivism underlie the form or technique of Wilder's drama. *Our Century*, a short "occasional" piece written in 1947 for the one hundredth anniversary of the Century Association of New York (of which Wilder was a member) is an exception. It consists of three short scenes depicting the amusingly distorted or stereotyped impressions of the association held by the members' families and other outsiders. The contrasting subjective points of view are more of a "gimmick," however, than an indication of expressionist leanings on the playwright's part. In any case, the entire piece is more a clever skit than a true, serious work that should be included in Wilder's dramatic canon. In the dramatist's major plays, the subjectivist element is all but nonexistent.

One might interpret as a form of subjectivism the implication in Wilder's plays that the individual can, to a certain extent, conquer the immensity of the cosmos by realizing that much if not all of that immensity can be encompassed within the imagination. Strangely, a passage by Schopenhauer, in which the philosopher asserts that the "vastness of the world" is merely an idea in the great cosmic mind, of which all individuals are fragments, provides support for this interpretation. Schopenhauer's essentially romantic thought, as Sokel notes (24–28), influenced the expressionists (as well as the symbolists and the naturalists), and his examination of this problem constitutes a useful third reference point with which to assess Wilder's exact position in this matter and its relationship to the expressionist ethos. Schopenhauer writes:

> If we lose ourselves in the contemplation of the infinite greatness of the universe in space and time, meditate on the thousands of years that are past or to come, or if the heavens at night actually bring before our eyes innumerable worlds and so force upon our consciousness the immensity of the universe, we feel ourselves dwindle to nothing; as individuals, as living bodies, as transient phenomena of will, we feel ourselves pass away and vanish into nothing like drops in the ocean. But at once there rises against this ghost of our own nothingness, against such lying impossibility, the immediate consciousness that all these worlds exist only as our idea, only as modifications of the eternal subject of pure knowing, which we find ourselves to be as soon as we forget our individuality, and which is the necessary supporter of all worlds and all times the condition of their possibility. The vastness of the world which disquieted us before, rests now in us; our dependence upon it is annulled by its dependence upon us. All this, however, does not come at once into reflection, but shows itself merely as the felt consciousness that in some sense or other (which philosophy alone can explain) we are one with the world, and therefore not oppressed but exalted by its immensity. (133)

Although Wilder, too, usually seeks to portray the individual as exalted rather than oppressed or diminished by the immensity of the cosmos, he never tries to abolish or resolve the tension between that immensity and individual finitude, as Schopenhauer does here, by characterizing time and space as mere notions in or functions of the individual beholder's mind—even at the transpersonal level. It is true that several seemingly unrelated elements in *Our Town*, when scrutinized together, seem to indicate that the dramatist is precisely echoing the philosopher in that play. In the address on the Jane Crofut letter, Wilder does present the cosmos as an idea of the "eternal subject of pure knowing"; and in the Act III assertion that the individual's identity ultimately fades away after death, the playwright implies that the core of every human being is a fragment of that "eternal subject." However, the entire play, and especially Emily's anguish in the last act, demonstrates how difficult it is for mortals to forget their individuality, as Schopenhauer would have them do, at least while they are alive or recently dead, and to sense their unconscious connection with all creation.

The expressionists, for their part, rarely concern themselves with Wilder's pet problem of the relationship between the individual and the immensities. However, one of the most common motifs in expressionist plays is the sundering or collapse of the rear wall of the set, an event that reveals either a vast landscape or the limitless expanse of the night sky.[5] This revealed vista clearly symbolizes the new possibilities beckoning to the protagonist after he or she has broken out of the stifling prison of stale convention, and the motif thus presents the physical immensity of the universe as a reflection of elements within the consciousness of the individual, if not as, in itself, a dimension of that consciousness.

If Wilder's use of the subjectivistic expressionist forms of the dream play and monodrama is limited, the structural resemblances between certain of his plays and the other characteristic expressionist dramatic forms are only slightly less so. True, his quartet of "journey plays," *The Flight into Egypt*, *Pullman Car Hiawatha*, *The Happy Journey*, and *Childhood*, exhibit a strong likeness to the Strindbergian dream plays, such as *To Damascus*, and to expressionist "*stationendramen*" or "stations dramas," such as Kaiser's *From Morn to Midnight* and Hasenclever's *Humanity*, that depict parallel physical and spiritual voyages of discovery or self-discovery. The partially symbolic nature of the journeys in *Pullman Car*, *The Happy Journey*, and *The Flight into Egypt* was pointed out in Chapter 2. In *Childhood*, the imaginary physical journey clearly parallels, symbolizes, and provides the occasion for a progression toward increased intimacy, rapport, and understanding by the family members. At the conclusion of the game, all three children take leave of the adults with the conventional comment, "I'm very glad to have met you" (84), which in the context of the play assumes added resonance. The play as a whole is strongly reminiscent of *The Happy Journey*. The inner voyage portrayed in both plays is not so much spiritual as emotional and ethical, but it does nonetheless provide, in expressionist fashion, a parallel to the physical (or, in one case, imaginary) voyage that constitutes the main external action of the play.

However, none of these four plays is truly an expressionistic or Strindbergian "stations drama." Rather than depicting a series of loosely related episodes occurring at successive stages, or "stations," of the journey, Wilder's plays present the journey in the form of a single condensed, but uninterrupted, flow. This technique is strikingly similar to that employed in a 1920 futurist dramatic piece (see Chapter 5), but it has little in common with expressionist practices. Even *Pullman Car*, which at times exhibits a kaleidoscopic structure similar to that found in numerous expressionist plays, portrays a steady forward movement on the journey, with incidents dovetailing smoothly into one another even as the focus leaps from one sphere to another (from the terrestrial to the astronomical to the chronometric). Even the comments of the Stage Manager assist in establishing continuity more than they serve to disrupt it.

In fact, markedly disjointed, expressionist-style episodic structure is, if not nonexistent in Wilder's plays, at any rate rarely encountered. His disregard for linear anecdote or intrigue (which was not so categorical as one might suppose, as *The Matchmaker* attests) never quite leads him into the splintered form that characterizes most European expressionist drama. In this respect, his expressionist tendencies, such as they are, have an American air about them. *Our Town* might, at first glance, appear to be an exception to this generalization, but upon closer examination it may be found that the structure or much of Acts I and II, which seem to be thoroughly fragmented, tends more toward the static symbolist pattern than the disconnected, but still dynamic, expressionist norm. The individual scenes in Act I, while brief and not expressly linked to one another in a causal, linear succession, are knitted together more tightly than the episodes in the typical expressionist play by the steady forward progress of the day on which the events depicted all occur, as well as by the Stage Manager's transitional comments. In the play as a whole, the disruptive effect of the occasional flashbacks and interruptions by the Stage Manager (some of which actually enhance the continuity) is counteracted by the repetitions of the daily routine, which help to create a sense of predictability from act to act.

Repetition also serves to unify the structure of *The Skin of Our Teeth*. The play appears episodic in that one act does not lead directly or causally to the next. However, the repeated pattern of disaster and narrow escape—a pattern explicitly discussed by the fortuneteller Esmeralda in Act II—gives the play a form that is readily identifiable—even obvious and almost abstract. Moreover, the acts are longer structural units than the episodes in a typical expressionist play, which makes Wilder's drama appear less discontinuous than expressionist pieces. Finally, there is a continuity of mood, if not of action, from act to act. The hopeful, cooperative, earnest atmosphere at the end of the first act is carried over and expanded into the jubilant, self-congratulatory mood with which the second act begins. The decadent, frenzied, and terrifying tone at the conclusion of that act then leads smoothly into the tense, somber, yet cautiously hopeful postwar atmosphere of the third.

The Alcestiad is another play with a somewhat episodic structure, since each of its acts constitutes a more or less autonomous unit—or at least depicts an autonomous action. However, again, continuity is provided—not only by the figure of Alcestis, with her lifelong quest to know the meaning of her existence (which might have a close parallel in the quest of the protagonist in a typical expressionist monodrama or stations drama), but also by the repeated "frame" for each act, the morning rounds of the palace watchman. Once again, also, the action is presented in full-length, continuous acts, with each supposedly depicting the events of an entire day, rather than in brief expressionistic scenes or episodes. The play is, in fact, patterned after the trilogic form of Aeschylean tragedy, with each act corresponding to a single Greek play, and the relative autonomy of the individual acts is due entirely to this circumstance.

Although in their structure, then, several of Wilder's plays or portions of them partially or superficially resemble one or more of the major expressionist forms—dream play, monodrama, and stations drama—Wilder's overall conception of dramatic form is more conventional than that of the expressionists, reflecting his deep veneration of, and love for, literary and theatrical tradition. He characterized himself as "not an innovator but a rediscoverer of forgotten goods and [hopefully] a remover of obtrusive bric-a-brac" (*AC* 111). True, the expressionist stations drama is a form based on ancient theatrical tradition—the medieval German passion plays depicting Christ's progress through the stations of the Cross—but the expressionist version is a form that depicts progress as occurring in separate, distinct stages. Wilder always felt, and attempted to convey, a sense of continuity with the past, which was not for him a series of "leaps" from one plateau to the next, but rather a cycle of "eternal recurrence," in which progress occurred, if at all, in a spiral pattern. Conversely, he recognized and preserved in the form of his plays the traditional *dis*continuity between the individual and external reality, subject and object. It is these two traditional biases that prevent his dramatic works from displaying fuller formal affinities with the structurally looser, more subjectively inspired expressionist types.

On the other hand, a few of the specific theatrical techniques or devices commonly employed in expressionist drama find virtually exact counterparts in Wilder's plays, especially *The Skin of Our Teeth*. It is these devices, more than anything else, that give these plays their expressionistic flavor.

The playwright's borrowings from the expressionists' technical storehouse are, in some respects, as limited as the structural resemblances between his plays and theirs. Distortion and exaggeration, the twin pillars of the expressionist style in all the arts, are almost totally absent from all elements of Wilder's plays. Characters may be generalized, as they normally are in expressionist drama, with their ordinariness emphasized or some one quality heightened, but they are never the mere nameless ciphers or simplified types that so abound in expressionist plays. The grotesque, a stylistic element related to distortion and exaggeration and frequently found in expressionist drama, holds no place in Wilder's dramatic vision either. The naturalistic matrix of that vision militates against such fantastic deformations of material reality on any level.

Bearing these qualifications in mind, however, one can still discern a number of characteristic expressionist devices and techniques in several of Wilder's plays. The expressionist theatre, like that of the symbolists, sought to incorporate a wealth of subsidiary arts into its performances, although not necessarily to synthesize them all into a harmonious *Gesamtkunstwerk* as the symbolists wished to do. In fact, expressionist productions could easily develop into orgies of sensory assault, utilizing not only the commoner constituent arts of the theatre—scenic architecture, painting, music, dance, poetry, and the like—but also masks, puppets or animated figures, film projections, and, especially, spectacular, unusual lighting effects. The instances of comprehensive aesthetic synthesis among Wilder's plays were discussed in Chapter 2. The amalgamation in such plays as *Pullman Car* and *The Skin of Our Teeth* may be looser or more freewheeling, and therefore more expressionistic, than the symbolist ideal, but the verbal component is ordinarily paramount for Wilder, as it is for the symbolists. In the expressionist synthesis it is the visual element that dominates.

On the other hand, some typically expressionistic elements or aesthetic "languages" are identifiable within the comprehensive synthesis in some of Wilder's plays. Foremost, and perhaps most immediately obvious, among these are the novel lighting effects, especially projections. This device is confined primarily to *The Skin of Our Teeth*, the first two acts of which begin with the projection of a series of lantern slides on a screen hung in the middle of the act curtain. The slides form a sort of droll newsreel (narrated by an unseen announcer), which serves as a technique for delivering exposition, introducing the dramatis personae succinctly, efficiently, and humorously, and establishing from the outset the play's mythical-historical, "all times and all places" premise. The device of the newsreel, which has been inaccurately ascribed to the influence of Olsen and Johnson's *Hellzapoppin'*, also implies a pretense, however, (albeit flimsy, in this instance) of journalistic objectivity, which consequently requires that the slides themselves be restricted to images of relatively mundane, realistic subjects. They are not conspicuously fanciful and surrealistic, for example, as are the cinematic sequences in Ivan Goll's *Methusalem*, which depict the protagonist's dreams and include, among other things, images of the dreamer talking at a table in a restaurant to a woman who changes every minute. Instead, they are essentially naturalistic in spirit.

Other lighting effects—both in this play and in *Our Town*—may impart an expressionistic air to the scenes in which they occur, but the effect is temporary in all cases, and the link with expressionist style is tenuous in any event. Near the conclusion of Act II of *Skin*, "Strange veering lights start whirling about the stage" (205) in the darkness that heralds the approaching deluge. In *Our Town*, the lighting is employed in a more definitely "expressionistic" way on at least two occasions, when it is used either to isolate a character or to shift the focus to a certain part of the stage. Lighting is used to indicate scene changes and to direct focus in the first act of Sorge's *The Beggar* (the first genuinely expressionist play) and throughout Hasenclever's *Humanity* and the American expressionist play *Roger Bloomer*, by John Howard Lawson. In Wilder's play, during the Stage Manager's discussion of the time capsule sealed into the cornerstone of the Cartwrights' new bank, "the lights gradually dim to darkness, leaving only a spot on him" (31). In the final act, as Emily's return to life for her twelfth birthday commences, although the "stage at no time in this act has been very dark; . . . the left half of the stage gradually becomes very bright—the brightness of a crisp winter morning" (93). The change in lighting, besides indicating a new scene, emphasizes Emily's reentry into another plane of existence, just as the changes in lighting in expressionist plays accentuate mood shifts in addition to signaling changes of focus or of scene.[6] However, only in these few isolated instances does Wilder use such quasiexpressionistic lighting in his plays. On other occasions where he calls for special lighting effects, those effects—for instance, the fiery red glow offstage in Act III of *Skin* and the projected stained-glass window in the wedding scene in *Our Town*—are invariably realistic in nature. Moreover, it is difficult to justify classifying the former effects as unequivocally or exclusively expressionistic, since innovative lighting techniques have been incorporated into nearly all theatrical endeavors in the twentieth century.

Moving scenery (especially walls), another feature of numerous expressionist plays, is also incorporated into *The Skin of Our Teeth*. The flying and precariously leaning walls or flats of Act I may owe more, as critics usually assert, to *Hellzapoppin'* (which Wilder claimed never to have seen) (Goldstein 119) than to any expressionist influence, direct or indirect. However, one moment at the end of the play is strikingly similar to those in *The Beggar*, *Humanity*, August Stramm's *Awakening*, and *Roger Bloomer*, in which the back wall either divides or collapses to reveal the larger dimensions of the cosmos. In Act III of *Skin*, as Antrobus reminisces about the nights in the war when he would give the hours the names of philosophers, the back wall of the set disappears, "revealing the platform" (248) on which the people impersonating the hours are to cross the stage as they deliver their quotations. Although the procession of the Hours constitutes a somewhat different vision from the night skies and open landscapes typically revealed in the expressionist plays mentioned above, the ultimate implications of the vision remain essentially the same as those in expressionist examples of the use of the device. Moreover, "Mr. Fitzpatrick," the Stage Manager, informs the audience earlier in the act that they are to imagine the planets "singing in this scene. Saturn sings from the orchestra pit down here. The Moon is way up there. And Mars with a red lantern in his hand, stands in the aisle over there" (218). Although the singers representing these planets have been taken ill and therefore cannot appear as planned, the playwright notifies the audience, through Mr. Fitzpatrick's description, of his intention of representing symbolically, not only the hours, but the night sky as well, following the disappearance of the back wall. The quotations themselves that are read by the Hours also lead the mind from the "occurrences of daily life" (in the passage from Spinoza) to affairs of state (the passage from Plato), the attributes of God and their reflection in human beings (Aristotle), and finally to the cosmic vision of Genesis 1:1 with its evocation of heavens and earth, darkness and light.[7] Thus, the basic pattern of the expressionist device (walls sundering, disappearing, or collapsing to reveal a transcendent, cosmic vision) is followed closely in Act III of Wilder's play.

In some of Wilder's plays, one may also find the expressionist device of embodying metaphorical conceits or figures of speech in literal, concrete stage images—a device that extends at least as far back as Strindberg's *Ghost Sonata*, with its depiction of characters literally "haunted by the memory of their past sins," and which may also be found in such expressionist plays as Oskar Kokoschka's *Job* (in which the title character literally has his head turned by a young woman) and O'Neill's *All God's Chillun* (in which the walls of the protagonist's room actually begin to close in on him and his wife as the two come to feel progressively more imprisoned in their marriage). Wilder may be said to have utilized the device in *Skin*, since Mrs. Antrobus and Sabina are shown literally "setting their house in order" after the war by pulling on a rope hanging from the "ceiling" and thereby causing the fallen walls of the set to rise and move into place once again. In *The Long Christmas Dinner*, the "feast of life" is literally represented onstage, and in a comment to her mother (quoted in Chapter 2), Genevieve even explicitly makes the connection between life and the dinner. In the same play, the common phrase, "the portals of death" is given concrete, visible embodiment in the dark portal standing at stage left throughout the play. Finally, the "music of the spheres" is actually heard in *Pullman Car*, in both the nonverbal murmurings of the planets and the "orchestral" or "symphonic" passages conducted by the Stage Manager. Such examples could doubtlessly be multiplied, but these are the most immediately obvious and significant ones.

Although expressionist playwrights, in keeping with their aim of representing dreams and other self-contained, subjective experiences, rarely destroy the "fourth-wall" illusion in their plays, there are some precedents in expressionist theory and practice for Wilder's "theatricalism": his frank acknowledgement of—and insistence on the audience's recognition of—the artificial nature of the dramatic event they are witnessing. For instance, in *Methusalem*, a man in the audience at one point interrupts the play by laughing, is addressed from the stage, and leaves in a huff. The entire incident bears an unmistakable resemblance to the scene in *Our Town* in which "members of the audience" ask Editor Webb about the extent of drinking, political awareness, and "culture" in Grover's Corners. Especially reminiscent of the spectator in Goll's play is the Belligerent Man in the back of the auditorium, the spokesman for Michael Gold's faction, who, after asking why nothing is done in the town to eliminate or reduce social injustice, leaves "without waiting for an answer" (25).

It might be said that the minimalist elements in Wilder's dramaturgy (which were examined in Chapter 2) constitute almost as much of an expressionist feature as they do a symbolist one, since the expressionists too tended to eliminate particularizing or localizing details in their settings, characters, and even dialogue. However, just as his minimalism—wedded as it is to theatricalism—differs in important ways from that advocated and practiced by the symbolists, so it diverges from expressionist norms and practices at certain critical points. The expressionists placed comparatively little emphasis on pantomime, for instance, although it does appear in some of their plays. The expressionist vision generally is more grounded in phenomena and less contemplative than that of Wilder or the symbolists. Wilder's minimalism might be termed primarily *metaphoric*, since he tends to suggest objects and settings by substituting roughly comparable or similarly shaped items. The expressionists' minimalism, on the other hand, is more *synecdochic*, (with, for example, a single distorted piece of furniture conveying the nature and atmosphere of an entire room). In addition, the minimalist vision of an expressionist director such as Leopold Jessner is more architectural in essence than that of Wilder. There are no fixed, immobile flights of "*Jessnertreppen*" ("Jessner Steps"), leading from one level platform or landing to another on Wilder's bare stage. The closest he comes is the "balcony or bridge or runway" (*LCD* 49) set against the back wall of the stage, with a short flight of steps at either end descending from it to the stage floor, which is used for the "pageant" processions in both *Pullman Car Hiawatha* and *The Skin of Our Teeth*. There are also some low platforms called for in some plays—one suggests the pulpit during the wedding in *Our Town* and another represents the outlines of the automobile in *The Happy Journey*. However, all these "scenic elements" have more in common with Vsevolod Meyerhold's utilitarian, constructivist "machines for acting" than they do with Jessner's architecturally unified arrangements of steps and plateaus. Meyerhold's skeletal "jungle gyms," consisting of ladders, ropes, ramps, chutes, and a wooden framework, find a faint reflection in the ladders used to suggest the second stories of the Gibbs and Webb houses in *Our Town* and in the "ladder-like" steps descending from the Hours' balcony in *The Skin of Our Teeth.* Wilder's use of steps and platforms, then, in addition to being more limited than Jessner's, is also more austerely pragmatic.

Similarly, Wilder's bare stage is less a neutral void, like that created in a number of noteworthy expressionist productions by the suspension of black curtains on three sides of the stage, than it is a "constructivist" (or Brechtian, Pirandellian, or simply "theatricalist") machine for acting, in which the mechanics of theatrical make-believe and the workings of the dramatic imagination are themselves exposed to view.[8] On this point, the expressionists' minimalism seems close to that of the symbolists, and Wilder's, approximately equidistant from both.

The language in Wilder's plays, too, exhibits few of the traits characteristic of expressionist linguistic minimalism. There are no passages in his plays in the true expressionist "Telegram Style," wherein articles, adjectives, and conjunctions are omitted, and his dialogue is never liberally sprinkled with screams and cries, as are the expressionist pieces that led hostile critics to label the movement's dramatic style "*schreidrama*" ("scream-drama"). One exception might be *Infancy*, which could be said to contain instances of both the "Telegram Style" and the *schreidrama* technique. Understandably, the babies' limited experience condemns them to having an impoverished vocabulary and imperfect grasp of language in general. Naturally, their syntax is distorted and primitive and reduced in places to its essential components and punctuated, especially at the end, by cries and screams of frustration or terror. Examples of the elliptical "Telegram Style" include the following exchange between one of the infants and his nursemaid:

TOMMY: Wanta make a house!

MILLIE: Wants to be petted, yes!

TOMMY: (*Violently*) Wanta make a bay-bee!

MILLIE: Miss Millie's lil lover wants a little attention.

TOMMY: (*Fortissimo*) Chawclut. Chawclut. Wanta eat what you're eating. Wanta eat what you smell of . . . chawclut. (7)

The "scream-play" technique, which is hinted at in a number of passages, becomes more evident when Tommy lifts his head above the rim of his carriage and sees the policeman and the nursemaid kissing. His response is an outraged "Ya! Ya! Ya! Ya! Ya!" (9). However, within the context of the play, such language and accompanying nonverbal outbursts appear, not as distortions, compressions, or abstractions of normal speech, as they do in expressionist plays, but rather as realistic or naturalistic—if also comic—attempts to render verbally the stream of consciousness of a typical infant.

The majority of the babies' dialogue follows perfectly ordinary speech patterns, although the thoughts that are expressed tend to be jumbled.

Like his scenic minimalism and linguistic compression, Wilder's method of character drawing, while somewhat resembling that of the expressionists, nevertheless differs materially from it. One of the most striking features of expressionist drama is that its characters, with the occasional exception of the protagonist, are nameless types or abstractions, distinguished, if at all, only by their occupation or relationship to the protagonist. Wilder's characters, on the other hand, while generalized or typical, not only are almost always given names—and realistic, if commonplace, names at that, in contrast to the tongue-in-cheek generic designations used in some American expressionist plays—but also are at least rudimentarily individualized in the various ways described in the previous chapter.[9] Many of the secondary characters in *Pullman Car* are nameless, yet even some of these, such as the engineers, are given first names. The Insane Woman has a name, too, and the other passengers are, in any case, more than mere abstractions or typical representatives of their professions or social classes.

One character who rarely has a name is the Stage Manager, but an exception is the man in *Pullman Car*, who is granted that much of an identity when one of the Hours addresses him as "Mr. Washburn" (62). Even in those cases (*Our Town* and *The Happy Journey*) in which the Stage Manager remains anonymous, his anonymity is a function more of his protean nature, his ability and readiness to assume numerous roles, than of any perceptible abstract or typical quality in his character. In fact, the Stage Manager in *Our Town*, with his omniscience and contemplative bent, is far more than just a typical stage manager, although it might be difficult to say the same for his counterpart in *The Happy Journey*, who, except for one scene, simply reads the lines of other characters, without any attempt at characterization, and helps to move the automobile on and off the stage. Even "Mr. Washburn" in *Pullman Car* exhibits a protean nature rather than an abstract and typical one, since he briefly assumes other roles in the course of the play's action. Moreover, in his interference at various points in that action, he displays an impatience and eagerness that further help to define him as a distinct, autonomous individual.

The most generalized characters in Wilder's drama are the Antrobuses and Sabina in *Skin*, representing as they do all of humanity, past and present (and future). However, their universality, which is built up out of cultural and mythological "correspondences," is entirely distinct from the generalized featurelessness or anonymity of the typical expressionist character. Their multidimensionality is at the opposite pole from the abstract one-dimensionality of the subsidiary characters in the average expressionist play. The expressionist protagonist, it is true, is frequently an "Everyman" or "Everywoman" figure, but he or she is typically either an unremarkable, downtrodden victim of the status quo or a visionary outcast, and not a vigorous, "mainstream" paterfamilias identified with the Biblical Adam and Noah, like George Antrobus. In any case, in expressionist plays, the "Everyman" or "Everywoman" protagonist is the only character even to approach three-dimensionality. As if to underscore the fundamental differences separating the five major characters in *Skin* from the usual nameless expressionist types, the playwright gives four of the five (all except Gladys) *several* names and identities, including, in the case of Sabina, the name of the fictitious actress supposedly playing the role.

Wilder's "expressionism," then, lies not in a profound sympathy with the movement's fundamental premises or vision, its subjectivism and revolutionary leanings, or its visionary intensity and ecstatic religious emotionalism, but rather in certain possibly coincidental formal or structural traits that portions of some of his plays share with common expressionist dramatic types; in particular themes, motifs, and incidents in his plays that are echoed in expressionist ones; and finally, in some stylistic similarities, which are also possibly coincidental, but in any case, limited. The main impulse shared by Wilder and the expressionists—and probably the main attraction that the movement held for him—was an impulse to abandon or transcend the conventional realistic/naturalistic style that dominated the theatre of the time. That impulse, in turn, may have sprung in both cases from an urge to probe beneath surface appearances and discover and convey inner truth, an urge shared by the symbolists as well. Wilder's tendency in general, however, was to adapt expressionist dramaturgical devices, motifs, and techniques—or portions thereof —to suit the needs of his own, fundamentally different, dramatic vision, in somewhat the same manner as he used and modified naturalistic techniques to transcend naturalistic philosophy.

Not surprisingly, given the fact that Bertolt Brecht's dramaturgical roots lie in expressionism, Wilder's theatre stands in a relationship to Brecht's roughly comparable to its relationship to that of the expressionists. The resemblances are technical and stylistic rather than thematic, philosophical, or teleological, except that Wilder is even more distant philosophically from Brecht than from the expressionists. However, the two playwrights' names have frequently been linked in print as kindred spirits in matters of dramaturgy (e.g., Kuner 104, 125, 138; A. N. Wilder 17, 70–71, 77; Wixson 112–24; Papajewski 96). Moreover, Wilder's plays (especially *The Skin of Our Teeth*) were enormously popular in Germany after the war (A. N. Wilder 77–85; Frenz 123–37; Fussell 394–95)—more so even than Brecht's—a phenomenon possibly attributable to the fact that audiences there perceived Wilder's work as inspired by, or related to, that of such native but long-suppressed playwrights as Brecht and the expressionists.

Wilder certainly became aware of Brecht's work at some point, as Brecht did of his, but it is difficult to determine just when that point was or precisely how familiar with both Brecht's plays and his theories Wilder was at any given time. In all likelihood, the resemblances between the two playwrights' dramaturgical styles are the result of coincidence rather than direct influence or even shared beliefs and concerns. It is possible that Wilder and his sister, when visiting Germany in 1928, saw the original production of *The Threepenny Opera*, which opened in August of that same year, but there is no evidence in "Playgoing Nights" to support such speculation. Nor is there any record of Wilder's having attended any of the American productions of Brecht's plays during the years when he was writing his own major dramatic works (1930–1942).[10]

At one point during Brecht's years of political exile in the United States (1941–1947), the German playwright approached Wilder with a proposal that they collaborate on an English adaptation of *The Good Person of Setzuan*, an offer that Wilder declined (Esslin 78; Wixson 112). Apparently, Brecht had learned that Wilder knew German (and perhaps knew that he had lived in China as a boy), and he must have felt that the obvious parallels between their theatrical techniques made the author of *The Skin of Our Teeth* and *Our Town* a likely choice as a translator for *Good Person*. Wilder's negative response to Brecht's proposal may have been due to the fact that he was sufficiently familiar with Brecht's work and beliefs to perceive the philosophical gulf separating the two men, but it may also have been due to nothing more than a lack of available time. As far as published indications are concerned, the only indisputable piece of evidence that Wilder knew Brecht's plays, and the only indication of how he regarded them, is a footnote in a 1972 article by Douglas Charles Wixson, Jr., comparing the two playwrights. The note mentions a letter, dated 8 July 1969, from Wilder to Wixson, in which the dramatist "refers to the 'heavy, didactic hammering' of Brecht's plays" (113n), clearly with disapproval. A 1956 letter to Wilder from American director Alan Schneider contains an enthusiastic discussion of the work of the Berliner Ensemble, which Schneider had just witnessed in Europe, and the terms of the discussion imply a knowledge on Wilder's part of at least the basic gist of Brecht's theories (ts., Wilder papers, YCAL). That he was acquainted with those theories and the plays in 1956 or 1969 is no indication that he knew them while he was writing his own, though, and the extent of his familiarity with them even in 1969 remains uncertain.

Setting aside questions of "influence," however, there are striking, if largely accidental, similarities between the dramatic styles of the two playwrights. At the same time, the differences between them are equally striking and significant. In fact, a comparison of the two playwrights' works and intentions can provide a useful picture of the curious manner in which the same or similar dramaturgical devices may be made to serve two entirely different, and even diametrically opposed, purposes.

On a very general level, Wilder's and Brecht's purposes resemble one another. The aim of both dramatists' theatrical work is, broadly speaking, didactic. Brecht acknowledged, sometimes in their very titles, the didactic purpose of several of his early Marxist plays, including *The Flight of the Lindberghs*, *The Didactic Play of Baden*, and *The Mother*. Even after he came, in 1948 or so, to accept entertainment as a valid—indeed, the only valid—function of the theatre, he still conceived of true, worthwhile entertainment as inevitably possessing an instructional dimension (*BOT* 185–86). Wilder, who spent much of his life lecturing and teaching in colleges, universities, and secondary schools, had a natural urge to instruct, which he sought to inhibit in his writings with varying degrees of success. He was originally drawn to the theatre because it was "freer from the 'editorial presence' " than the novel (Parmenter 10). However, as he himself admitted in the *Paris Review* interview, his efforts to maintain an objective tone and aesthetic distance in his works are primarily attempts to counteract a didactic tendency, which is, nonetheless, still apparent in them (Goldstone, *Writers* 111). Even his most "commercially oriented" play, *The Matchmaker*, ends with the youngest character, Barnaby Tucker, pronouncing the "moral" of the story.

In "Some Thoughts on Playwrighting," Wilder justifies his inclination to use his plays as instructional vehicles by stating that the playwright must be "a born storyteller" (*AC* 118). Such an attribute consists, for him, not merely in the capacity to spin a good yarn, but, more importantly, in the instinct for "coupling . . . idea and illustration" (118). He writes:

> The myth, the parable, the fable are the fountainhead of all fiction, and in them is seen most clearly the didactic, moralizing employment of a story. Modern taste shrinks from emphasizing the central idea that hides behind the fiction, but it exists there nevertheless, supplying the unity to fantasizing, and offering a justification to what otherwise we would repudiate as mere arbitrary contrivance. (118)

Wilder's didacticism is thus, like much of his art, inextricably linked to his Neoplatonic habit of thinking.

Brecht, too, had an instinctive fondness for parable. He designated *The Good Person of Setzuan* and *The Caucasian Chalk Circle* as "parables for the theatre," and as early as 1934, he was referring to his plays in general as "parables" (*BOT* 67, 100, 130). However, the main thrust and content of Brecht's teaching contrast starkly with those of Wilder. Brecht is preaching revolution, whereas Wilder is concerned with acceptance and appreciation of everyday life and familiar things—that is to say, with acceptance and praise of what *is*.

In addition to their generally didactic aims, Wilder and Brecht share an interest in promoting the audience's imaginative participation in performances of their plays. Describing his production of *Mother Courage* at the Berliner Ensemble in 1949, Brecht wrote, "Paul Dessau's music for [the play] is not meant to be particularly easy; like the stage set, it left something to be supplied by the audience; it was up to them to link voice and melody aurally" (*BOT* 216). Analyzing in general the work of Caspar Neher, his favorite designer, he stated, "he is always content to give indications [i.e., use suggestion] wherever something 'plays no part.' At the same time these indications are stimulating. They arouse the spectator's imagination, which perfect reproduction would numb" (*BOT* 232). Wilder's interest in arousing the spectator's imagination was examined in detail in Chapter 2. In another passage, the playwright discusses the role played by convention in the theatrical art, and refers to the vital and arresting quality of the *Medea* as performed in its original setting in the ancient Greek theatre. He remarks:

For the Greeks . . . there was no pretense that Medea was on the stage. The mask, the [symbolic] costume, the [distorted] mode of declamation were a series of signs which the spectator interpreted and reassembled in his own mind. Medea was being re-created within the imagination of each of the spectators. (*AC* 123)

In his own plays, of course, Wilder uses conventions involving suggestion—of objects, settings, and (in *The Long Christmas Dinner*) personal characteristics such as age—to elicit this same imaginative participation from his audiences. Despite this similar concern on the part of both Brecht and Wilder, however, there is at least one intriguing difference between their methods. Brecht restricts his use of suggestion to music and settings, noting explicitly in his theoretical writings that the properties for his plays need to be real, since "here the audience's imagination can add nothing" (*BOT* 219–20). For Wilder, suggestion—including the actor's suggestion of objects through pantomime—has a Platonic function in addition to its task of stimulating the audience's imagination, whereas for Brecht, who was ever the materialist, "The truth is concrete."[11] Thus, an apparently minor difference between the two dramatists is actually based on a profound disagreement between their respective outlooks.

A somewhat Brechtian aura is imparted to certain of Wilder's plays, notably *Our Town* and *The Skin of Our Teeth*, by a similarly minor element, the announcement that audience members are free to smoke in the lobby, if they wish, during intermissions or other unavoidable pauses in the action. Although these invitations to smoke help to create a relaxed atmosphere in the theatre, such as Brecht wished to establish, the German playwright also wanted the spectators to be free to smoke in the auditorium itself during the performance, as were the patrons at sporting events.[12] The difference is again a minor one, but it does illustrate the contrast between Brecht's ever-present desire to alter existing conditions and Wilder's readiness to accept and defer to traditional practices.

Finally, the most important and obvious similarity between Brecht's and Wilder's theatres is the common "theatricalist" bias that both playwrights share. Both dramatists seek to destroy the illusion that what is being presented on stage is a fragment of reality—whether "inner" or "outer." Many of the "theatricalist" or anti-illusionistic devices that Wilder employs in his plays—direct address, visible scene shifts, a bare stage with visible rear wall, interruptions of the action, and the temporary metamorphosis of certain characters without the benefit of makeup or costume change—are identical or nearly identical to "alienation effects" utilized by Brecht in his work. However, there the resemblances end. Each playwright applies this theatricalism or presentationalism to ends diametrically opposed to the other's. Wilder seeks to destroy the theatrical illusion in order, paradoxically, to facilitate the spectator's "belief" in the truths underlying the events depicted. His objections to the naturalistic theatre include the fact that, in his opinion, "You don't have to pay deeply from your heart's participation" (*AC* 108) in the drama.

Although Brecht also, naturally, wishes his audiences to "believe" in the fundamental truths that his stories illustrate, he is staunchly opposed to making them "pay deeply from [their] heart's participation" in the story. Indeed, with a few important qualifications, he wants to minimize that participation, albeit without eliminating it altogether.[13]

In fact, Wilder's attempt to increase empathy or belief by destroying the theatrical illusion occasionally causes him problems, since it can lead him to work at cross-purposes, especially in *The Skin of Our Teeth*. In the play's second act, immediately prior to the Antrobuses' arrival on stage in the scene on the boardwalk, the fortuneteller Esmeralda tells the audience, "They're coming—the Antrobuses. Keck. Your hope. Your despair. Your selves" (174). Thus, an anti-illusionistic, "alienating" device, direct address, is employed by Wilder to induce his audience to identify themselves with the central characters in the drama, a response Brecht generally sought to avoid at all costs.[14] Direct address, it is true—in the form of asides, prologues, epilogues, and the like—has been used throughout history to draw audiences into the action of a play, so the device itself is not expressly, or even primarily, Brechtian. Brecht himself recognized that alienation effects could be used for purposes other than his own. In the "Little Organon for the Theatre," his most comprehensive theoretical statement, he writes that the masks of the classical and medieval theatres and the musical and pantomimic "alienation effects" of the Asian theatre "were certainly a barrier to empathy, and yet this technique owed more, not less, to hypnotic suggestion than do those by which empathy is achieved. The social aims of these old devices were entirely different from our own" (*BOT* 192). However, the fortuneteller's statement is an appeal for the spectators to *identify* themselves with the Antrobuses, which is an unlikely result given the distancing device she employs. It is with the *speaker* of an aside that a spectator will be likely to feel empathy, if at all. The awkwardness of the moment may not, it is true, be due to Wilder's un-Brechtian use of a Brechtian technique. Instead, the feeling of clumsiness may be the result of the gypsy's melodramatic diction or the playwright's heavy-handed statement of his intention. In either case, though, the passage serves to show the gulf that separates the basic aims of Wilder the dramatist from those of Brecht.

The first act of *Skin* contains an equally un-Brechtian, and even more maladroit, use of a closely related alienation technique. Wilder takes great pains in the act to undermine the audience's emotional involvement in the "story" being told and to inhibit its ability to empathize with the mythic-archetypal characters. The spectator is confronted with scenic "accidents," missed cues, actors dropping out of character, cartoon-style makeup, and compound anachronisms—a veritable barrage of reminders, in fact, that the only "reality" he or she is witnessing is the reality of a theatrical performance. At the end of the act, however, as the actors are feverishly building up the fire in an effort to stave off the deadly cold accompanying the advancing wall of ice, Sabina "comes down to the footlights and addresses the audience" (159), saying: "Will you please start handing up your chairs? We'll need everything for this fire. Save the human race.—Ushers, will you pass the chairs up here?" (159). As the "Ushers rush down the aisles with chairs and hand them over" (159), the act ends with Sabina's line: "Pass up your chairs, everybody. Save the human race" (160).

Wilder appears to be working at cross-purposes here. The distance between audience and characters created by the "alienation" devices is substantially reduced by the action preceding and accompanying Sabina's appeals. Henry's struggles to stay awake and recall the multiplication tables, Gladys and her mother's recitation of the first verse of Genesis, and the refugees' soft singing in the background are plainly intended to draw the spectators into the characters' predicament. However, the fire itself is imaginary, and the notion that the spectators' contribution of a few hundred chairs will indeed "Save the human race" is blatantly absurd. Moreover, the dramatist reminds the audience, in the very moment of Sabina's asking for its chairs, that the entire crisis is a fiction. If his purpose is merely facetious—if he intends simply to wink at the audience as he cleverly juggles with ideas of "illusion" and "reality"—then he is undermining the stirring mood he himself has sought to create, along with the possibility that the spectators will experience any "heart's participation" in the drama (although Sabina's call is implicitly for just such a response, and for practical assistance as well). The device appears, in any case, no more than a pointless theatrical gimmick, jarring and forced, since no truly effective action on the part of the audience is possible or even, surely, expected. In this respect, the moment is far less effective theatrically, and less engaging, than those instances in, say, Tudor interludes, in which spectators are drawn into the world of the play by being asked to hold a character's bundle or purse while the character is engaged in a more important task.

In contrast to Wilder's technique, Brecht's use of such devices is always more consistent with his stated aims and with the natural tendencies and capacities of the device itself. He never asks his audience to believe and join in the world of the play but instead presents the play to them as a mirror to help clarify their perceptions of reality. His intention is to motivate them, ultimately, to alter that reality, and not to induce them to enter the world of the *play*, as Wilder asks them (tongue-in-cheek) to do. Thus, in *The Measures Taken*, the Control Chorus exhorts the audience to "Change the world, it needs it!" (*Jewish Wife* 97). Similarly, at the end of *The Exception and the Rule*, the actors in unison admonish the spectators,

> What here is common should astonish you
> What here's the rule, recognize as an abuse
> And where you have recognized an abuse
> Provide a remedy! (*Jewish Wife* 143)

The didactic, hortatory tone that the playwright uses might alienate (in the wrong sense) an otherwise neutral auditor, but at least the device of directly appealing to the spectators to take action is used in a manner consistent with Brecht's larger aims. Where, as in *Our Town*, *The Happy Journey*, and *Pullman Car Hiawatha*, Wilder refrains from attempting, even in jest, to arouse his audience to concrete, outward action but rather is content to let their participation in the theatrical event remain on a mental level, his use of "alienation effects" is more successful and, to a certain extent, more Brechtian.

At any rate, some of the more Brechtian of the anti-illusionistic devices in Wilder's plays include direct address, which Brecht uses in *The Measures Taken*, *The Exception and the Rule*, *The Good Person of Setzuan*, and several other plays; a narrator or narration that sets the scene or provides straightforward exposition, as in Brecht's *The Caucasian Chalk Circle*; and the filmed material discussed earlier in this chapter.[15] It need only be noted here, with respect to Wilder's use of slides in *The Skin of Our Teeth*, that in his predilection for "factual" rather than fanciful filmic material, he is closer to Brecht than to such expressionists as Goll. However, inasmuch as the "facts" presented in Wilder's "newsreel" are only pseudofacts, "true" only within the fictive context of the play itself, his use of pictorial projections cannot be said to have a great deal in common with Brecht's use of the same device. For *Galileo*, Caspar Neher projected maps and Renaissance documents on a screen behind the set (*BOT* 203), and in Brecht's production of *The Mother*, Neher flashed actual prices of basic foods on a screen during a scene in which the high cost of living was discussed (Esslin 133). For Brecht, then, projections—other than projections of song lyrics and titles and scene summaries—were a means of bringing the real world into an immediate relationship—either ironic or supportive—with the world of the play. They constituted a technique for presenting the audience simultaneously with two perspectives on the action, that of external reality and that of the characters themselves. In contrast, Wilder's projections in *Skin* are merely devices for giving exposition efficiently. They precede the live action on stage but do not accompany it. If they supply a second perspective on the action, it is the perspective of the Antrobuses as public figures, as opposed to the view of them as private citizens that the live action largely provides. However, Wilder does not make much of the contrast.

For Brecht, the episodic structure that he gave some of his plays was itself an alienating or distancing device as well. In Wilder's most episodic plays—*Our Town*, *The Skin of Our Teeth*, and *Pullman Car Hiawatha*—though, the American dramatist's principles of construction remain somewhat different from Brecht's. The question of the extent to which Wilder's plots can be called "episodic" in the Aristotelian (and expressionist) sense has already been treated. The short vignettes of Act I of *Our Town*, although relatively discrete, loosely linked units, do not depict complete, self-contained actions with sharply defined beginnings, middles, and ends, as do most of the scenes in Brecht's most characteristic epic works, such as *Mother Courage*, *The Good Person of Setzuan*, and *Puntila*. The drug-store scene and wedding in Act II are more "Brechtian" in this respect, as is the final scene depicting Emily's twelfth birthday. However, although these latter three scenes are all relatively autonomous units of action, they deviate from Brecht's theories (if not from his practices). Brecht wrote that he wished each scene in his epic dramas to stand on its own rather than to "make the next one" (*BOT* 37), as is the case in conventional, "Aristotelian" drama. In Wilder's play, the drug-store scene, along with the rest of Act II, prepares the way directly for the wedding scene, and Emily's reliving of her birthday grows naturally and smoothly out of the scene of her funeral and flows directly into the concluding scene on the hillside. Similarly, the vignettes that make up the bulk of *Pullman Car Hiawatha* are little more than cinematic impressions, which succeed one another seamlessly as the play flows smoothly toward its end. The one scene that constitutes a relatively complete action is the scene of Harriet's death, but the play as a whole does not proceed via discontinuous leaps, as do most of Brecht's works. In *Skin*, again, individual scenes blend seamlessly, for the most part, into full-length acts, even though on the level of dramatic action, the acts themselves are loosely connected, at best.

Both Wilder and Brecht favor a dramaturgy that minimizes the element of suspense in the plot. However, Wilder never resorts to the Brechtian device of summarizing in advance for an audience the action of a scene, even though he does have the Stage Manager in *Our Town* provide in his first monologue some information (largely irrelevant to the main action of the play) regarding the future lives (and deaths) of Dr. and Mrs. Gibbs and others. He also has the same character deliver a broad hint at the beginning of the second act concerning the subject matter of the third. In none of these passages does he actually summarize the central action to be depicted, though, as Brecht did by means of placards in his productions. It is the cyclical form common in many of Wilder's plays that weakens the suspense in those plays, and that form makes their conclusions seem predictable. Brecht, on the other hand, strove mightily to undermine his audience's sense that the endings of his dramas were fated or inevitable. He fought assiduously, at least in his theories, against the notion that human life is, or has to be, eternally and everywhere the same, with all people facing the same basic options and forced to undergo the same recurrent experiences. In fact, Brecht's plays tend to be more linear, and thus to generate *more* suspense regarding their outcomes, than do Wilder's cyclical dramas. Most of Brecht's dramatic works have fairly conventional structures, with rising actions, climaxes, and resolutions. Wilder does undermine the sense of inevitability in his plays, but his methods do nothing to destroy the "eternal" patterns established by the circular action.

Other structural resemblances between the two dramatists' works can be seen, however. Although there are no original songs incorporated into Wilder's plays, as there are in nearly all of Brecht's, the action in some of them is frequently interrupted in Brechtian fashion by the Stage Manager, who functions (in part) as narrator in two plays. In *Our Town*, of course, several of the interruptions provide the audience (and the Stage Manager himself) with the opportunity and motivation to ruminate about the larger implications of the action, which is what Brecht wished his audiences to do during the songs and other interruptions of the action in his plays. In *Pullman Car Hiawatha*, the Stage Manager breaks into the dialogue between the passengers in the berths to give the audience a chance to hear those passengers thinking; then he signals them when the thinking aloud has gone on long enough. He interrupts the scene of Harriet's death in order to initiate the consideration of the car's geographical, meteorological, astronomical, and theological positions and even interjects comments in the midst of the recitations by the Hours. In *Skin*, Sabina's asides to the audience as "Miss Somerset" break up the direct forward movement of the story, and the main action stops completely for the rehearsal of the stand-ins for the Hours, as it does for the analysis by the actor playing Henry of the reasons for his emotional identification with the character during his confrontation with Antrobus. Whatever the other effects of these various interruptions may be, though, they do not tend to induce the spectators to want to change society, nor are they evidently intended to arouse such a response.

More unequivocally "Brechtian," in any case, are those theatricalist devices in Wilder's plays that expose the mechanical workings of the theatre itself—in both the technical and the human spheres. First of all, the visible rear wall of the stage called for in *Our Town*, *The Happy Journey*, *Pullman Car Hiawatha*, and *The Skin of Our Teeth* corresponds quite closely, in nature and effect, to the visible lighting instruments used by Brecht in his productions. Even more Brechtian are the visible scene shifts employed in these same four plays. Brecht commonly used the half-height curtain in his productions to allow scene changes to remain partly visible to his audiences. In *Our Town*, two ladders are pushed on stage in the middle of the first act to represent the upper stories of the Gibbs and Webb houses, and in the second act, the scene shifts that establish Mr. Morgan's drug store and the church in which the wedding is held are both accomplished before the audience's eyes. In *The Happy Journey*, the Stage Manager pushes the family's "automobile" (a platform supporting four chairs) onstage prior to their departure from their home, and after they arrive at their destination, he removes it. In *Pullman Car*, finally, the actors carry on and arrange the chairs that are to represent their berths and compartments.

Wilder also follows, after a fashion, Brecht's recommendation that "The element of rehearsal in the acting and of learning by heart in the text" remain perceptible even in the epic actor's finished performance (*BOT* 122). Brecht meant simply that the actor in his plays, rather than seeking to appear "natural" and spontaneous in his or her role, ought to play with virtuosity, openly displaying to the audience, through the confident and fully conscious execution of difficult and unusual maneuvers, the skill, training, and hard work that have been necessary parts of the preparation for the performance. Wilder, on the other hand, actually shows a "rehearsal" on stage in the last act of *The Skin of Our Teeth* and makes manifest to the audience the element of "learning by heart in the text" by dramatizing its absence in Mrs. Antrobus's "missed cue" in the first act, which forces Sabina ("Miss Somerset") to "improvise" some remarks in character to cover the "error," a task to which she quickly finds herself unequal. In addition, the presence of a Stage Manager makes *Our Town*, *The Happy Journey*, and *Pullman Car* all seem like rehearsals of plays rather than finished performances. In *Pullman Car*, the Planets and Hours enter too soon and must be sent offstage again by "Mr. Washburn," and when they finally do appear on cue, he must request adjustments in pitch and volume from Saturn and Jupiter and changes of tempo and volume from "Miss Foster" as "Twelve O'clock." In addition, of course, he plainly and actively controls the sequence of incidents, telling the actors when they must move on to another section. In *Our Town*, not only does the Stage Manager have to act as moderator during Professor Willard's remarks, suggesting the points he ought to cover and those he ought to omit, but he also must wait for Editor Webb to appear immediately thereafter since, as Mrs. Webb reports, "He just cut his hand while he was eatin' an apple" (23).

These techniques that make visible "the element of rehearsal in the acting" do not render the plays more Brechtian, however. Rather than decreasing the sense that the action exhibited is occurring spontaneously, they increase it. Brecht, on the other hand, writes of the epic actor that "he need not pretend that the events taking place on the stage have never been rehearsed, and are now happening for the first and only time" (*BOT* 194). For his own part, Brecht advocated a style of acting in which the actor "narrates the story of his character by vivid portrayal, always knowing more than it does" (*BOT* 194). Such a style necessitated a fundamental change of attitude on the actor's part, whereby, " 'I am doing this' has become 'I did this,' and now 'he did this' has got to become 'he did this, when he might have done something else' " (*BOT* 195). Wilder, on the other hand, accepts the more traditional view, observing in "Some Thoughts on Playwrighting" that one of the primary distinguishing features of the theatrical medium is that the "action takes place in a perpetual present time" (*AC* 115, 124–25). Elsewhere he notes, "it is precisely the glory of the stage that it is always 'now' there" (108), and he objects to the naturalistic theatre on the grounds that its emphasis on the accurate representation of place thrusts the action back into the past, with the resulting implication that the characters are all dead before the story begins (108). Ironically, such "alienation" of the action by means of historical distance would undoubtedly have met with Brecht's approval, although the same cannot be said of the naturalistic style itself. Brecht wished his actors to perform as if they were merely "reporting" an action that occurred at another time and place (*BOT* 142). In contrast, the rehearsal-like quality of Wilder's plays tends, especially in *Our Town* and *The Happy Journey*, to make the performance itself, as well as the action, appear to be occurring in a "perpetual present time," as the playwright intended. Despite his opposition to the naturalistic style, Wilder's plays are themselves illusionistic in their presentation of seemingly genuine rehearsal conditions and apparently unforeseen, unrehearsed interruptions of the performance. In this respect, his theatre is closer to Pirandello's than to Brecht's (see Chapter 5).

On the other hand, one device that gives *The Happy Journey* its air of being a rehearsal has more in common than the devices already mentioned with the technique of epic acting developed by Brecht. In Wilder's play, the Stage Manager does not intervene in the action or attempt to shape it, but in addition to moving the few required properties on and off the stage, "he reads from a typescript the lines of all the minor characters. He reads them clearly, but with little attempt at characterization [except when he plays a service station attendant], scarcely troubling himself to alter his voice, even when he responds in the person of a child or woman" (101). He is, thus, merely "demonstrating" or "reporting" the words and actions of these minor characters, as Brecht might wish, without seeking to identify himself with his roles. However, when Brecht writes of "demonstrating" or "reporting" a role, he does not have in mind a style of acting that ignores or eliminates characterization entirely, but rather one in which the actor comments subtly on the character he or she is demonstrating. Nonetheless, the Stage Manager's "reporting" of his characters' words in *The Happy Journey* does constitute a rudimentary Brechtian technique for alienating the actor from his or her role. It is, in fact, a technique Brecht taught his actors to use in rehearsal (*BOT* 137–38, 241). On the other hand, all the other characters in Wilder's play are meant to be performed in the conventional way.

The device of having the Stage Manager assume different roles, with or without characterization—which is used not only in *The Happy Journey* but also in *Pullman Car Hiawatha* and *Our Town*—has itself a parallel in Brechtian practice. In *The Measures Taken*, four Communist agitators reenact (before a "Control Chorus" whose members act as judges) the story of the reasons for their execution of a young comrade who worked with them but could not keep his compassion from interfering with the demands of his work of subversion. The four telling the story don masks at the beginning of their reenactment and then divide among them—without changing costumes or masks—the roles of the young comrade, the local Communist Party leader, an overseer and two coolies, two textile workers, a trader, and a policeman.

Another, more tenuous, link is Wilder's literal depiction of some of his "actors' " attitudes toward their roles in *The Skin of Our Teeth*. In the last act, after the play has been stopped in order to prevent "Henry" from actually strangling "Antrobus," the actor playing Henry apologizes, saying:

> I don't know what comes over me. . . . It's like I had some big emptiness inside me—the emptiness of being hated and blocked at every turn. And the emptiness fills up with the one thought that you have to strike and fight and kill. Listen, it's as though you have to kill somebody else so as not to end up killing yourself. (238–39)

Antrobus shortly thereafter replies in his "own person, with self-condemnation, but cold, and proud":

> It's not wholly his fault that he wants to strangle me in this scene. It's my fault, too. He wouldn't feel that way unless there were something in me that reminded him of all that [his unhappy childhood]. He talks about an emptiness. Well, there's an emptiness in me, too. Yes,—work, work, work— that's all I do. I've ceased to *live*. No wonder he feels that anger coming over him. (240)

Significantly, however, in both cases the actor's commentary on the role concerns his near-total *identification* with the character, to the point where actor becomes *indistinguishable* from role, rather than entailing the sort of critical detachment or "alienated" perspective that Brecht wished his actors to adopt toward their characters. In Antrobus's speech, it even becomes difficult to tell whether the actor is referring to his own addiction to work or that of the character. More Brechtian, then, is "Miss Somerset's" refusal to play one scene with Antrobus in the second act because, as she explains, "there are some lines in that scene that would hurt some people's feelings and I don't think the theatre is a place where people's feelings ought to be hurt" (191). The actress's hypocrisy becomes immediately evident when, shortly thereafter, she "accidentally" quotes some of the objectionable lines in passing, but the scene remains unplayed. This method of having an "actor" comment explicitly and verbally on his or her role does not correspond to Brecht's notion of having the real actors "comment" implicitly on their roles *while "in character,"* but it does provide the audience with a quasi-Brechtian critical perspective on the characters themselves, delivered from the standpoint of the "actors" playing them. Again, the *illusion*, rather than the reality, of a critical perspective is what Wilder, in Pirandellian fashion, provides. It might almost seem as if here, as in the case of the Stage Manager in *The Happy Journey*, he borrowed (albeit unwittingly) some of Brecht's *rehearsal* techniques for alienating the actor from the role—in this case, the extended critical analysis of the role by the actor—and incorporated them directly into his own finished plays.

In keeping with their shared didactic aims, Wilder and Brecht agree to a limited extent on the immediate purpose or desired effect of all these "alienation" techniques in their plays. In Wilder's case, the devices just enumerated are designed to make the spectator look at the familiar world with new eyes, just as Brecht's alienation effects are motivated by a desire to turn "familiarity . . . into awareness" by stripping "the familiar . . . of its inconspicuousness" (*BOT* 144). However, as John Willett points out in *The Theatre of Bertolt Brecht*, Shelley, Schopenhauer, and Cocteau all perceive such estrangement of the familiar to be one of the basic functions of all art, not just the socially committed variety (177). As might be expected, the ultimate aim of Wilder's and Brecht's respective attempts to strip the familiar of its inconspicuousness—appreciation in the one case and a radical questioning of conventional wisdom in the other—could not be more different.

Given this philosophical and temperamental abyss dividing the two playwrights, it is not surprising that the major Brechtian themes and motifs are not encountered to any great extent in Wilder's plays. If there is a strong dialectical tension in Wilder's drama, as there is in Brecht's, it is not between reason and instinct or emotion (the two pillars upon which Brecht's drama is built), but rather between the individual's claim to significance and the cosmic immensity that tends to deny the claim—two poles that are not even precisely antithetical. The conflict between reason and the irrational does surface in *The Skin of Our Teeth*, in the various confrontations between Antrobus (representing rationality) and his wife and Henry (representing constructive and destructive forms of instinct or emotion, respectively), but the conflict is a secondary concern of Wilder's at best, whereas it is central to Brecht's vision, as Martin Esslin has demonstrated (19–20, 238–55). In none of Wilder's plays does one find characters who are "expressionistically" split into two opposing personalities by the force of this dialectical conflict (or any other), as are Brecht's Shen Te, Galy Gay, Sergeant "Bloody Five" Fairchild, and Puntila. Wilder's plays, like Brecht's, contain numerous impressive mother figures, perhaps the chief among them being Maggie Antrobus and Ma Kirby. However, Brecht's mothers, such as Shen Te ("The Good Person of Setzuan"), Anna Fierling ("Mother Courage"), Grusha

Vashnadze (in *The Caucasian Chalk Circle*), and Pelageya Vlassova (in *The Mother*), all exist on the periphery of the established power structure and are, in fact, forced to fight it—and fight it alone—in order satisfactorily to raise their children (who are frequently illegitimate—or illegitimately adopted). Wilder's mothers, on the other hand, remain firmly ensconced within the traditional bourgeois family structure and preserve and promote traditional bourgeois values for their children. Moreover, except for Ma Kirby (and Dolly Levi and Alcestis, who are not primarily mothers), they are not the central figures in their plays, as Brecht's mothers are in theirs.

A major cause of the thematic distance separating Wilder from Brecht is the former dramatist's conventional, bourgeois conception of both the theatre's function and humanity in general. Wilder's admiration for, and support of, middle-class values has already been demonstrated. Brecht's condemnation, as a Marxist, of those same values is abundantly evident in his writings. Wilder's traditional Christian skepticism regarding the fundamental goodness of humankind has also already been explored. He even once (apparently only half-jokingly) told an interviewer (Lewis 56) that the "message" of *The Skin of Our Teeth* was contained in Sabina's line, "We're all just as wicked as we can be, and that's the God's truth" (240). Brecht's assertion of the fundamental goodness of human beings is evident not only in *The Good Person of Setzuan*, where it is a central element, but also in his often-quoted poem about the Japanese demon-mask that hung on his wall and showed him "How great a strain it is to be evil."[16]

However, the irreconcilable differences between Wilder and Brecht can perhaps most clearly be seen in their respective conceptions of human history and the nature of human personality. In a statement quoted in Chapter 3, Wilder registers his disagreement with "These radical critics [like Michael Gold]" who view man as "solely the product of the economic order under which he lives. . . . If my characters are not starved," he contends, "if they have a little something for their stomachs, then they will be much the same in any environment" (qtd. in Simon 87). Obviously, such an assertion is diametrically opposed to Brecht's view that:

> a man will respond differently according to his circumstances and his class; [that] if he were living at another time, or in his youth, or on the darker side of life, he would infallibly give a different response, though one still determined by the same factors and like anyone else's response in that situation at that time. (*BOT* 190)

Brecht might even seem to be attacking Wilder's theatre specifically when he writes that:

> The bourgeois theatre emphasizes the timelessness of its objects. Its representation of people is bound by the alleged "eternally human." Its story is arranged in such a way as to create "universal" situations that allow Man with a capital M to express himself: man of every period and colour. All incidents are just one enormous cue,

and this cue is followed by the "eternal" response: the inevitable, usual, natural, purely human response. (*BOT* 96–97)

Brecht condemns the bourgeois theatre for being "unhistorical," an adjective that admirably fits Wilder's drama and that he would doubtlessly be pleased to see applied to it. When Wilder sets one of his plays in the past (*Our Town* or *The Matchmaker*, for example), it is usually a relatively recent past, which his audience will tend to regard with nostalgia rather than objectivity. He never seeks, as Brecht does, to use his depiction of the past as a means of making the present appear strange to his spectators. Rather, he uses it to persuade them of precisely the converse, namely, that "The human adventure is much the same in all times and all places" (Wilder, "Thoughts," 779–81, qtd. in Haberman, *Plays* 54). Nothing could be more un-Brechtian than such an assertion.

Although later in life, Wilder came to consider himself something of a "crypto-Marxian" (Harrison 351, 361, 380), nothing of these beliefs or concerns is evident in his plays. The resemblances between his theatre and Brecht's, while occasionally striking, are wholly technical and superficial, and even there, the fundamental irreconcilability of the two dramatists' *Weltanschauungen* is so deep and complete that it is reflected in their use of technical devices that are otherwise nearly identical.

NOTES

1. For instance, Driver (339). See also Fulton, Sokel (1), Goldstein (75–76), and Styan, *Expressionism* (2, 115, 165).

2. See, for instance, Kuner (104, 125, 138), A. N. Wilder (70–71) (quoting a speech by Franz H. Link), Wixson, Papajewski (96), and Oppel (discussed in A. N. Wilder, 17).

3. This very phrase serves as the title for a collection of stories by the expressionist writer Leonhard Frank, and in Ernst Toller's play *Masse-Mensch*, a debate on the same topic between the protagonist and a priest is ultimately resolved implicitly in favor of the protagonist's point of view (which is the same as Frank's), when two other characters reveal their basic decency following the protagonist's execution.

4. Although in some later expressionist plays, such as Werfel's *Mirror Man*, and other writings, such as the same author's *Not the Murderer*, the father is presented sympathetically in intergenerational confrontations, the protagonist is still the son, and the father, although portrayed with compassion and understanding, is never really admirable, as Antrobus is meant to be here.

5. Expressionist plays incorporating this motif include Hasenclever's *Humanity*, Sorge's *The Beggar*, John Howard Lawson's *Roger Bloomer*, and Stramm's *Awakening*, to name just a few.

6. For one scene change in *Methusalem*, the playwright calls for a radical alteration in the color of the illumination, from sulfurous yellow to a more realistic blue and red.

7. The passage from Plato was actually an invention of Wilder's. No such passage exists in Plato's works.

8. For instance, the black curtains were used in the most famous expressionist production ever mounted, Jürgen Fehling's 1921 staging of Toller's *Masse-Mensch*, and in Reinhardt's 1917 production of *The Beggar* at the Deutsches Theater.

9. Such generic designations include, for example, the "Zeros," "Ones," "Twos," and "Threes" in Elmer Rice's *The Adding Machine* and "Richard Roe" and his companions "Thomas" and "Harry" in Sophie Treadwell's *Machinal*.

10. These productions included stagings of *The Flight of the Lindberghs* (1931), *The Threepenny Opera* (1933), *The Yea-Sayer* (1933), *The Mother* (1935), and *Señora Carrar's Rifles* (1939—in San Francisco). List compiled by Walter Nubel, cited in Esslin (353–54).

11. A sign bearing this inscription customarily hung in Brecht's study-workroom.

12. While he was *dramaturg* at Reinhardt's Deutsches Theater (1924–1925), Brecht proposed that all Reinhardt's theatres be renamed "epic smoking theatres" (Esslin 25).

13. In 1949, Brecht wrote that the epic theatre "by no means renounces emotion, least of all the sense of justice, the urge to freedom, and righteous anger; it is so far from renouncing these that it does not even assume their presence, but tries to arouse or reinforce them. The 'attitude of criticism' which it tries to awaken in its audience cannot be passionate enough for it" (*BOT* 227).

14. He did eventually come to acknowledge that empathy, the spectator's emotional identification with one or another character on stage, was permissible in his theatre and even socially useful in certain instances (*BOT* 125, 221). Such instances were definitely rare, however. The one character in his plays with whom he thought it might be beneficial for the spectator to identify was Kattrin, the mute daughter of Mother Courage.

15. Brecht frequently referred to the narrative—as distinct from dramatic—character of his "epic" theatre.

16. This is the last line of Brecht's poem, "Die Maske des Bösen," trans. by Eric Bentley, in *The Playwright as Thinker: A Study of Drama in Modern Times* (228).

Chapter 5

A "Passion for Compression," a "Multiplication of Pretenses": Echoes of Futurism and Pirandello in Wilder's Theatre

Commentators in at least two sources (Kirby 67–68; Brockett and Findlay 530, 533) point out the intriguing and pronounced similarities between certain aspects of Wilder's dramaturgy and the theatre aesthetics of the Italian futurists, and one writer[1] even suggests a possible direct futurist influence on Wilder. However, the most arresting similarities between Wilder's work and that of the futurists are, in all likelihood, purely fortuitous. Any influence the movement had on his dramatic imagination was almost certainly indirect, transmitted to him by way of Pirandello who, although he was acquainted with the futurists' work and is known to have had a direct, if largely superficial, influence on Wilder, did not incorporate many expressly or identifiably futurist elements into his plays. In fact, although Wilder can by no stretch of the imagination be considered a true futurist, his theatre ultimately exhibits more—or more obviously—"futurist" traits than does Pirandello's. As it does with those of Brecht and the expressionists, Wilder's theatre shows striking stylistic or structural resemblances to the theatre of the futurists, despite radical differences between his and their philosophies, underlying assumptions, and basic aims.

Futurism, it is true, appropriated many ideas, beliefs, and attitudes from the French symbolists—and was, in fact, partly, a direct descendant of the earlier movement. Filippo Tommaso Marinetti, the founder and guiding spirit of futurism, had lived in Paris as a youth (Goldberg 9), lectured in Italy on the symbolists in his prefuturist days (Cary 106), translated Mallarmé into Italian even after the futurist movement had been launched (106), and incorporated the declamation of Mallarmé's late poem, "Un Coup de Dès," into a futurist performance of 1920 in which he took part (Kirby 68). However, taken as a whole, futurism possessed its own distinctive character and outlook, a character as unlike that of symbolism as it was that of expressionism. Curiously, though, it is not the symbolist or quasi-symbolist elements in futurism that one finds mirrored in Wilder's theatre, but rather those that are non- or even antisymbolist.

The actual extent of Wilder's acquaintance with the work of the futurists is unknown. He was a student in Rome, at the American Academy in 1920–1921, when the movement, although perhaps past its prime, was nonetheless still active and vigorous. Michael Kirby speculates that Wilder might have seen the futurist theatre piece, *Public Gardens*, a work that bears a partial resemblance to *The Happy Journey* and other plays by Wilder (67–68). However, such a possibility seems more than remote, given what is otherwise known of the future playwright's movements at this time. *Public Gardens* opened in Naples on September 30, 1921, by which time Wilder was in the United States, ready to assume his new teaching duties at the Lawrenceville School in New Jersey. On the other hand, it is not impossible (although nowhere recorded) that Wilder might have seen other futurist performances during his year in Rome. It is even conceivable, although somewhat unlikely, that he read or read accounts of some of the Italians' brief theatre pieces, known as *sintesi*. Again, however, there is no "hard" evidence of his having done either. The primary evidence for his exposure to these works is the startling and extremely precise resemblance between certain of his favorite technical devices and those employed by the futurists in some of their *sintesi*.

At the same time, however, his basic beliefs and aims could scarcely be more different from those of the futurists. Futurism, as the name implies, entailed an effort to break utterly with the past and with the artistic and cultural legacy it had bequeathed to the twentieth century. In his 1909 announcement of the movement's birth, "The Founding and Manifesto of Futurism," Marinetti proclaimed, "We will destroy the museums, libraries, academies of every kind" (42), and elsewhere he writes, "Our Futurist theatre jeers at Shakespeare" (127) and scoffs at "the ridiculous inanity of the old syntax inherited from Homer" (84).[2] Wilder, of course, not only invokes Shakespeare and the Greek dramatists at every turn, holding them up as hallowed precedents for his own dramaturgical experiments, but he also conveys, through the mouth of George Antrobus, his reverence for Homer, Moses, and all the past accumulated wisdom of humanity that sustains the race in its recurrent struggles. In Act I, Antrobus instructs his wife to "burn everything except Shakespeare" (124). The "futurist" Henry, with his contempt for "old books," is the enemy of all the dramatist holds sacred. The futurists themselves would doubtlessly have branded Wilder a "*passatista*"—one of the worst, in fact—using a term of opprobrium that they coined to describe the pathetic admirers of humanity's past achievements who frequented museums and libraries.[3] Although Wilder observes in the Preface to *Three Plays* that "The theatre has lagged behind the other arts in finding the 'new ways' to express how men and women think and feel in our time," he goes on to call himself "not an innovator but a rediscoverer of forgotten goods" (*AC* 111). For the futurists, innovation possessed an absolute value.

Similarly, despite their connection with symbolism, the futurists exhibited no real Platonist or Neoplatonist leanings. They were, for the most part, uncompromisingly materialistic. Indeed, their attitude toward the physical world verged on the worshipful. Marinetti coined the term "*fisicofollia*" ("matter-madness" or "physicality-madness") to denote the infatuation with objects in themselves—without reference to their function or past history or possible symbolic meanings—that he and his followers cultivated. He also described this same "madness" as "the lyrical obsession with matter" (qtd. in Cary 104).

As far as the theatre was concerned, this non- or anti-Platonist attitude was translated into a call for a theatre that was "*Autonomous, alogical, unreal*" (Marinetti 127), a theatre that, in Marinetti's conception, "will not be subject to logic, will pay no attention to photography; . . . will be *autonomous*, will resemble nothing but itself, although it will take elements from reality and combine them as its whim dictates" (127). This radical, "nonobjective" form of theatre, which has much in common with contemporary "performance art," remained largely an unattained ideal for the futurists. Most of their theatre pieces, including some of the most experimental, eccentric, or outrageous ones, convey discursive meanings of one sort or another—in many cases, intentionally. Nevertheless, the stated aim, along with the entire concept of *fisicofollia*, indicates a fundamental ideological gulf separating the Italians from Wilder. If, for example, Wilder destroys the theatrical illusion or exposes the "agreed-upon falsehoods" on which it rests—as the futurists gleefully, frequently, and imaginatively did—it is never simply for the sake of flying in the face of convention or obliterating a work's reference to an extra-theatrical reality, but rather "to enhance the one truth that is there—the truth that dictated the story, the myth" (*AC* 102). In accordance with his Platonic beliefs, Wilder considers plays inescapably to have a significative dimension. In this respect, he is clearly an anti-Marinettian.

Marinetti even went so far, in his search for "meaninglessness," as to originate a verbal style that was known as "*parole in libertà*" or "words in freedom," which lived up to its name in its complete disregard for syntax, verb forms, and ultimately, actual words themselves. Its syntactical deformations reportedly influenced the expressionists in their development of the "Telegram Style." It resembles a primitive, artless (or undisciplined) form of stream-of-consciousness writing, except where it abandons words altogether (which it frequently does) and becomes a cascade of proto-Dada nonsense syllables or "sound language," wholly devoid of discursive meaning. Such self-referential "language," needless to say, lies entirely outside Wilder's dramaturgical idiom.

He does, it is true, exhibit a regard for the phenomenal world in his efforts to increase his audiences' awareness and appreciation of the objects and natural wonders around them. Moreover, at least one of his techniques for accomplishing this goal, the personification of material phenomena, is closely related to futurist practices that were directed toward a roughly equivalent end. The futurists' *fisicofollia* often manifested itself in the *sintesi* in a fondness for the personification, or at least the animation, of inanimate objects. For example, Marinetti's *sintesi*, *They Are Coming* (termed by the author a "drama of objects"), ends with the exit of nine chairs from the stage, apparently under their own power; and the furniture in another piece, *The Little Theatre of Love*, speaks, relating information about the weather, the offstage doings of human beings, and its own condition. Similarly, a 1914 futurist performance piece titled *Printing Press* involved nothing more than the simulation by the performers of the movements of the various components of a rotary printing press. A short ballet performed in 1925 depicted *The Love of Two Locomotives for the Stationmaster*, the locomotives being played by two dancers in costumes composed mainly of cardboard (or metallic) cylinders that completely obscured the body and head (Kirby 92–94).

As the last two examples indicate, the material objects most likely to be personified or brought to life by the futurists (preoccupied as they were with modernity and the future) were machines, and especially machines that moved. In pointed contrast to both the symbolists and the expressionists, the futurists enthusiastically embraced the machine age. In an often-quoted passage from the "Founding and Manifesto of Futurism," Marinetti argues that "A racing car whose hood is adorned with great pipes, like serpents of explosive breath—a roaring car that seems to ride on grapeshot—is more beautiful than the *Victory of Samothrace*" (41). One of the hallmarks of futurist art is an admiring fascination with machines, and perhaps the single most characteristic feature of futurist painting and sculpture is the artist's attempt to communicate a sense of motion via an inherently solid, immobile medium.[4] This latter feature constitutes one of the most important and striking points of intersection between Wilder's theatre and futurist aesthetics, but Wilder reveals in his writings no infatuation with machines themselves. If, in order to convey a sense of the wonders of the physical universe, he animates or personifies inanimate objects or entities, those objects or entities are either natural features of the landscape (the marsh in *Childe Roland* and the field in *Pullman Car Hiawatha*) or human communities (the towns in *Pullman Car*). Furthermore, the futurists, rather than characterizing inanimate objects anthropomorphically, as Wilder does in *Pullman Car*, tend to lean in the opposite direction, favoring the animation of such objects by means of dehumanized, mechanized, or "objectified" human performers.

Wilder is also sharply at odds with the futurists on a number of more serious issues. The acknowledged aim of much futurist poetry, for example—especially that of Marinetti himself—and other futurist art was the chauvinistic glorification of the Italian spirit, particularly as it was revealed in war, which Marinetti termed "Futurism intensified" (123) and "the world's only hygiene" (42). Many of the movement's leading figures—notably Marinetti, the painter and sculptor Umberto Boccioni, and the painter Luigi Russolo—enlisted and fought enthusiastically in World War I, and nearly all those who remained in the movement in its later years—or remained under the influence of Marinetti—became ardent Fascists in the 1920s (Cary 100; Kirby 4). In keeping with this aggressive, masculine orientation, the movement also adopted an attitude of undisguised misogyny and scorn for conventional romantic love.[5] Wilder, for his part, is far from advocating a narrow, aggressive nationalism, despite his admiration and love for his native land, and indeed looks forward to an imminent epoch of "world literature" and global consciousness. Although he may accept war as a necessary evil, and although he himself enlisted in World War II, he by no means seeks to glorify armed conflict. Finally, far from exhibiting disdain for women, Wilder for the most part admires them, as is evident in the passage in *Skin* in which Mrs. Antrobus, preparatory to throwing her letter into the sea, sets the record straight on the subject of women and calls down a curse on any man who would harm them. In *Our Town*, too, the Stage Manager reminds the audience of the strength, diligence, and dedication of Mrs. Gibbs and Mrs. Webb who, like countless other late-Victorian–era women, cooked and cleaned for their families day in and day out without a word of complaint. Last, Wilder unequivocally idealizes romantic love in the drug-store scene of the same play and, to some extent, in *The Matchmaker* as well.

Given the profound differences separating Wilder and the futurists, which are even sharper in some instances than those dividing him from Brecht, it is all the more remarkable that the resemblances between his theatre and theirs should be so pronounced and distinct. However, these resemblances all reflect three basic impulses or tendencies shared by Wilder and the Italians: a fondness for the radical compression of time and space, a penchant for exposing and emphasizing the artificiality of theatrical conventions and the theatrical medium itself, and a related interest in the simultaneous, side-by-side juxtaposition on stage of physically separated locales. The first of these tendencies is the most readily apparent and significant of the three.

The futurists' interest in the acceleration or compression of time follows naturally from their glorification of dynamism and forward motion in general, a function, in turn, of their orientation toward the future. Wilder first acknowledged his "passion for compression" in the Foreword to *The Angel That Troubled the Waters and Other Plays* (*AC* 96). Indeed, their brevity causes the "three-minute" plays to resemble, in a general way, the futurist *sintesi*, few of which were as long as five minutes in performance. However, the subject matter with which Wilder's playlets deal bears little relation to futurist concerns, and the *sintesi*, for their part, are nearly all designed for live performance, as Wilder's little pieces are not.

Wilder's compression of time and space in such plays as *The Flight into Egypt*, *Hast Thou Considered My Servant Job?* *The Happy Journey*, *The Long Christmas Dinner*, *Pullman Car Hiawatha*, *The Skin of Our Teeth*, and *The Alcestiad* has been discussed in Chapters 3 and 4. However, there are uncanny resemblances between some of these plays and certain specific futurist *sintesi*, and the analogies, therefore, deserve extended comment here. First, the parallels between *The Long Christmas Dinner* and at least one *sintesi*, *Sempronio's Lunch*, are astonishing. The title character in the Italian piece is shown consuming, at different ages and in different places, what appear to be the courses of a single meal. Each course is served in a different setting by a different servant or attendant, but each has been ordered by Sempronio during the preceding scene. The courses—soup, boiled meat, a roast with vegetables, fruit, and coffee—follow one another in apparently unbroken succession and in the same order as would be followed in a single meal. Each brief scene, which shows Sempronio at a certain age and in a certain place eating a certain course, is separated from the next by a period of darkness. In this manner, the character's life, from age five to age ninety, and his global peregrinations, which take him from his childhood home to a restaurant, an African plantation, and a Parisian cabaret, are compressed into less than five minutes of stage time. Except for its changes of setting and periods of darkness between scenes, the futurist piece strikingly prefigures Wilder's play in its use of what seems to be a single, continuous meal as an accompaniment to and symbolic reflection of the accelerated, "time-lapse" passage of nearly ninety years. *Sempronio's Lunch* could almost be regarded as a preliminary sketch or study for *The Long Christmas Dinner*. The same could be said of two other *sintesi* as well, *Education* and *Old Age* (or *Passéism*), both of which, like Wilder's play, make use of repeated dialogue in order to indicate in accelerated fashion the passage of many years. In the former piece, a professor is shown at ages thirty, forty, and sixty delivering, in a progressively more bored and mechanical manner, the opening sentence of the same lecture on Dante. The brief individual tableaus making up the piece are separated from one another by several seconds of either silence or darkness, and in the last one, the lecture is finally interrupted by a student who asks, "Why?" The entire work emphasizes not so much the repetitive, cyclical passage of the years, however, as the poverty of imagination characteristic of those *passatistas* or "passéists" whose unreflecting veneration of "classics" causes them to resemble broken phonograph records. A similar technique is used in *Old Age* (or *Passéism*) (*Passatismo*), in which an old couple is shown repeating exactly the same banal conversation on three separate dates, which are mentioned in the dialogue: January 10, 1860; January 10, 1880; and the same day in 1910. Each of the "acts" is separated from the others by darkness, to indicate the passage of time, and only the mention of the date in each one reveals the amount of time represented by the darkness.

Wilder condenses both time and space in such "journey" plays as *The Happy Journey*, *Pullman Car Hiawatha*, and *The Flight into Egypt*. Although there is among the *sintesi* no exact equivalent to the technique used by Wilder for compressing space in these plays, his attempt to represent forward motion in an essentially static medium is in harmony with the futurist spirit, as expressed in futurist paintings and sculpture, and there is one case in which the Italians employ a technique almost identical to Wilder's for representing motion. In *Public Gardens*, in the midst of various unrelated actions, five actors pretend to be in a car and indicate through pantomime and appropriate sounds that they are taking a ride. The resemblance to *The Happy Journey*—and, by extension, to *Pullman Car Hiawatha* and *Childhood*—is obvious, and it is not difficult to see why Michael Kirby should have suspected that Wilder saw the piece.

However, as was indicated above, the compression of time and space in the futurist *sintesi* is rarely assigned a larger significance, as it is in Wilder's plays. *Sempronio's Lunch* makes no statement regarding the swiftness or poignancy of time's flight—outside of an implied assertion that it is indeed swift—nor any comment about either the extent of Sempronio's awareness of his condition or the need for him to be aware of it. The work is, for the most part, a purely formal construction, an elegant stunt or tour de force, although its technique alone causes it—perhaps unintentionally—to convey a sense of the poignancy of the human condition. Nor does either *Education* or *Old Age* make a coherent statement about time. Instead, both simply reveal the boredom inherent in the values and existence of the "passéist."

In Wilder's plays, on the other hand, the compression of time and space is consciously used to imply a number of other ideas: the difficulty of realizing and appreciating life and loved ones while one is alive, the poignancy of human mortality, and, conversely, the ability of the individual imagination to transcend spatial and temporal limitations and thus to experience a connection with far-flung lands and peoples of the past, present, and future. Repetition is used by Wilder not to convey a sense of the sterility or banality of ordinary life, but rather to suggest the universality of the repeated actions and perceptions and, ultimately, the common, eternal ties binding all humanity together.

Like Wilder's penchant for compressing time and space, his predilection for shattering the stage illusion, which is the second major similarity between his theatre and that of the futurists, has been examined in previous chapters (especially in Chapter 4). For the futurists, the destruction of the theatrical illusion was simply one small prong of their assault on all ossified, effete conventions in modern culture and society. Their methods of achieving that destruction include not only direct address (which Wilder also employs, of course), but also a multitude of techniques aimed at involving the audience directly in the "action" on stage. Marinetti writes enthusiastically of the ability of music halls, circuses, and other forms of popular entertainment to evoke

> the audience's collaboration. It [the audience] doesn't remain static like a stupid *voyeur*, but joins noisily in the action, in the singing, accompanying the orchestra, communicating with the actors in surprising actions and bizarre dialogues. (118)

In a later manifesto, too, he advocates eliminating "THE PRECONCEPTION OF THE FOOTLIGHTS BY THROWING NETS OF SENSATION BETWEEN STAGE AND AUDIENCE; THE STAGE ACTION WILL INVADE THE ORCHESTRA SEATS, THE AUDIENCE" (128). He even proposes directly provocative measures, such as selling the same seat to several patrons in order to spark fights, spreading glue on some seats, and sprinkling sneezing or itching powders throughout various parts of the auditorium. Indeed, the relationship between the futurists and their audiences was, from the earliest days, a mutually antagonistic one. The futurists themselves were commonly pelted with vegetables and other missiles hurled from the house when they recited their poetry.

In their *sintesi*, the futurists employ a host of devices designed to provoke a less perilous or sadistic form of audience participation. A favorite technique for destroying the theatrical illusion was to eliminate the physical separation between audience and action by allowing the latter to move into the auditorium or "penetrate" the audience's traditional sovereign territory. *Sintesi* frequently require that performers be scattered throughout the house pretending to be spectators. For example, one piece consists of nothing but repeated calls for "Lights!" by a group of such performers sitting in the darkened auditorium, in an attempt to induce the real spectators to join them in their demand. In Marinetti's *The Great Remedy*, the central character leaves the stage at one point and passes before the first row of spectators, so close to them that she may "almost graze" them with her hands. The dramatist stipulates that the first row is to be "occupied by very beautiful women, abundantly decolleté" (qtd. in Kirby 48), who were apparently performers rather than actual spectators.

More subtle, complex techniques of audience involvement were used as well. For example, one piece is set in a hospital and begins as a wholly realistic slice of life. A patient with an injured arm and leg is revealed discussing with his mother and the doctor his present condition and the prospects for his recovery. Suddenly, the patient, who has been staring fixedly at one spectator for a long time, drops out of character and shouts that the man in the audience is the murderer of the actor's brother. He tries to leap from the stage, is restrained by the other actors and stagehands, and is carried away by force as the Stage Director enters and calls for the curtain to be lowered. Finally, the patient returns, humbly confesses he was mistaken, and apologizes to the entire audience for interrupting the performance, which he declares will begin again immediately. Such Pirandellian goings-on point the way, not only to the master himself, but also to his American disciple, Wilder.

The most "futurist" of the latter's anti-illusionistic practices are, in fact, his experiments with the "penetration" of the audience's space by the actors. In *Our Town*, of course, several "spectators," after being invited to question Mr. Webb about life in Grover's Corners, inquire from the auditorium about the extent of drinking, awareness of social injustice, and appreciation of "culture" in the town. The introduction of counterfeit "spectators" recalls not only the passage in Goll's *Methusalem* (see Chapter 4), but also the *sintesi* in which the performers attempt to goad the spectators into calling for lights. Similarly, at the end of the wedding in Act II of Wilder's play, the bride and groom exit by running up the aisle of the theatre, and the Antrobuses leave the boardwalk in Act II of *Skin* by the same route which, in this instance, represents a pier. Also in *Skin*, at the end of Act I, the ushers run down the aisles to hand chairs up to Sabina. Moreover, the Stage Manager explains in Act III that the scene with the Hours is meant to include the planets singing from various parts of the stage and auditorium, although the scene cannot actually be performed that way. Apparently, the playwright's intentions here (although he was probably unaware of the similarity) are "futurist," even though his practices are not. *The Great Remedy* is perhaps the closest of the *sintesi* to Wilder's plays in this respect. At the same time, an unpublished note by Wilder states unequivocally that he borrowed the idea for his use of the auditorium as acting area from Pirandello (note, n.d., YCAL).

An even closer parallel, however, may be discerned between *The Skin of Our Teeth* and *Gray+Red+Violet+Orange*, the *sintesi* in which an actor drops out of character when he believes he recognizes his brother's murderer in the audience. The action is similarly interrupted by a number of surprising, unforeseen occurrences in *Skin*. Perhaps the closest analogue in Wilder's play is "Miss Somerset's" refusal to play Sabina's love scene with Antrobus in Act II. She refers to "a personal guest" of hers in the audience whose feelings might be hurt by some of the sentiments expressed in the scene, and both the Stage Manager, "Mr. Fitzpatrick," and her colleague playing Antrobus must turn her attention away from her unhappy friend and persuade her to resume her character and continue the performance from the point immediately following the objectionable passage. This incident in Wilder's play contains nearly all the major elements found in the Italian *sintesi*: an interruption of the action by an actor who drops out of character, reference to a personal relationship between that actor and a particular member of the audience—a relationship that motivates the interruption—and the intervention of fellow actors and backstage personnel to try to salvage the performance.

Again, though, the destruction of the stage illusion in futurist *sintesi*, by whatever means, is rarely endowed with any wider significance, as it is in Wilder's play. It provides ironic commentary on theatrical convention, but little else. In *The Skin of Our Teeth*, on the other hand, the precariousness of the theatrical illusion echoes the precariousness of human existence which is the play's subject. Again, too, the countless reminders that Wilder gives his audiences (in *Our Town*, *The Happy Journey*, *Pullman Car*, and *The Long Christmas Dinner*) that they are watching plays rather than transcriptions of everyday reality are intended to turn their attention away from the "exhibited individual action" and toward "the realm of idea and type and universal" (*AC* 108). This idealistic, Platonic purpose accords ill with the materialistic futurist spirit, although some futurists, such as Boccioni (127), pay lip service to a "spiritual" dimension—in their case, meaning an immediate, emotional essence or "spirit"—of their art.

The last major area of resemblance between Wilder's theatre and that of the futurists, the presentation of simultaneous actions and settings side-by-side on stage, is similarly an incomplete or superficial—and, furthermore, not particularly significant—one, although it is related in futurist thinking to the "invasion" of the auditorium by the actors. The futurists' employment of this device, which Marinetti termed *compenetration*, usually involved actions and settings totally unrelated to one another, whereas in Wilder's plays, such scenes are invariably connected to each other as parts of a coherent whole. The futurists' practice may be seen in the piece *Public Gardens*, in which, alongside the "automobile ride," "two lovers [kiss] on a park bench [and] a 'typical invert' . . . [saunters] about effeminately" (Kirby 67). It is even more clearly apparent—and more typical—in Marinetti's *sintesi*, *Simultaneity* and *The Communicating Vases*, in which two or more entirely different locations, containing wholly separate actions or situations, share the stage. In the former piece, the dressing table of a beautiful cocotte is set in the middle of a bourgeois family's living room, but for the bulk of the play cocotte and family remain unaware of one another's presence and act out their separate dramas in complete isolation. In the latter work, the stage is partitioned into three different, unrelated settings—a mortuary chapel, the street outside an inn, and a rural battlefield—with the first two displaying actions appropriate to the settings and the third one empty. At certain points in both *sintesi*, the separate actions do "penetrate" one another; the cocotte in *Simultaneity* "invades" the living room (of which she has hitherto been unconscious) and a thief and a company of soldiers in *The Communicating Vases* move freely from one setting to the next, even enacting in the process a "linear," cohesive story. The partitions separating the three settings are eventually broached by the soldiers, also, as they charge across the stage from their trenches in the battlefield. However, this particular "penetration" flies directly in the face of logic and credibility, obliterating all plausible connection between action and setting.

In Wilder's plays, by contrast, the rationale behind the "simultaneity" is, in all cases, realistically valid and readily apparent. In *Pullman Car Hiawatha*, for example, a watchman in a tower near Parkersburg, Ohio, appears on stage next to the car to announce that he is awake and the signals are all right for the train, which is at that moment at some distance from the town. A mechanic then enters to deliver a weather report. Earlier, the towns and fields outside the car have been brought on stage, represented by whimsical or eccentric figures. However, although all these moments might be considered to entail the simultaneous depiction of physically separate locales, none of the announcements delivered by the seemingly extraneous characters is unrelated to the main action, the journey of the Pullman car itself, and all the personified exterior "locations" appear just as the car is supposedly passing or approaching them, thus following a natural, "realistic" progression. In *Our Town*, two separate households are exhibited side-by-side throughout Act I and much of Act II. Moreover, several different locations in the town and in the Gibbs and Webb residences themselves—the church, George's and Emily's bedrooms, and the lower stories of both houses—are shown simultaneously on the stage (including the orchestra pit) at the end of Act I; and the hillside cemetery and Emily's childhood home occupy the two halves of the stage throughout the bulk of Act III. However, again, not only are the settings themselves—at least in Acts I and II—in effect merely components of a single larger locale, the town; but in all cases, the actions depicted in these physically separate environments are interrelated and help to produce a single, coherent, integrated picture of life in that town.

Other resemblances between Wilder's theatre and that of the futurists are few and vastly more approximate than the ones discussed here. Different historical periods are juxtaposed, as they are in *Skin*, in one *sintesi* in which a man in modern dress interrupts a thirteenth-century love scene to ask for a match. However, the futurist piece is designed, not to make a point about the universality of human experience, as *Skin* is, but rather to expose the falseness of sentimental love, the idealization of women, and the depiction of these values in old-fashioned romantic melodrama.

Thus, overall, the resemblances between Wilder's work and that of the futurists, uncanny though some of them are, seem largely due to coincidence or accident. At the same time, perhaps "coincidence" is not quite the appropriate word to describe the phenomenon. Once a playwright has decided to abandon the narrowly realistic style in favor of more unconventional, fanciful modes, he or she is faced with a limited number of options if the work is still to depict recognizable, relatively coherent dramatic actions. It is therefore hardly surprising that Wilder, in his efforts to create a nonrealistic dramatic style suited to the expression of his favorite themes, should have explored pathways that had previously been discovered and trodden by members of a movement dedicated exclusively to innovation. In fact, some futurist "innovations"—especially their anti-illusionistic strategies of mingling audience and actors—were nothing of the sort, having been commonplace practices in the medieval and Elizabethan theatres, among others. As in the case of Brecht, however, a comparison of the theatres of Wilder and the futurists provides, more than anything else, a graphic demonstration of the ways in which strikingly similar dramaturgical devices and techniques can be utilized for radically different or diametrically opposed ends. In such cases, context determines meaning.

Pirandello's name, like Brecht's, is frequently linked with Wilder's in critical discussions of the latter's writings for the stage (Goldstone, *Portrait* 175; Modic 59; Harrison 186; Kuner 137–38, 148). Unlike Brecht's, however, Pirandello's theatre is known to have influenced Wilder's work directly, although the similarities between the two writers' respective dramatic idioms may not be as extensive or significant as at first appears.

Wilder saw Elsa Merlini's production of *It* Is *So*! (*If You Think So*) while he was in Rome in 1921 (unpub. note on Pirandello, ms. and ts., Wilder papers, YCAL), and from 1921 to 1927 he sought out and read all the Pirandello plays he could find in the Princeton University library. He wrote in a letter to a friend, after having read a review of Georges Pitoëff's Paris staging of *Six Characters* in 1923, that he wished the two of them could have been there (letter to B. Pemberton, 20 May 1923, copy in letter bk., ms., Wilder papers, YCAL). In an unpublished statement regarding Pirandello's influence on his work, Wilder acknowledges that the Italian writer was "indeed an influence—not so much for his metaphysical ideas, but for his liberation of the play from the 'box set' " (Pirandello note, first ms. and ts., Wilder papers, YCAL). Wilder wrote, in addition, that Pirandello's "concern with identity and the clash between the social fiction and the subjective self was of deep interest but not among T. W.'s [*sic*] influences" (Pirandello note, second ms. and ts., Wilder papers, YCAL).

Wilder's assessment here is accurate. Despite the fact that the development of Wilder's theatrical vision owes a lot to Pirandello, the influence was, again, more in the realm of technique than in that of theme, content, or underlying philosophy. Pirandello succinctly summarized his main thematic concerns as a dramatist in a Preface to *Six Characters* written nine years after the play's première. As described by the playwright, those concerns consist of the following:

> the impossibility of mutual understanding that is irrevocably based on the empty definition of words [i.e., the relative nature of human truths, or the impossibility of arriving at a verbally—or otherwise—communicable truth about one's inner being]; the multiple personality that each of us has corresponding to the possibilities of being to be found in each of us; and finally the inherent tragic conflict between life (which is always moving and changing) and form (which holds it immutable). (qtd. in Gilman 173; see also Matthaei 80)

As the third theme indicates, Pirandello's artistic vision, like Brecht's, is essentially dialectical, being founded on a preoccupation with paradox and antithesis, which finds expression in his plays in an unresolvable conflict between fluidity and fixity, these latter abstractions manifesting themselves respectively as either Life and Art, Feeling and Reason, Face and Mask, Actor and Role, Present and Past, or even Individual and Society.

Wilder's drama, in contrast, does not focus primarily or substantially on any of these concerns. If there is a dualistic aspect to his theatrical vision, it is the tension between the individual and the cosmos, between the "here-and-now" and "everywhere and always." This tension is not exactly dialectical, but even if one wishes to consider it as such, it is still a far cry from the central, and, in fact, obsessive, concern of Pirandello—the perennial struggle between mutable life and rigid, but illusory, form.

Wilder is acutely aware of the poignancy inherent in human life within the stream of time, as is evident in *The Long Christmas Dinner* and the final act of *Our Town*, in which Emily protests that she cannot properly appreciate life because "It goes so fast" (100). Her anguish, it is true, is largely due to the fact that her earthly existence, being finished, is now irrevocably fixed and immutable, while her consciousness remains "alive" and capable of growth and change. Conversely, too, she is attempting to fix and preserve each fleeting moment so as to be able to hold and savor it forever, an attempt that the play shows to be doomed. However, Wilder's point has more to do with the blindness of living mortals to what is around them than with the mind's futile attempts to make order out of chaos. Furthermore, in contrast to Pirandello, Wilder does not perceive form as illusory, a mere product of the human imagination—whether individual or collective. The Italian dramatist, writing of the perpetual conflict he perceives occurring within every individual's consciousness, asserts that

> The forms in which we try to stop and fix this continuous flow [of life] are the concepts, the ideals, within which we want to keep coherent all the fictions we create, the conditions and the status in which we try to establish ourselves. ("On Humor" 52)

Elsewhere he writes, "Reality is a continuously illusory construction" (48). Wilder, on the other hand, with his Platonic bias, is far from viewing life as unpredictable, mutable, and impossible to fix in words, images, masks, concepts, or other forms. Instead, he discovers everywhere examples of the eternal, changeless patterns and verities of human existence. Instead of regarding life (that is to say, mutability) as the ultimate truth—a fluid, unstable truth—and concepts or ideals as fictions, as Pirandello does, Wilder propounds the opposite, Platonic point of view: namely, that the unstable world of time and the senses is illusory and that Pure Forms or Ideas embody ultimate reality and truth.

Not surprisingly, then, Wilder's conception of the personality also differs sharply from Pirandello's. Wilder nowhere depicts the ego as a fundamentally plural entity. In *The Skin of Our Teeth*, the central characters' names or identities may change. The Biblical Cain has assumed the new name of Henry Antrobus; Sabina, the maid of Act I, metamorphoses into Lily-Sabina Fairweather, the beauty contestant, in Act II, and Sabina the camp follower in Act III; and beneath their twentieth-century façades, George and Maggie Antrobus are, in fact, Adam and Eve. However, the archetypal dimension of the characters, which is established in large measure by this very proliferation of identities, provides them with a fundamental unity of essence, and their natures indeed remain constant beneath the shifting masks, that constancy being one of the playwright's main points.

By having Sabina and Henry and Antrobus drop out of character at times, and by thus playing with the dichotomy/identity between actor and role, Wilder does endow his play with a decidedly Pirandellian aura. However, even on this level, he attempts to preserve the impression that his characters and the "actors" playing them are merely different aspects of larger, integral entities. In a letter to Tallulah Bankhead, who played the first Sabina, the playwright advised the actress about how he wished her to treat "Miss Somerset's" intrusions into the primary role. "It's so necessary for the play," he wrote, "that each of your changes of mood and especially the 'break-throughs' to the audience come through with such spontaneous inner reality that they don't seem to the audience to be author's contrivances but pure SABINA NATURE" (qtd. in Bankhead, letter to M. Myerberg, Wilder papers, YCAL; qtd. in Haberman, *Plays* 82).

Similarly, when Henry and Antrobus are forced in Act III to drop the masks of their characters after "Miss Somerset" has stopped them from playing the scene that reportedly culminated in a near-murder "last night," both actors express sentiments in their "own persons" that seem entirely in character for their respective roles as well. The very reason why "Miss Somerset" must stop the scene is that the actor playing Henry identifies so strongly with his role at that point that he is liable to strangle in earnest the actor playing Antrobus if he comes near him. He blames his overidentification with Henry on an unhappy childhood, but that version of his childhood is itself a fabrication according to "Miss Somerset," who knew the Henry-actor's family and denies that his father took the whip to him, locked him in his room on Saturday nights, or neglected to feed him properly. Apparently, the actor has "inhabited" his role to such an extent that he has developed the same persecution complex or paranoia his character exhibits—or else, he has found it convenient to resort to lying, as Henry does, in order to excuse his objectionable behavior. This confusion regarding the actor's true experiences and true childhood introduces the genuinely Pirandellian theme of relativism: the difficulty of establishing the objective truth about human beings, given the natural human capacity for, and tendency toward, self-delusion. However, Wilder no sooner introduces this theme than he abandons it. "Miss Somerset" merely contradicts the actor's story, and the matter is allowed to drop. The truth remains hidden, as it would have done for Pirandello, but Wilder's interests obviously do not lie in examining the paradoxes or inconsistencies of human behavior and perception.

Like the actor playing Henry, though, in this scene the man playing Antrobus also seems to identify completely with his role. He confesses that he is to blame for working too hard, and this self-accusation brings to mind the Antrobus of Act II, who, thinking that all deserved a rest from their labors of previous epochs, proclaimed the motto of his tenure as President of the Human Race to be, "Enjoy yourselves" (164), and whom Sabina seduced with the sympathetic remark, "Mr. Antrobus, you work too hard" (189).

This identification of actor with role is certainly a favorite motif of Pirandello's; it appears in *Enrico IV*, *As You Desire Me*, and *Tonight We Improvise*. In the second play, although the heroine knows she is not the missing wife of the man she has accompanied from Berlin to northern Italy, who is persuaded that she *is*, she nonetheless willingly assumes the borrowed robes of the other woman's identity in order to escape from a sordid, degrading life. In *Tonight We Improvise*, the leading actress identifies so strongly with the role she is creating improvisationally that she actually faints when the character dies. However, once again, Wilder's use of this motif increases the impression that his characters are indivisible, multifaceted wholes, rather than unstable, pluralistic personalities, since there is no indication that the actors have *altered* their "true" natures in identifying with their roles.

Some approximation of the Pirandellian view of the individual personality may perhaps be seen in *Queens of France*, in which each of the successive "queens" obviously assumes a different personality or demeanor once she becomes convinced she is truly the heir to the French throne. The airs the women give themselves hardly lead one to conclude that their essences are wholly fluid or unstable, however. Each reacts in a different way to the belief that she is of royal descent, but this is the only play of Wilder's in which role-playing or the assumption of new identities is a central motif or subject. The origins of the work can, in any case, more justifiably be traced to Thomas Mann's doorstep than to Pirandello's.

Even in *The Long Christmas Dinner*, with its graphic portrayal of the headlong rush of time, the characters' personalities remain wholly intact in the face of its onslaught. The individual Bayards gradually change in subtle ways: Genevieve is transformed over the years from a carefree teenager into a sardonic, disillusioned spinster, and her brother Charles, having been an eager, energetic youth, settles down to become, in his mature years, a conservative, slightly pompous businessman. However, these are no more than the ordinary changes associated with aging, and the core of all the characters remains unaltered over the course of time, as is made evident by their regular repetition of familiar thoughts, sentiments, and phrases.

Other Pirandellian themes or motifs are also largely absent from Wilder's plays. Neither mirrors, masks, nor madness, the three most commonly recurring motifs or metaphors in Pirandello's plays, occupy an especially prominent place in Wilder's dramatic universe. The Insane Woman in *Pullman Car Hiawatha* plays a crucial role in the overall scheme of that play, but she is the only character in the major, published plays to be afflicted with madness, and even she can scarcely be considered a Pirandellian figure. The exact nature of her delusion is never revealed, nor is her perception of truth shown to be in direct conflict with that of any sane character, as it would almost certainly be if she were in one of Pirandello's works. Both Harriet and the woman agree on the identity and business of the archangels, for instance, although their initial reactions to the celestial visitors are diametrically opposed. Wilder thus does not use madness, as Pirandello does in *Enrico IV*, *As You Desire Me*, and *It* Is *So*! (*If You Think So*), to make any point about the relativity of truth or the impossibility of determining it.

On the other hand, the related Pirandellian theme of the difficulty of interpersonal communication does find its way into several of Wilder's plays. The Insane Woman herself complains at one point, "At last I understand myself perfectly, but no one else understands a thing I say" (65). The observation is something of a cliché in the case of a psychotic, but the central action of both *Infancy* and *Childhood* is the frustrating and frustrated (and doomed) efforts of one or more "normal" characters to establish communication with members of another generation. In the latter play, the father and mother fail to establish complete trust between themselves and their children in their shared dream-game, but the make-believe journey does provide both generations with the opportunity to present their points of view clearly. In *Infancy*, the frustration of the two babies is largely a result of their inability to communicate their desires. The babysitter Millie misinterprets Tommy's cries for chocolate as a need for affection, and similar misunderstandings punctuate the entire play. Nor are these two plays and *Pullman Car* the only plays by Wilder in which this theme is treated. In *Our Town*, Emily's suffering in the final act is caused by her mother's absorption in her mundane tasks and consequent inability really to see and appreciate her daughter. Wilder examines the difficulty of interpersonal communication in many of his novels as well, especially *The Bridge of San Luis Rey* and *Heaven's My Destination*, where it constitutes a central concern. In all these cases, however, the difficulties tend to be due to generational barriers or differences in spiritual condition, rather than, as for Pirandello, the innate imprecision of language and the individual's inescapable subjectivity, conceived of as a condition of human existence.

As far as the most characteristic of Pirandello's favorite motifs, the conception of theatre as a metaphor for life, is concerned, Wilder does not explicitly present or explore it in his plays, although it might be considered an implicit, secondary meaning in such "theatricalist" plays as *Our Town*, *Pullman Car Hiawatha*, *The Happy Journey*, *The Long Christmas Dinner*, and *The Skin of Our Teeth*. Richard Gilman calls Pirandello "the great modern playwright of the theater, or the theatrical, as *subject*"; observing that "in his work the full, radical questioning of the stage as a place of formal pretending begins" (157). Wilder, in contrast, evinces little interest in exploring such matters. He does, it is true, touch on the subject of role-playing in calling for the assumption of various minor roles by the Stage Managers in *Our Town*, *The Happy Journey*, and *Pullman Car Hiawatha*; and the parallels between the theatrical catastrophes in *The Skin of Our Teeth* and the natural or political cataclysms threatening the characters suggest that the theatre is, in many respects, *like* life. However, the parallels do not thereby make the natural disasters appear to be mere stage effects. In fact, in his use of the theatre as a metaphor for life, Pirandello never questions the truth or reality of physical phenomena. It is *human truth* that is elusive and ultimately uncertain. In a passage from his theoretical essay *On Humor*, he writes: "The sea is true, yes, and the mountain is true; the rock is true; the blade of grass is true; but man? . . . he cannot stop posing, even in front of himself, in some way" (qtd. in Driver 398). Wilder is not suggesting, in *Skin*, that life is an insubstantial pageant enacted by self-deluded poseurs. Indeed, he once observed that the play seems to come alive best in times of crisis (*AC* 110), a clear indication of the extent to which he intended "objective," external reality to anchor or color the viewer's experience of his theatrical fantasy, rather than vice versa. Similarly, the mere fact that the Stage Managers in his other three plays assume various roles does not, in itself, suggest that those plays are primarily (or even in part) *about* role-playing per se.

An examination of Wilder's and Pirandello's respective views of the theatre can help to clarify further the differences between the two in this matter. For Wilder, the theatre offers a means of presenting a story objectively, freed of the "editorial presence" that inevitably is found in works of fiction, whereas Pirandello questions the very idea of "objectivity" and has no scruples about allowing his own point of view and beliefs—or a part of them—to intrude into his plays through the mouths of his *raisonneurs*, such as Lamberto Laudisi in *It* Is *So*! (*If You Think So*), Diego Cinci in *Each in His*

Own Way, and the Father in *Six Characters*. Wilder, it is true, allows the Stage Manager in *Our Town*, whom he terms "a hang-over from a novelist technique" (Parmenter 10), to guide the audience toward the desired interpretations of the various actions presented; and George Antrobus, with his reverence for books and all the past accomplishments of his race, begins to sound very much like Wilder himself, especially in the final act of *Skin*. However, Pirandello's use of *raisonneurs* is much more extensive and unapologetic than Wilder's, in keeping with his more subjectivist philosophy. Pirandello, in fact, considered himself a "philosophical" playwright (*Masks* 365), and his fondness for including spokesmen for his point of view in his plays follows logically from this perception of himself and his purpose. On a general level, too, this self-characterization constitutes a link between him and Wilder, since the latter playwright could justifiably be characterized in the same way, although his philosophy is quite different from Pirandello's. Perhaps his more limited use of *raisonneur* figures springs from similarly "philosophical" intentions.

In any event, even "Miss Somerset" serves as something of an inverse *raisonneur* in *Skin*, and her sarcastic comments at Wilder's expense about the incomprehensibility and pretentiousness of his play recall Pirandello's practice of poking fun at his critics by including typical and exaggerated anti-Pirandellian comments in his own plays (for example, *Six Characters*, *Each in His Own Way*, and *Tonight We Improvise*). However, Molière indulged in precisely the same form of theatricalist joking, and in fact, the practice of juggling with illusion and truth in the theatre—one way of using the art form as a metaphor for human existence—is almost as old as the theatre itself. Tom F. Driver points out that Pirandello's originality lay, not in his exploitation of the theatrical metaphor, but in the purpose to which he applied it. In earlier instances of its use—by Shakespeare, Jonson, Beaumont, Calderón, and others—the playwright's point about the theatrical character of real life has to do with the impermanence of human beings, their actions, and their institutions, compared to the imperishability of the supernal realm (Driver 392). Pirandello, for his part, is making no metaphysical or religious point in his equation of life with theatre, but rather a psychological one. His primary interest is in the "masks" that individuals reflexively assume in order to fix their identities. If Wilder, on the other hand, is suggesting in any of his plays that "All the world's a stage," his implication is the same as that offered by the Elizabethan and Spanish Golden Age dramatists, in Driver's analysis: that the phenomenal world is merely a reflection or imitation of a higher, truer realm.

The play *Childhood* provides a crucial perspective on the distinctions between Wilder's and Pirandello's respective ways of regarding the theatre. Wilder's play implies that theatrical activity is little more than an institutionalized form of make-believe, of the naïve but wholly conscious and intentional sort engaged in by children. It is not, as it is for Pirandello, an extension of the instinctive or reflexive, unavoidable human activity of self-masking. Wilder's play depicts role-playing or make-believe as a means of arriving at a deeper understanding of other people, but it does not take role-playing as its primary subject, as do Pirandello's *Enrico IV*, *Cecè*, *Tonight We Improvise*, and *As You Desire Me*, nor does it present it as a universal, perpetual human activity. Significantly, Wilder's characters (even the children) easily and consciously fall into and drop out of their roles, as Pirandello's, almost without exception, seem unable to do.

In one other thematic area, the treatment of time, Pirandello's *Enrico IV* bears a superficial resemblance to *The Skin of Our Teeth*. However, once again, Wilder's purpose and vision differ markedly from those of his Italian predecessor. In *Enrico*, as in *Skin*, several historical "layers" are simultaneously depicted on stage. Pirandello's interest, however, lies not (as Wilder's does) in revealing the continuing presence of eternal truths and patterns in human history, but rather in portraying once again the conflict between fixed form (the past) and fluid life (the present). Wilder does not perceive time as wholly static in *Skin*, even though all ages are simultaneously present in that play, but in his conception "life" or change is less volatile, unpredictable, and dizzyingly chaotic than it is depicted as being in *Enrico IV*, where the title character at one point vividly describes the men of the twentieth century as "torturing themselves in ceaseless anxiety to know how their fates and fortunes will work out" (*Masks* 195). In *Skin*, humanity's survival may not be a foregone conclusion, but the synchronic presentation of time in the play implies that the race's experiences follow familiar, predictable scenarios. Moreover, the historical "layers" in Pirandello's play, which juxtapose the eleventh and twentieth centuries, all fit into a carefully established realistic framework, whereas it is impossible to reconcile, on a realistic level, Antrobus's identity as suburban commuter with his depiction as a caveman, Noah, and General Eisenhower.

Similar discrepancies between Wilder's and Pirandello's plays appear when one begins to examine their respective dramaturgical techniques, although Wilder clearly borrows a number of devices and methods from his Italian predecessor. In the matter of dramatic structure, the two playwrights share some common ground but also differ significantly on several points. Pirandello's plays are, for the most part, conventionally constructed and even illusionistic, although not as carefully crafted and polished as, say, Ibsen's. It is only in his "trilogy of the theatre in the theatre" (*Six Characters in Search of an Author*, *Each in His Own Way*, and *Tonight We Improvise*) that he attempts to embody his ideas on life and form in the structure of the dramas. In those three plays, however, a distinct pattern emerges. In each work, the "inner" action—the play-within-the-play—is interrupted a number of times until the whole performance finally collapses in chaos and confusion, as unbridled "life" sweeps away "form" for good. In *Tonight We Improvise*, it is true, the action is played out to the end, but there is still an element of confusion and uncertainty in the leading actress's loss of consciousness at the moment when her character dies. The playwright does not indicate whether she is to regain her senses or not. Wilder nowhere—except in the "three-minute" play *Proserpina and the Devil* (*ATW* 27–30), which he wrote as a teenager—employs an ending depicting the utter, chaotic collapse of the central action. He does, through the use of a cyclical structure in *Queens of France*, *The Long Christmas Dinner*, and *The Skin of Our Teeth*, create an "open-ended," unresolved action. However, the impression given in all three plays is that the exhibited action will be indefinitely prolonged and will follow the same predictable course as has already been shown rather than collapsing in confusion.

On the other hand, seemingly spontaneous, unforeseen interruptions and accidents destroy the continuity of the central action in such plays as *Our Town*, *Pullman Car Hiawatha*, and *The Skin of Our Teeth*. These interruptions collectively constitute a major parallel between the playwrighting techniques of Wilder and Pirandello, but they also link Wilder's dramaturgy with that of Brecht (treated in detail in Chapter 4). At the same time, Wilder's use of the technique is, in many respects, closer to Pirandello's than it is to Brecht's, since it is still illusionistic on a deeper level. The interruptions in Wilder's plays, as in Pirandello's, are only apparently spontaneous and accidental. In fact, they are carefully planned and controlled. The supposedly "improvised" dialogue in *Tonight We Improvise*, for instance, along with the "interruptions" of it by the *régisseur*, Dr. Hinkfuss, has been completely written out by Pirandello in the form of a conventional script. The interruptions of the action in Brecht's plays are carefully controlled and planned, too, but there is no pretense that they are not.

Some specific stylistic and technical resemblances (and fundamental differences) between Wilder's drama and Pirandello's have already been discussed. There are others, but most resemblances are relatively incomplete—that is to say, Wilder seems to use, in any given play, only one or two facets of the Pirandellian devices that he borrows. All these devices have to do with making visible the inner workings of the theatre. For instance, the audience at *Six Characters*, upon entering the theatre, sees the curtain raised on a bare stage, with some actors already in place, just as the audience at *Our Town* or *The Happy Journey* does. A "Manager" (actually the stage director) enters in Pirandello's play and proceeds to coordinate the action on stage, just as the Stage Managers do in *Our Town* and *Pullman Car Hiawatha*. However, none of the characters in the Italian play acknowledges the audience's presence, as the Stage Managers (and other characters) do in Wilder's two plays, and the stage is bare for a thoroughly mundane, realistic reason: the fictional action to be presented at first is a play rehearsal taking place in any empty theatre. Although Wilder's plays often give the impression of being rehearsals or partially improvised, spontaneous performances, in none of them that utilizes a bare stage, including *Love and How To*

Cure It, does the dramatist present the illusion of an actual rehearsal occurring in an empty theatre. Wilder does include an "actual" rehearsal in *Skin*, of course, but here, too, there is no pretense that the theatre is empty. Pirandello appears to be the more conventional, "illusionistic" playwright in this respect. In *Tonight We Improvise*, Pirandello employs direct address by a "Master of Ceremonies" who is comparable to Wilder's Stage Manager in *Our Town*, but in Pirandello's play, the stage does not remain bare, except perhaps in the final act.

All such distinctions are obviously minor, and it is plain that much of Wilder's technical vocabulary as a dramatist is drawn from Pirandello. For example, a number of other devices in *Tonight We Improvise* are echoed in one or more of Wilder's plays, as well as in those of Brecht and the futurists. The visible scene changes in Pirandello's play (and in *Six Characters*) anticipate the similar changes in *Our Town* and other plays by Wilder, just as they anticipate the partly visible scene shifts incorporated by Brecht into his productions for the purpose of "alienation." The interruptions of the interior play by Dr. Hinkfuss (the "Master of Ceremonies") closely resemble the similar interventions by the Stage Managers in *Our Town* and *Pullman Car Hiawatha*, who, like Hinkfuss, are ostensibly responsible for the overall shape and pacing of the evening's performance. The introduction of filmed material, although not an especially original or "experimental" device in 1930, when Pirandello's play was written, nevertheless points forward to Wilder's use of slides in *The Skin of Our Teeth*. However, Pirandello, like Brecht, combines simultaneous film and live action instead of separately presenting the two modes in consecutive sequences, as Wilder does in *Skin*. One other technical element in Pirandello's play also reappears in some of Wilder's, namely the destruction of the aesthetic boundaries between stage and auditorium by means of actors who impersonate members of the audience and engage in dialogue with those on stage, and by means of the extension of the stage action itself into the auditorium (chiefly the theatre aisles). These techniques both have precedents in futurist practice, of course, but Wilder explicitly acknowledged that Pirandello's example inspired him to employ these devices (second note on Pirandello, ms. and ts., Wilder papers, YCAL).[6] Finally, the scene in *Tonight We Improvise* in which the leading actress, in preparation for her death scene in the final act, applies her old-age makeup with the help of her friends, in full view of the audience, constitutes a rough parallel to the moments in *The Long Christmas Dinner* at which certain characters "simply and without comment" (1) adjust wigs of white hair on their heads to indicate advancing age.

Thus, despite the direct influence that Pirandello had on his American admirer, the relationship between the two men's theatres is very similar to that between Wilder's theatre and that of the expressionists, the futurists, and Brecht. The same or similar technical means are used to explore and elucidate fundamentally different governing concerns, beliefs, and underlying visions. In the case of Wilder and Pirandello, many of the stylistic resemblances—such as the use of a bare stage and exposure of the processes involved in theatrical production—are the result of borrowing by Wilder.[7] At the same time, in utilizing the older playwright's techniques for his own purposes, Wilder maintained his integrity as an artist and (as Brecht, too, was able to do) converted his borrowings into raw material for the construction of his own unique theatrical idiom.

NOTES

1. See Kirby (67–68). A futurist influence on Wilder is also postulated by Rosa Trillo Clough in her study, *Futurism: The Story of a Modern Art Movement, A New Appraisal* (200, 207, 208). Clough, like Kirby, also points out that Wilder was in Rome at a time (1920–1921) when futurism was very much in evidence and considers that the concept of "simultaneity" found its way into his dramatic vision as a result of his (hypothetical) contact with the movement.

2. Marinetti, "Technical Manifesto of Futurist Literature," trans. R. W. Flint, in Marinetti (84). See also Marinetti, "The Free-Word Style," trans. Arthur A. Coppotelli, in Marinetti (164).

3. The term is usually translated as "passéist." See Kirby (14), and Marinetti (55, 63).

4. The best-known example of this phenomenon is perhaps Umberto Boccioni's sculpture, *Unique Forms of Continuity in Space*, but nearly all futurist painting and sculpture exhibits the same quality.

5. Marinetti, for instance, in his "Founding and Manifesto of Futurism," declares that the movement will promote "contempt for woman" and will combat "moralism, feminism, and all the opportunistic and utilitarian forms of cowardice" (Goldberg, 8 [photo]; author's translation).

6. Wilder writes, "Pirandello's continued use of the theatre (aisles and lobby) as setting was certainly an influence."

7. Harrison (186) states categorically that Wilder's use of the bare stage was a direct result of the influence the 1921 production of *Six Characters* (which Harrison contends that he saw) had on him, as well as of the influence of the Elizabethan and Spanish Golden Age theatres.

Chapter 6

"The Sign of Kierkegaard": Existentialist Aspects of Wilder's Theatre

Like Pirandello's dramaturgy, existentialist thought (principally that of Kierkegaard and Sartre) directly influenced Wilder's own thinking and perceptions and the development of his creative vision. The writer even explicitly identified Kierkegaard as the primary source of inspiration for his novel *The Ides of March,* a work that marks the beginning of a recognizably "existentialist" or "Kierkegaardian" period in the author's career: the twenty years following the end of World War II (Wilder interview with Robert van Gelder, qtd. in Haberman, *Plays* 139n). During that time, he produced, along with *Ides,* the Kierkegaard-inspired novel *The Eighth Day* and the play *The Alcestiad,* along with its accompanying "satyr play," *The Drunken Sisters*. On the other hand, Wilder's acquaintance with Kierkegaard (apparently only a nodding one at first) dates from as early as 1920–1921, the same period in which he was first exposed to Pirandello. It was at that time that he met the American Kierkegaard scholar and translator, Walter Lowrie (A. N. Wilder 32), who was then rector of the American church, St. Paul's, in Rome and who remained a friend of the playwright for many years (Haberman, *Plays* 41; Simon 42). Moreover, many of Wilder's plays—all the major ones, in fact—written prior to his avowedly existentialist period of 1948–1967 contain both embryonic and full-blown existentialist elements, indicating a susceptibility on his part to the influence of the movement after it became known to him.

At the same time, he never (except possibly in *The Ides of March* and perhaps *The Eighth Day*) created a work of art consistent in all particulars with existentialist doctrine. Some of his stated beliefs and presuppositions—chiefly, his ingrained Neoplatonist habit of mind—are irreconcilable with the whole basic thrust of existentialist thought, and in most of his works he deviates in significant, if subtle, ways from the straight and narrow pathways of that thought. In the unresolved tension in Wilder's plays between the particular and the general—between the individual and the universal—the existentialist elements in those plays, like the naturalistic ones, add weight to the former pole.

Although existentialism, unlike the movements examined in previous chapters, was not primarily an aesthetic school, it served to systematize and synthesize certain currents, tendencies, and assumptions, buried or apparent, within many of the aesthetic movements already discussed. Existentialist tendencies in symbolism include the symbolists' antirationalist bias, their emphasis on the use of "private," obscure symbols whose meaning is determined by the individual poet or artist rather than by convention or consensus, and Mallarmé's fascination with the void—especially his belief that he was himself a void through which the truth spoke (see Chadwick 35).

In addition, the belief of Proust and Maeterlinck that habit dulls the consciousness and prevents it from fully and intensely experiencing life and the world has much in common with existentialist ideas, especially those of Heidegger. The naturalists share with the existentialists a conception of the universe as fundamentally unintelligible and an orientation toward immediate sensory and psychological data as the sole valid foundation and repository of truth—in other words, toward descriptive or ontological rather than speculative or cosmological thinking. Nietzsche, who is ordinarily classified as an existentialist, exerted a powerful influence on a number of naturalistic writers, such as London and Norris, and both naturalists and existentialists subscribe to the theory of moral relativism, although for different reasons—those reasons being the power of determinism in the case of the naturalists (which relieves individuals of responsibility for their actions) and the primacy of subjectively assigned values in the case of the existentialists. Moreover, despite the naturalists' view of human beings as entirely consubstantial with the rest of nature, the penchant of certain naturalistic writers for exploring the individual's behavior in hostile or unfamiliar environments can be seen as preparing the way for the existentialist characterization of *all* individuals as "forlorn," "abandoned" exiles in an alien, incomprehensible universe. The expressionists' obsession with subjective perceptions and the unique vision of the individual artist may be considered a link between them and the existentialists, just as the futurists may be regarded as "existentialist" in their categorical rejection of the authority of inherited cultural tradition and their delight in action and the dynamic projection of will and consciousness toward the future. Brecht shares with the existentialists a recognition of the vital importance of choice and the conscious commitment of all one's energies to a specific course of action. Like them, too, he considers the human personality to be fluid or contingent, although for Brecht, the particular configuration met with at any given time is determined largely by biological or social exigencies rather than, as for the existentialists, by the individual's free, conscious choice. Finally, Pirandello's convictions that human beings lack a fixed "essence" and that they are irremediably isolated from one another by the subjective basis of their consciousness are quintessentially existentialist.

All the same, the existentialist or quasiexistentialist elements in Wilder's plays are distinct, for the most part, from those features that link his work with one or more of the movements and playwrights already examined in this volume. The existentialist dimension of Wilder's drama must therefore be outlined and explored separately, in its own right. The first step in that exploration is to trace briefly the development of his acquaintance with existentialist thought.

Wilder renewed his acquaintance with Walter Lowrie, whom he had met in Rome, in 1925, when both men were at Princeton (Wilder as a graduate student in French and Lowrie as a faculty member), and the two remained friends for many years. Although few works by Kierkegaard were available in English translation before the early 1940s, Wilder attended some of Lowrie's "Kierkegaard evenings" while at Princeton in 1925 (Simon 42) and presumably thereby acquired at least a superficial familiarity with the basic ideas of the Danish thinker. Wilder reportedly studied Kierkegaard seriously for the first time in the late 1940s (Haberman, *Plays* 40), but his work before that time displays sufficiently striking existentialist tendencies to warrant assuming, if not a general or subconscious Kierkegaardian influence stemming from his friendship with Lowrie, then at least a strong philosophical kinship with the Danish master.

The spark that ignited Wilder's renewed and intensified interest in Kierkegaard was provided by Sartre, whom Wilder met while the French writer was on a lecture tour of U.S. universities following World War II. Wilder was undoubtedly intrigued by Sartre's ideas, since he translated the latter's play, *Les Morts sans Sépulture* (*The Victors*) into English in 1948 (Goldstein 21), a translation that was never published but was performed off-Broadway. However, Sartre's atheism, not surprisingly, made Wilder uncomfortable, and he naturally sought out a more congenial version of existentialism through which he could expand his acquaintance with the movement. Sartre's influence is strongest in *The Ides of March*, which contains many echoes of Sartrean utterances and a protagonist, Caesar, who, in his devotion to action and total involvement in human affairs, appears to typify the Sartrean hero (rather than the Kierkegaardian "knight of faith," who may be largely indistinguishable from the Philistine and whose commitment is largely inward). However, Wilder himself claimed in an interview that the novel had been inspired by

Kierkegaard; and *The Alcestiad* (including *The Drunken Sisters*) and *The Eighth Day* are both far more obviously Kierkegaardian than Sartrean in inspiration.

Wilder also knew some of the ideas of a third major existentialist, Nietzsche, but few if any of Nietzsche's ideas found their way directly into the playwright's work or are discernible in it.[1] Sartre and Kierkegaard were the primary sources through whom Wilder became acquainted with the movement, and his familiarity with their respective corners of it is well documented.

Acquaintance with a creed and full acceptance of it are two different things, however, and Wilder's acceptance of the existentialist view of the universe and of the human condition, at least, is limited, even in some of the works that are otherwise explicitly inspired by existentialist ideas. It is true that, as concerns the individual's situation in the cosmos, Wilder's point of departure is close to that of the "first existentialist," Pascal, who was struck with fear and astonishment at the thought of himself as a tiny, finite creature, "swallowed up in the eternity before and after" his life span and "engulfed in the infinite immensity of spaces" which were ignorant of him, as he was of them (61). This perception of the individual as dwarfed by the rest of creation lies at the heart of Wilder's dramatic vision. However, that perception or concern is not unique to the existentialists and Wilder.

Moreover, in no work prior to *The Ides of March* does Wilder imply that the universe is without a priori meaning or that its meaning—or the meaning of human life—is inherently unintelligible. For the atheistic existentialists, of course, the ultimate meaninglessness of both the world and human existence is axiomatic; and even the theistic existentialists, who assert on faith the existence of an objective meaning, acknowledge that that meaning is not objectively knowable, is not "revealed" incontrovertibly or explicitly to human beings. One critic (Goldstein 122–23) writes that God is effectively absent from the world depicted in *The Skin of Our Teeth*, but such an assertion entails an excessively literalistic misreading—even a distortion—of the play's second act (see Chapter 3). God speaks through the mouth of the Fortuneteller Esmeralda, as well as in the storm signals that warn the heedless merrymakers in Atlantic City of the imminent end of the world, and the Deity's hand may be discerned in the "fortunate chance" that allows a boat to be tied up at the end of the pier, ready to carry the Antrobuses to safety. It is these omens, in fact, that set the play at odds with existentialist doctrines, since they imply that the universe—and human life—not only have a meaning and a preconceived purpose, but that that meaning and purpose are intelligible to ordinary mortals. Moreover, and perhaps most significant of all, the omens imply that there are certain universal, divinely sanctioned moral values, transgressors against which are duly punished by Heaven. Sartre, in contrast, observes:

> Nowhere is it written that the Good exists, that we must be honest, that we must not lie. . . .
>
> [W]e find no values or commands to turn to which legitimize our conduct. So, in the bright realm of values, we have no excuse behind us, nor justification before us. We are alone, with no excuses. (*Existentialism* 22–23)

Kierkegaard, it is true, would accept that certain values may have divine sanction, but *knowledge* of such sanction could be acquired only *subjectively* by the individual, through a "leap of faith" in the face of objective uncertainty, and not through unequivocal, universally decipherable direct communiqués from the Almighty.

On the subject of omens themselves, Sartre writes: "No general ethics can show you what is to be done; there are no omens in the world. The Catholics will reply, 'But there are.' Granted—but, in any case, I myself choose the meaning they have" (28). In contrast, the meanings of the Fortuneteller's pronouncements and other signs and portents in Act II of *Skin*—including the black disk that announces "the end of the world," (183)—are clearly stated and objectively determined. The conveeners may choose to *ignore* the warnings they receive, but they do not choose their meanings, which, as the play's action demonstrates, are absolutely and objectively correct.

God may seem more remote or incomprehensible in the play's third act, but war is a more exclusively human disaster than those depicted in the other two acts, and one for which human beings alone must bear full responsibility. Furthermore, Antrobus comments late in the act that God has always given him and his family the chance to build new worlds, and the passage from Genesis that concludes his vision of the Hour/Philosophers implies that the Almighty is indeed present, even in war. Finally, Mrs. Antrobus proclaims in Act III that she "could live for seventy years in a cellar and make soup out of grass and bark, without ever doubting that this world has a work to do and will do it" (232–33). This expression of faith may, in an existentialist sense, be her attempt to impose a meaning of her own choosing on a fundamentally meaningless world, but there is no evidence that the playwright intended it to be taken this way. In any case, the suggestion of a predetermined task or (in Sartre's terminology) "project" or purpose for the world—to say nothing of the certainty expressed that that task *will be accomplished*—carries the statement itself out of the realm of existentialist ideology.

Similarly, there is little evidence in *Our Town* that the playwright regards the universe as fundamentally meaningless or its meaning as utterly or inherently inaccessible to human understanding. The action of the play is set in "the Mind of God," and although the precise nature of that mind is never specified or even explored in the dialogue, there are indications that it is not beyond the reach of human reason. When the Stage Manager comments that "he" is in the ministry perhaps because he believes nature is interested in quality as well as quantity, he is contending that God's presence and purpose are perceptible in the very order of nature, which is itself wholly accessible to reason, in the form of scientific investigation. In contrast, even for a Christian existentialist such as Kierkegaard, reason is powerless to apprehend the true nature or intentions of God. God is referred to by Kierkegaard as the "Unknown," which is defined by the philosopher as "the limit to which Reason repeatedly comes, and in so far, substituting a static form of conception for the dynamic, it is the different, the absolutely different" (*Fragments* 55). The order of nature, by contrast, is certainly not "absolutely different" from human beings. The Stage Manager's belief that nature is interested in quality or perfection is an expression of faith rather than a rationally derived insight, but the implication is still that in nature, God can be seen at work. However, for Kierkegaard, faith is not simply an extension of reason but must often contradict or overcome it. The philosopher writes:

> But even if [the Reason] obtains . . . knowledge [of the Unknown from the Unknown itself] it cannot understand it, and thus it is quite unable to possess such knowledge. For how should the Reason be able to understand what is absolutely different from itself? (57)

Thus, in its attempt to understand God, the reason, for Kierkegaard, is everywhere confronted with "scandals" or offenses to itself, and faith or understanding must be achieved "by virtue of the absurd" (*Fear* 47)—that is to say, through confronting that which is directly contrary to reason. In the last act of Wilder's play, Emily and her mother-in-law agree that the living do not understand life, by which they mean simply that the earth holds more and greater wonders than all but the saint or poet can appreciate fully, and not that the universe is inherently without meaning or that that meaning is beyond the power of reason to grasp.

Existentialism, on the other hand, is in fact rooted in a vision of human beings as irremediably alienated from the world in which they exist, "abandoned" (Sartre's term) or "thrown" (Heidegger's term) into a meaningless or incomprehensible void and left to make their way as best they can, without reliable guidance or aid from above. Nowhere in *Our Town* or any of Wilder's other early plays does the playwright endorse or propound this view of the human condition. Antrobus, in the final act of *Skin*, praises the voices or authorities—both divine and human—that have guided his and his family's footsteps during their long journey, and the very harmony between the inhabitants of Grover's Corners and their natural environment implies a deeper harmony between them and the entire cosmos. They may remain insufficiently aware of that harmony and of the deeper significance of their lives, but in Wilder's plays it is not anguish, "fear and trembling," and alienation that the person who pierces through the veil of the world's appearances experiences, but rather wonder and awe and connection or identification. Sartre, by contrast, in his novel *Nausea* describes in the following terms the experience of the protagonist, who sees beneath the surface appearances of the world of objects for a brief moment:

> The diversity of things, their individuality, was nothing but an appearance, a varnish. This varnish had melted. What was left were monstrous soft masses in disorder, naked in frightening nudity. (qtd. in Olson 39)

Of course, Emily experiences anguish at the very marvelousness of the world, and the Stage Manager confirms her suspicion that the earth is, perhaps, too wonderful for anyone to realize completely. However, this anguish bears no resemblance to that of Sartre's hero, which is the classic existentialist angst. It is caused by alienation, it is true, but Emily's alienation is potentially remediable and is experienced on the interpersonal, not the cosmic, plane. It is presented as a conditional circumstance that could be reduced by an expanded awareness on her and her mother's part, difficult though such awareness might be to achieve. The same harmony between individual and cosmos that one finds in *Our Town* is evident in *Pullman Car Hiawatha* and *The Happy Journey*, too. Even though, in the former play, the sleeping passengers fail to perceive the wonders that surround them, they still form an integral part of the "chorus" of sounds symbolizing universal harmony that constitutes the accompaniment to and auditory content of Harriet's epiphany. Thus, Wilder cannot be said to be presenting an existentialist universe in these plays.

On the other hand, a quasiexistentialist view of the universe and the individual's place in it is enunciated, on a much simplified level, by Ma Kirby in *The Happy Journey*. Comforting her oldest daughter in Camden over the stillbirth of a baby girl, Ma says: "God thought best, dear. God thought best. We don't understand why. We just go on, honey, doin' our business" (121). Granted, the thought is conventional, unoriginal, and even expected, but the bare outlines of the basic existentialist creed, that individuals must dedicate themselves to sustained action in an unintelligible universe, are plainly visible, too. The passage in a very general way even calls to mind Kierkegaard's paradigmatic "knight of faith," Abraham, who was ready to sacrifice his son Isaac if it was God's will, without understanding why.

It is in *The Alcestiad*, however, that Wilder first pointedly and systematically (and consciously) constructs a picture of a universe whose meaning is hidden from ordinary human consciousness and reason. The playwright told an interviewer that the play "On [one] level . . . is a comedy . . . about the extreme difficulty of any dialogue between heaven and earth, about the misunderstandings that result from the 'incommensurability of things human and divine' " (qtd. in Cubera 595–96; cited in Burbank 124). Thus,

Hercules, upon learning that Apollo has spent a year living incognito, in the guise of a mortal herdsman, with Alcestis and Admetus, exclaims: "who can understand [the gods]? We shall never understand them. When I try to think of them, I start trembling; I get dizzy" (63). Moreover, when Alcestis concludes despairingly, because of the god's inscrutability, that mortals are alone and without aid in the world, she receives the following reply from one of the four herdsmen (of whom one is said to be Apollo in disguise, although none of the four believes it):

> If they did exist, these gods, how would they speak to us? In what language would they talk to us? Compared to them, we are diseased and dying and deaf and blind and busy as clowns. Why, there are some who even say that they love us. Could you understand that? What kind of love is that, Princess, when there is so great a gulf between the lovers? . . . That would be an unhappy love, no doubt about that. (31)

Hercules and the herdsman, it is true, are not depicted as possessing the most exalted of intellects, but even the more sophisticated and comprehending characters in the play find it difficult to perceive a meaning in existence or the universe. Teiresias, the blind prophet, lives in a state of perpetual befuddlement, continually forgetting the identity of those to whom he is speaking and getting the particular message he is supposed to deliver thoroughly muddled. The herdsman himself is amazed that the gods should have chosen such a "half-witted, crumbling old man" for their messenger and asks, "Can't they say what they have to say in any clearer way than this?" (30). Teiresias himself articulates the converse of this question when he asks rhetorically, "what use is Delphi if men and women cannot learn to listen?" (25). Finally, Alcestis herself is searching throughout the play—or the first two acts—for the meaning and purpose of existence—both her own and others'. In the first act, which occurs on the day of her wedding to Admetus, she is on the point of refusing to marry the king, since her lifelong ambition has been to serve Apollo as his priestess at Delphi. When the herdsmen arrive and she tries to speak directly to the god—although without knowing which of the four is actually Apollo—she seeks above all to learn the meaning of her life and is nearly forced by the god's silence on this question to adopt the position of the atheistic existentialists. She tells him:

> You know that I have wished to live only for you: to learn—to be taught by you—the meaning of our life.
>
> *No answer.*
>
> Are we human beings to be left without any sign, any word? Are we abandoned?
>
> *She waits another second above the embarrassed silence of the HERDSMEN, then turns toward the palace, and says to herself, bitterly:*

Then we must find our way by ourselves . . . and life is a meaningless grasping at this and that; it is a passionate nonsense. (28)

In the play's final act, she has discovered a meaning in life, although she still has extreme difficulty communicating that meaning to other mortals, being compelled to resort to cryptic allusions and oblique hints in order to make her points. To the tyrant King Agis, who has invaded Thessaly, overthrown and killed Admetus, murdered two of her three children, and enslaved her and now has lost his daughter, Laodamia, to the plague, Alcestis explains that "the last bitterness of death . . . is the despair that one has not lived. It is the despair that one's life has been without meaning. That it has been nonsense; happy or unhappy, that it has been senseless" (101). When Agis protests that Laodamia loved him and that the love was enough for the two of them, Alcestis contends:

Love is not the meaning. It is one of the signs that there is a meaning. Laodamia is in despair and asks that you help her. That is what death is—it is despair. Her life is vain and empty, until you give it a meaning. (102)

Agis asks what meaning he can give her life, and Alcestis replies enigmatically, "Today you have begun to understand that" (103), although she has already implied that the way for him to give Laodamia's life a meaning would be to return to his own country and reform himself, dedicating his own life to love and charity rather than brutality, cruelty, and power. In one sense, Wilder is deviating from strict existentialist dogma here by implying that one individual can determine the meaning of another's life or endow it with a meaning it lacked. Alcestis does imply that Agis can give Laodamia's life a meaning *for Laodamia*, and in so doing she introduces a nonexistentialist note. However, her deeper implication—that Agis must assign his daughter's life and death a meaning *for himself*, incorporating that meaning into his own life—is consonant with existentialist beliefs. Moreover, concerning the meaning of human life in general, she can tell him nothing definite, and with this implicit recognition by the playwright of the limits of human understanding, the universe of the play remains a basically existentialist one.

Wilder's immediate inspiration for the view of the human condition presented in the play was a series of passages in Kierkegaard's *Philosophical Fragments* (Harrison 322), a work dealing with the question of the extent to which human beings can know "the Truth."[2] In one of these passages, Kierkegaard asserts that God, being "absolutely unlike" human beings, must remain forever unknowable. Alcestis' reference to her desire to learn from the god and be taught by him recalls Kierkegaard's characterization of God as a teacher (*Fragments* 28–45, 58–59), and the philosopher's discussion of the love of God for humanity is clearly the source for the Herdsman's speech quoted earlier, as well as for ideas set forth in the cited speeches of Hercules and Teiresias. Kierkegaard writes:

> Moved by love, the God is thus eternally resolved to reveal himself. . . . His love is a love of the learner, and his aim is to win him. For it is only in love that the unequal can be made equal, and it is only in equality or unity that an understanding can be effected, and without a perfect understanding the Teacher is not the God, unless the obstacle comes wholly from the side of the learner, in his refusing to realize that which had been made possible for him.
>
> But this love is through and through unhappy, for how great is the difference between them! It may seem a small matter for the God to make himself understood, but this is not so easy of accomplishment if he is to refrain from annihilating the unlikeness that exists between them. (30–31)

The desired union, Kierkegaard states, "might be brought about by an elevation of the learner" (35), and the Herdsman in Wilder's play echoes this thought when he tells Alcestis that in order "to bridge that gulf" (31) between themselves and the mortals they love, the gods might try to "find a way to bring those they love up—up nearer to them" (31). Kierkegaard argues that such a solution is untenable, however, and that:

> In order that the union may be brought about, the God must therefore become the equal of such a one [as the learner], and so he will appear in the likeness of the humblest. But the humblest is one who must serve others, and the God will therefore appear in the form of a *servant*. But this servant-form is no mere outer garment, like the king's beggar-cloak, which therefore flutters loosely about him and betrays the king. . . . It is his true form and figure. For this is the unfathomable nature of love, that it desires equality with the beloved, not in jest merely, but in earnest and truth. (39)

Although Kierkegaard is referring to Christ here, it is plain that Apollo's incarnation as a herdsman in Wilder's play is an instance of the god's appearing "in the form of a servant." In Act II, Alcestis is reported to have called herself "the servant of the servants" (66), and the fact that Apollo's presence in one (or more) of the Herdsmen is completely undetectable—even by them—clearly indicates that the god has assumed the servant-form not as a "mere outer garment," but as "his true form and figure."

Seemingly departing from Kierkegaard, though, Wilder implies in his play that in making himself "the equal of the humblest," Apollo has, in fact, prepared the way for an attempt to raise human beings a little nearer to his own level, as the Herdsman suggests. At first glance, such an implication seems at odds with Kierkegaard's denial that an exaltation of the mortal beloved to the level of the divine lover can be satisfactorily effected. However, Kierkegaard elsewhere admits that "when the God implants himself in human weakness, . . . man becomes a new vessel and a new creature!" (*Fragments* 43). The Herdsman in *The Alcestiad* contemplates the possibility that the gods might seek to bridge the chasm separating them from mortals by drawing the latter a little nearer to them and observes: "The world changes; it changes slowly. What good would this world be, Princess, unless new kinds of men came into it—and new kinds of women?" (32). He concludes, "And wouldn't that be, maybe, the way those unhappy lovers (*He points upward.*) would try to throw a bridge across the gulf I was talking about?" (32).

Despite the massive debt that *The Alcestiad* obviously owes to the *Philosophical Fragments*, however, the playwright undermines the existentialist "purity" of his presentation in one significant way: he introduces Apollo himself into the play and allows him to explain his aims, feelings, and motivations—in exceedingly clear, colloquial language, moreover—in a pair of dialogues with Death, who also appears as a character. Wilder uses these dialogues to help clarify the meaning of his play, but he thereby implicitly contradicts those of his characters who insist that the "radical incommensurability" of gods and humans makes all dialogue between the two orders of beings, if not impossible, at least inescapably subject to gross misunderstandings. In addition, when Death asserts that human beings will never understand divine beings, Apollo replies: "They have begun to understand me.... In thanks they discovered speech, and I gave them song. These were signs and they knew them. First one, then another, knew that I prompted their hearts and was speaking" (8–9).

Thus, even in his most explicitly existentialist play, Wilder apparently finds it impossible to accept wholeheartedly the orthodox existentialist principle that human life occurs in any inherently incomprehensible universe. The radical incommensurability of the human and divine spheres is apparently, for the playwright, not so much an inescapable "given" of human existence in the world as a temporary inconvenience, which it should be possible some day to circumvent.

It is true that Sartre introduces Zeus as a character in *The Flies*, but this Zeus is merely a proponent of the conventional religious point of view, an image of the gods as human beings conceive of them and not an actual divine being in whom the atheist Sartre might believe. Wilder certainly did not believe in Apollo, but he uses him as a Christ surrogate in the play. Moreover, Sartre's play is not, like Wilder's, about the difficulty of communication between the divine and human spheres, so his depiction of the god involves no self-contradiction, as Wilder's does. It seems that the same rationalistic, positivistic turn of mind that prevents Wilder from being a true symbolist—the lack of enthusiasm for mystery and paradox and enigma—also prevents him from being a whole-hearted existentialist insofar as his conception of the universe is concerned.

Wilder's views regarding other aspects of the human condition within that universe, besides the fundamental one already treated here, also deviate from those of the existentialists. Wilder does examine the problem of the individual's isolation from his or her fellow human beings. Several of the more manifestly isolated characters—the Insane Woman in *Pullman Car Hiawatha*, Genevieve in *The Long Christmas Dinner*, and the children in *Infancy* and *Childhood*—were mentioned in preceding chapters. In addition, the artist's or exceptional individual's isolation from the rest of humanity is explored in *Nascuntur Poetae* and *The Angel That Troubled the Waters*, although this form of isolation is perhaps more characteristically "romantic" than "existential." Harriet in *Pullman Car Hiawatha* may be considered a better example of the existentially lonely individual. She is nearly as isolated as the Insane Woman, since the other characters are all too absorbed in themselves to be aware of her suffering and death. At the same time, she contributes to that isolation by trying to disturb no one unnecessarily, and all the other passengers are asleep when she dies and hence not really accountable for their indifference. Nevertheless, she, for her part, seems blinded by her sickness to everything about her fellow travelers except the superficial details of their appearances or identities—especially the fact that one of them is a doctor. It is only after she has died that she perceives all the others as desirable companions in Paradise. Here again, however, as in the cases of the Insane Woman and the children in *Infancy* and *Childhood*, the character's isolation is due more to immediate, unique, or transitory circumstances than to limitations inherent in the human condition itself, although it might be argued that illness and, especially, death are indeed inevitable features of the human condition and inevitably isolate the individual.

One character who seeks unsuccessfully to isolate himself from the rest of humanity is Henry in *The Skin of Our Teeth*. In Act III, after he has lost the war, as his father points a revolver at him, he tells him to shoot, declaring: "You don't have to think I'm any relation of yours. I haven't got any father or mother, or brothers or sisters. And I don't want any. . . . I'm alone, and that's all I want to be: alone" (235). When, shortly thereafter, he again tries to deny his relationship to the family, Antrobus points out that he nevertheless returned to his childhood home as if drawn by a magnet. At the end of the play, also, Henry appears on the periphery of the scene, "brooding and unreconciled, but present" (249). His "loneliness" is thus more wishful thinking than existential fact, and withdrawal from human contact is not generally advocated by existentialist writers. (Quite the reverse, in fact, is the case.)

A more truly existential conception of human isolation, in any case, is discernible in the final act of *Our Town*. Emily's overwhelming sense of separation from her mother is what leads her to cry out to her in anguish, as she relives her twelfth birthday, "*Let's look at one another*" (99). Emily's acute awareness of her isolation at that moment may be largely due to the fact that she is now dead and knows it and is thus irrevocably sundered from her mother as the latter was when both of them were alive (for, presumably, they will meet again when Mrs. Webb dies). However, the *fact* of her isolation while she *herself* was still alive is graphically demonstrated by the scene itself. In Mrs. Webb's absorption in her petty tasks, Emily sees a reflection of her own self-enclosure. Thus, although the implicit message of the play is a plea for greater awareness, a degree of blindness and, hence, of isolation from others may be an inescapable component of the human condition (except, perhaps, for that of the saints and poets) as it is presented in this play.

The existentialist dimension of Wilder's plays, such as it is, resides not, however, primarily in the view of the universe and the human condition that those plays present, but rather in certain features of the playwright's conception of the individual and, even more strongly, in his notion of the nature of that individual's existence and his or her relation to others. In fact, the most unequivocally existentialist elements in the plays—at least in those written prior to *The Alcestiad*—are certain statements by one character or another on the subject of interpersonal relations and ethics.

The playwright's appreciation of, and reverence for, the individual as individual is itself a broadly existentialist tendency. His respect for uniqueness per se is apparent in at least one line from *The Happy Journey*, as well as in a number of his essays. In the early play, the Kirbys' married daughter, Beulah, after learning that her father has bought her a present, protests to Pa that he ought not to have gone to all the trouble and expense. He thereupon justifies his extravagance with the observation that "There's only one Loolie in the world" (120). The infinite value of every individual's life is in direct proportion to his or her uniqueness. In an essay on Joyce, Wilder makes an explicit connection between this component of his vision and existentialism. He writes:

> Now, you and I and everybody live a complete life under unique occasions. Every single moment of our life is unique in that sense. Every human being lives only unique occasions, just as we all die one death—our death and no one else's. Likewise, of the millions of times that "I love" has been said, each time it is really said just once. The participation in essential love or essential death is, as they are now saying, "existential"—totally individual. (*AC* 1974)

The Platonistic reference to "essential love" and "essential death," of course, carries Wilder away from the existentialist position, since for the existentialists there is, as Sartre puts it: "no love other than one which manifests itself in a person's being in love. There is no genius other than one which is expressed in works of art. . . . A man is involved in life, leaves his impress on it, and outside of that there is nothing" (*Existentialism* 32–33). Still, the passage does show that Wilder (correctly) identifies existentialism with a recognition of the primacy, value, and validity of the individual's experience. Sartre notes that "Subjectivity of the individual is indeed our point of departure" (36). On the other hand, for the existentialists, the individual's value derives not so much from his or her uniqueness per se as from his or her own active, purposeful assertion of that uniqueness in the face of the emptiness, incomprehensibility, and indifference of the universe. Moreover, he or she is of value primarily to him- or herself, and not to relatives (as Beulah is to her father) or humanity as a whole.

The matter is complicated even further by Wilder's fondness for universalizing the characters, situations, settings, and overall meaning of his plays. This fondness is apparent in an earlier passage in *The Happy Journey*, where it seems implicitly to contradict the tenor of the sentiments expressed by Pa to Beulah, as well as those in the Joyce essay just cited. Arthur, the youngest Kirby child, is made aware by the journey of the immensity and populousness of the earth and comments on these facts to his mother in a passage worth quoting in full:

ARTHUR: Ma, what a lotta people there are in the world, ma. There must be thousands and thousands in the United States. Ma, how many are there?

MA: I don't know. Ask your father.

ARTHUR: Pa, how many are there?

ELMER: There are a hundred and twenty-six million, Kate.

MA: (*giving a pressure about Arthur's shoulder*) And they all like to drive out in the evening with their children beside'm. (116)

This picture of a homogeneous mass of humanity sharing the same fundamental likes and attitudes stands in direct opposition to Pa's appreciation of his daughter's uniqueness. The thought of the millions who share with Ma a pleasure in the company of their children may be comforting to her and her family, but the suggestion that an individual's surpassing value derives from his or her uniqueness is logically inconsistent with an image that denies him or her any genuine uniqueness. A playwright is under no compulsion to produce logically consistent works, of course, and Wilder leaves the paradox unresolved—in this and in other plays—as part of the tension between the particular and the general that is central in his dramatic universe. In the Joyce essay, the playwright does resolve the contradiction, or at any rate attempts to address it, with the help of existentialist concepts and terminology. There, Wilder writes: "what end is there to any human thing in which you are not also companion to billions? It does not diminish your grief, but it orients it to a larger field of reference" (*AC* 175). Similarly, although the individual's fear or joy, "the existential thing pouring up in [him or her], is a real thing[,] . . . the intensity with which [he feels] it can be called absurd. It is absurd to claim that 'I,' in the vast reaches of time and place and repetition, is worth an assertion" (176). The belief in the individual's unique and infinite value cannot be founded on deduction or objective observation but, like religious faith—with which, for Kierkegaard, it is associated—must be arrived at through nonrational means. Such reliance on the nonrational is itself an "existentialist" (although again, not exclusively existentialist) trait. Kierkegaard especially stresses that "faith begins precisely there where thinking leaves off" (*Fear* 64).

At the same time, Kierkegaard would maintain that Ma Kirby's attempt to relate herself and her family to all other United States citizens through a supposedly shared love of family outings is cowardly and even "depraved." He writes:

> The more the collective idea comes to dominate even the ordinary consciousness, the more forbidding seems the transition to becoming a particular existing human being instead of losing oneself in the race, and saying "we," "our age," "the nineteenth century." . . . Each age has its own characteristic depravity. Ours is perhaps not pleasure or indulgence or sensuality, but rather a dissolute pantheistic contempt for the individual man. . . . Everything must attach itself so as to be a part of some movement; men are determined to lose themselves in the totality of things, in world-history . . . ; no one wants to be an individual human being. (*Postscript* 23)

The existentialists' assertion of the value and significance of the individual in the face of the "vast reaches of time and place and repetition" is in all cases more uncompromising, or less ambivalent, than is Wilder's.

As regards the nature of the individual self, too, Wilder is somewhat at odds with existentialist thought. The existentialist position is summed up in the Sartrean formula that "existence precedes essence," that "first of all, man exists, turns up, appears on the scene, and, only afterwards, defines himself" (Sartre, *Existentialism* 15). Wilder, for his part, is inclined to accept the idea that each human being is endowed a priori with an essence, but the question, too, is complicated by several apparently conflicting indications. Ultimately, it must be recognized that Wilder, as an artist rather than a systematic thinker, was not obliged to formulate a coherent, consistent theory of the human personality and did not indeed do so, but it will be useful to examine in greater detail his views on the subject as they are revealed in his plays.

First of all, the "essentialist" Wilder is perhaps most clearly visible in *The Skin of Our Teeth*. One of the underlying assumptions of that play is that each of the four "eternal types" that represent the human race or family in it is possessed of an inner nature that remains fixed and constant throughout all the superficial changes of identity the character undergoes. It might be argued that these four characters—George, Maggie, Henry Antrobus, and Sabina—are not really human beings but archetypes, and therefore, the manner of their depiction does not necessarily indicate anything about the playwright's conception of the living, breathing individual. Certainly, the play is not to be taken literally and the characters are emphatically not real people, but Wilder is nevertheless attempting to depict real human history—the history of the actual human race—albeit in allegorical, fanciful, or metaphorical terms. One need not claim that any one historical individual was ever wholly identifiable as "Antrobus" or "Henry" or "Sabina." It is enough simply to accept that some portion of every individual is in essence one or another of Wilder's characters, and the play clearly supports that view. In so doing, it implies, contrary to Sartre, that some form of archetypal essence precedes existence. Moreover, the playwright's note to Tallulah Bankhead regarding "Miss Somerset's" intrusions into the play indicates that he also considered the "real" actors and actresses to possess natures that partake of the fixed, immutable essences of his archetypal characters. Additionally, Wilder's practice of basing characterizations in all his plays on type and even stereotype indicates a more "essentialist" than existentialist bias.

Sartre, it is true, believes in a "universality of man." However, this is not given and does not define the human being forever but rather "is perpetually being made" (*Existentialism* 39), as the combined life projects of countless individuals modify and reinvent the various cultural configurations that humanity has established in the past in response to the basic "givens" of the human condition. Sartre identifies those givens as the necessity "to exist in the world, to be at work there, to be there in the midst of other people, and to be mortal there" (38). Wilder, on the other hand, tends to assume that the life *experiences* of all human beings are fundamentally similar, and thus, life in all times and places begins, for him, to look the same—even in externals—as it does today.

It might seem that Kierkegaard's distinction between the aesthetic, ethical, and religious modes of life constitutes an attempt to identify certain universal patterns in human life or universal categories into which all particular lives may, on any given day, be placed. There is some justification for this interpretation, but if the categories are universal it is only because they constitute broad alternatives available, in principle, to every living soul, and not because they are "categorical imperatives" that, individually or together, dictate the path each or any life, depending on the individual's basic "nature," must follow. Indeed, Kierkegaard's central point in *Either/Or* and *Fear and Trembling*, where he discusses these modes of being, is that except for the aesthetic mode, which consists in following the "path of least resistance" or seeking infantile self-gratification in all things, the individual must choose consciously which path he or she will take and pursue his or her goal actively, renewing the original choice continually and at every moment. The ethical is identified specifically as "the universal," but Kierkegaard is referring here to the universality of a conventional moral code that is freely and intentionally adopted and adhered to by the majority in a community and not to any truly universal element in human nature or in the life experience of the race. On the other hand, Wilder's typical characters, and especially the four central figures in *The Skin of Our Teeth*, are compelled by their very natures to be what they are and live as they do.

At the same time, however, many aspects of Wilder's play can be readily interpreted in terms of Kierkegaard's categories or modes of existence. First of all, Sabina clearly lives within the aesthetic mode, absorbed as she is in pleasure, sensuality, and the present moment. In Act II, she tells Antrobus: "Except for two things, pleasure and power, what is life? Boredom! Foolishness" (194). In Act III, she reveals that she has appropriated a number of beef cubes and at first refuses to turn them in to the proper authorities, who will distribute them where the need is greatest. Instead, she selfishly wishes to use them to purchase admission to a movie, reasoning that "after anybody's gone through what we've gone through, they have a right to grab what they can find" (245). Her very addiction to the movies is symptomatic of an aesthetic personality. Kierkegaard's aesthete is devoted to the theatre (as was the philosopher himself at one stage of his life). Henry's self-centeredness and his devotion to "fun," which includes his murderous escapades with his slingshot, also mark him as a Kierkegaardian aesthete, although of a more sinister type than Sabina. More significantly, Antrobus himself chooses temporarily to tread the primrose path of aestheticism when he proclaims, "Enjoy yourselves," to be the motto of his tenure as President of the Human Race. His belated recognition of his responsibilities to his family, followed swiftly by his decision to try to save them and the animals from the impending deluge, may be said to constitute a "leap" from the aesthetic to the ethical plane, where he remains for the entire third act. He never attains the religious plane, at least in Kierkegaard's sense, yet it may be said that his decision at the end of the play to carry on, and build new worlds despite his knowledge that he will inevitably encounter daunting obstacles and threats, is an act of faith—even blind, wholly irrational faith (although it is based on his recollection of past achievements).

Perhaps, then, Antrobus's nature or essence is more fluid and more subject to his conscious control, than those of the other main characters. One knows for a certainty, for instance, that Sabina and Henry will never rise above the aesthetic level, just as Mrs. Antrobus will never sink to it or rise to become religious in Kierkegaard's sense. Upon closer examination, though, Antrobus as well appears too fixed and constant to accord with the existentialist view of the individual. He perpetually contains within himself both aesthetic and ethical impulses. As his wife points out to Sabina in Act I, his adulterous adventures are a common occurrence and always end in his return to hearth and home and Sabina's banishment to the kitchen. His ethical side is also evident in the first act, in his sense of responsibility toward the "refugees," Homer, Moses, and the Muses, and in his anguish at Henry's former and present transgressions, which remind him of his own sins as well. Thus, his decision to abandon the aesthetic life in favor of the ethical one at the end of Act II is less a total, committed Kierkegaardian choice of himself than a single phase of a cyclical, eternally recurring behavior pattern.

The cause of Wilder's deviation from existentialist doctrine on this point lies not only in the fact that the characters in *Skin* are archetypal figures and not genuine flesh-and-blood individuals, but also in the playwright's ingrained Platonist habits of thought. Platonism, the original "essentialist" philosophy, is, as such, irrevocably and fundamentally irreconcilable with existentialism. If Wilder can assimilate both perspectives into his dramatic vision, it is partly because his acceptance of the existentialist point of view is restricted primarily to the sphere of human relations and partly because, again, he ultimately declines to resolve the underlying tension in his work between the general (associated with Platonism) and the particular (associated with existentialism—and naturalism as well).

However, one Platonic element in *Our Town* seems paradoxically to leave the way open as well for the adoption of an existentialist conception of the individual, but it is impossible, due to the ambiguity of the passage in question, to determine Wilder's exact beliefs or intentions on this point. His assertion that the individual identity does not survive indefinitely after death may be said to imply that the "eternal part" of each human being is actually a featureless, undefined core, which the individual may mold into or clothe with whatever sort of "self" he or she chooses. If this is indeed what Wilder is implying, then clearly here he is close to an existentialist view of the nature of the individual. However, it is possible that for Wilder, the individual's eternal part, while lacking what one normally thinks of as a unique personal identity, nonetheless partakes of a general, universal "human nature." The very fact that Wilder characterizes the individual's core as "eternal" leads him away from the existentialists who, as Sartre puts it, "will never consider man as an end because he is always in the making" (*Existentialism* 50). An examination of the "three-minute" playlet, *And the Sea Shall Give Up Its Dead*, which explores the same concept of the postmortal dissolution of the identity sheds little light on the problem. The three drowned souls rising on Judgment Day are all absorbed into the "blaze of unicity" (103) as they are "reduced to [their] quintessential matter" (102), in which state they are entirely indistinguishable from one another and even from the stars; however, there is no indication in the play that their former identities were entirely their own creation or that, within the context of the created universe (which Wilder pictures as being utterly annihilated on Doomsday), these souls had no fixed, preestablished essence that largely determined who they would be and how they would act.

Of course, Wilder depicts in *Queens of France* the power of a subjective "choice of oneself" to transform one's life and personality in important ways. The choice of the "queens" to accept the lie offered them by M. Cahusac is, in existentialist terms, "inauthentic" or escapist. However, the flexibility of each client's "essence" can be seen in the behavior and confessions of the second and third visitors, Mme. Pugeot and Mlle. Pointevin, and especially the former. A vulgar, shallow, and formerly somewhat hypochondriac *bourgeoise*, Mme. Pugeot reveals the change wrought in her by her new self-image when she remarks, in reply to the lawyer's polite query about her health, "I used to do quite poorly, as you remember, but since this wonderful news I have been more than well, God be praised" (37). She is still vulgar and shallow, but her new vigor is apparent in her every speech, as is a marked sense of mission in life. Her husband, who scoffs at her airs and pretensions, has told her she even cried out in her sleep, "*Paris, I come*" (38), an outburst she attributes to her concern over the imagined threat of an invasion of "her" realm by Bismarck. Not only has her health improved, then, but in existentialist terms, she has embraced a fundamental project or plan.

Mlle. Pointevin, too, an impoverished schoolteacher, plays her role to the hilt, treating the lawyer with formidable condescension and sprinkling throughout her conversation such statements as "*La loi, c'est moi*" (42) and "Have they no bread? Give them cake" (42). However, according to Richard Goldstone (*Portrait* 86), the idea of the confidence man as benefactor of his "victims" was not derived by Wilder from any readings in existentialist philosophy but was borrowed, along with the basic outlines of the plot, from Thomas Mann's *The Confessions of Felix Krull, Confidence Man*.

On the other hand, Wilder comes remarkably close, at one point in the final act of *The Skin of Our Teeth*, to echoing Sartre's description of man as a being who contains Nothingness at his core and brings Nothingness into the world from within himself (Sartre, *Being* 56–59). After Sabina stops the scene between the actors playing Henry and Antrobus, the younger man apologizes for having lost control of himself the previous night and explains his reaction by saying:

> It's like I had some big emptiness inside me—the emptiness of being hated and blocked at every turn. And the emptiness fills up with the one thought that you have to strike and fight and kill. (239)

Shortly afterward Antrobus, too, comments: "He talks about an emptiness. Well, there's an emptiness in me, too. Yes,—work, work, work,—that's all I do. I've ceased to *live*" (240). As should be evident from these passages themselves, however, the emptiness in question in each case is contingent—a product of or reaction to certain transient conditions—rather than an inherent, universal fact of human existence, as it is for Sartre. Again, the playwright's distance from the existentialists on the question of the individual's essence is most evident in *Skin*. However, there are additional striking parallels between statements and motifs in the play and basic existentialist tenets, forming clear indications that the dramatist was in a frame of mind acutely receptive to the teachings of Sartre, whose influence was, indeed, to result in Wilder's next literary endeavor after *Skin*, *The Ides of March*.

Although Wilder's conception of the nature of the individual seems, then, to differ in important ways from that of the existentialists, his views regarding the individual's rights, prerogatives, responsibilities, purpose in life, and relations with others often exhibit a distinctly existentialist cast. First of all, several characters in different plays demonstrate by their words or actions that they regard self-assigned, subjectively established values and moral principles as a higher authority than those dictated by society or convention. Wilder, it is true, generally accepts the validity of conventional bourgeois moral standards and norms. He nowhere glorifies the antisocial, "existential" rebel as a hero. His recognition of the validity of what Kierkegaard terms a "teleological suspension of the ethical," the violation of the conventional moral code out of obedience to a higher, personally accepted authority, applies only to matters of sexual conduct or social convention, and never to complex or difficult, controversial moral problems. However, within these limits Wilder's characters come very close to enunciating genuinely existentialist (although perhaps not exclusively existentialist) ethical principles.

The earliest character to insist that, in matter of the heart, the individual's subjective values must take precedence over the conventional mores of society is the title character in the "three-minute" play, *Fanny Otcott*. The retired Irish actress's solitary reminiscences are interrupted by the arrival of a gentleman wearing a black hat and cape, whom she recognizes as George Atcheson, a former lover. He discloses that he is now the Bishop of Westholmstead, has married, and is the father of several sons. His love affair with the actress has troubled his conscience for some time and, wishing to confess his youthful transgression to his flock, he has come to ask her permission to make it known to them. She feels no remorse whatsoever and is contemptuous of his cowardly regard for public opinion. She admonishes him:

> Remember, George, the months you call sinful. It wasn't love, perhaps, but it was grace and poetry. The heavens rained odors on us. It was as childlike and harmless as paintings on fans. . . . Since then you have learned long names from books and heard a great many sneers from women as old as myself. You have borrowed your ideas from those who have never begun to live and who dare not. (38)

She dismisses him abruptly, telling him to say whatever he pleases to his congregations.

Similarly, in Act II of *Our Town*, Mr. Webb asserts obliquely that, in certain spheres at least, the individual is his or her own highest authority. Sensing George's craving, on the morning of his wedding, for an older man's guidance and reassurance, the Editor recalls the advice his father gave him before his own wedding to Emily's mother. The elder Mr. Webb counseled his son to assert his authority immediately and to treat his wife as if she were a child or servant so as to keep her cowed and submissive. When

George starts to protest that he does not think he could ever treat Emily in such a fashion, Editor Webb silences him with the comment, "So I took the opposite of my father's advice and I've been happy ever since" (58). Then he continues, "let that be a lesson to you, George, never to ask advice on personal matters" (58).

Ma Kirby, in *The Happy Journey*, also regards herself uncompromisingly as the ultimate authority for her own behavior. In fact, she functions throughout the play as a sort of "voice of existentialism" (at least, of a rudimentary, "popular" sort), despite the fact that she almost never gets beyond the level of cliché in her thinking or speaking and her values themselves are thoroughly conventional.

Her disregard for the authority of public opinion—in short, her ordinary American individualism—is evident at a number of points in the play. When the car carrying the family to Camden stops for a funeral and Ma's interest in the proceedings apparently, according to her children, arouses mirth in the passersby, she remarks, "I don't care what a lot of silly people in Elizabeth, New Jersey, think of me" (108). Her indifference to outside authority is again made manifest after her open camaraderie with a service station attendant (played by the Stage Manager) has again embarrassed her children. Her response to her daughter's plea that she be more reserved with strangers is to tell her, "Well, Caroline, you do your way and I'll do mine" (113). Her strongest demonstration that she allows her own subjective attitudes and concerns, rather than the attitudes of society at large, to determine the value she places on phenomena is prompted by Caroline's observation that Beulah lives on what appears to be a more affluent street than the Kirbys'. To this judgment, Ma replies majestically: "If people aren't nice I don't care how rich they are. I live in the best street in the world because my husband and children live there" (118). She also calls the car, "the best little Chevrolet in the world" (106) and Elmer, her husband, "the best driver in the world" (103). Both these latter assessments smack of fatuous provincialism as well as of endearing enthusiasm for what is hers, and Kierkegaard might regard them as evidence of worldliness, which for him consists in attributing infinite value to the paltry or inconsequential (*Fear* 166). However, it is not really *infinite* value that Ma attributes to the things and people that are near and dear to her, but merely transcendent or superior value, and to this extent she serves as a fine illustration of existentialist doctrine. Moreover, one of the paradoxical qualities of the "knight of faith" is that he or she is often indistinguishable from the crassest, most complacent bourgeois philistine. Kierkegaard writes, " 'he looks like a tax-collector!'. . . He takes delight in everything he sees, in the human swarm, in the new omnibuses, in the water of the Sound" (49–50).

Several Wilder characters besides Ma Kirby, Mr. Webb, and Fanny Otcott also reveal by their conduct or utterances that they believe that no outside temporal authority is qualified to dictate guidelines for their behavior.

Mrs. Molloy in *The Matchmaker* is one such character. In Act II, she tells her assistant, Minnie, "I can no longer stand being suspected of being a wicked woman, while I have nothing to show for it" (298). When her assistant protests that no one would dream of suspecting her of any improprieties, she declares that "All millineresses are suspected of being wicked women" (298). She complains that she can never allow herself to go to restaurants, balls, the theatre, or the opera because it would be bad for business. However, when circumstances conspire, later in the act, to compromise her reputation, leading Horace Vandergelder to break off his engagement to her, she decides to flout public opinion by being as "wicked" as she can and to have no regard for what people may say. She tells Vandergelder's clerks, who have been hiding in her shop and have thereby brought about her "undoing," that they must take her and Minnie out to an expensive restaurant in order to make up for all the trouble they have caused. She tells her assistant, "Minnie, you and I have been respectable for years; now we're in disgrace, we might as well make the most of it" (329). This response to her situation is reminiscent of Jean Genet's reaction, as described by Sartre, to being identified as a "thief" by "society" (in the person of his foster-mother) (*St. Genet* 237–40). Like the boy, Genet, Mrs. Molloy refuses to be intimidated by public opinion into accepting the usual values assigned by convention to certain modes of behavior. Although her "wickedness" is, in truth, extremely innocent, she nonetheless has, in existentialist terms, chosen (like Genet) first of all to recognize the truth—namely, that her reputation has been tarnished—and second, in spite of that recognition, to disregard the pressure to act in conformity with conventional values and injunctions and instead to take what others consider wickedness as her own good.

Mrs. Molloy has an "existentialist" antecedent in the "three-minute" plays as well: the title character in *The Message and Jehanne*. Jehanne, having been inspired by an accidental misdelivery of rings, decides to flee her home and family and the marriage and future they have arranged for her and to follow the promptings of her own heart, which has chosen to love an impoverished English scholar from Padua. Mrs. Molloy's decision to let Vandergelder depart and to marry someone she loves instead is roughly parallel to the choice of the young woman in the earlier play, and the device of an elopement appears in *The Matchmaker* as well, although in another plot strand, where it is used in part to make an "existentialist" point. In the latter play, however, the young woman, Vandergelder's niece, Ermengarde, although in love with the artist Ambrose Kemper (of whom her uncle disapproves) is in continual terror of offending against propriety and refuses to consider eloping with her suitor. She consents to meet him in New York, whither Vandergelder is sending her for safekeeping, only after she is persuaded to do so by Dolly Levi, who is to act as chaperone. Ermengarde's bondage to public opinion in personal matters is so complete that

Dolly and Kemper have much to do to convince her that there is no impropriety in dining in a restaurant. Thus, she is a foil for Mrs. Molloy and, by implication, Jehanne.

Certainly, decisions such as Jehanne's and Mrs. Molloy's to follow the dictates of feeling in affairs of the heart are by no means uncommon in works of literature, and especially dramatic literature. Indeed, they are a mainstay of comedy and romantic or sentimental drama. Thus, it may be stretching a point to label them "existential choices" rather than, say, "romantic literary conventions," especially when they do not apparently involve any serious, total commitment or rebellion in the name of subjective values on the part of the chooser, to say nothing of existential angst. Jehanne's choice does involve a serious commitment, however, and Mrs. Molloy consciously acts in the name of subjective values when she decides to flout the opinions of "society." In any case, the playwright's recurring emphasis on the subjective assignment of values, if only in the realm of love affairs, indicates indisputable existentialist tendencies and sympathies on his part.

Furthermore, there is a more unequivocally "existentialist" exploration of subjective values in *The Trumpet Shall Sound*, Wilder's first full-length play, which was produced professionally in 1926. Inspired by *The Alchemist*, it is set in the last century in a Washington Square mansion, several rooms of which have been illegally rented out to an assortment of shady characters by the maid, Flora, in the absence of the master of the house, Peter Magnus. One of the boarders is a former sea captain named Horace Dabney, who is revealed to have deserted a sinking ship of which he had command because he believed he had a mission to preach the gospel in America. All the passengers drowned; he alone was left alive. Although his action was undeniably reprehensible and he is depicted as somewhat self-righteous, his talk of a "higher mission" brings up the question of a "teleological suspension of the ethical." The fact that others would benefit from his preaching makes his decision to abandon the ship, not a true suspension of the ethical, but merely a substitution of a higher ethical good for a lower one: the salvation of souls for the saving of lives. Dabney is thus in a position similar to that of the tragic hero, as described by Kierkegaard, rather than that of the "knight of faith," Abraham, who attempts to achieve no social end with his sacrifice of Isaac. The tragic hero, such as Agamemnon, who must sacrifice Iphigenia so that the Greek fleet may punish Troy for the abduction of Helen, has merely placed the "national" interest above personal interests and the ethical injunction to love and preserve one's children. Dabney's avowed motivations for his choice to disobey conventional maritime ethics may be no more than a cowardly rationalization—and that possibility is expressly raised in the play—but the captain is not portrayed as contemptible. Magnus, returning home unexpectedly, forgives Dabney wholeheartedly for his crime and his intrusion into the house, being convinced that the captain was justified in deserting his ship. In any case, the seaman's discussion of his past introduces into the play the problem of subjectively assigned values that conflict with conventional ones, thus injecting typical existentialist issues into what is otherwise a thoroughly Platonist play.

A more explicitly existentialist feature of Wilder's drama is the role played by choice, that central concept in all existentialist thought, in determining the course of the action in several of the plays. Characters' momentous choices of course determine the outcome of countless plays created throughout the history of the drama, beginning with the Greeks. However, in the case of Wilder's work, the character's chosen course is nearly always in harmony with other basic existentialist (or at least Sartrean) values, since it entails the character's active involvement with the rest of humanity. First, in the final act of *The Matchmaker*, the title character, Dolly Levi, recounts directly to the audience the story of her decision to "rejoin the human race." She observes that "there comes a time in everybody's life when he must decide whether he'll live among human beings or not—a fool among fools or a fool alone" (395). Then she confides, "As for me, I've decided to live among them" (395).

It might be objected that Dolly's form of involvement amounts to intrusive meddling and interference, but that would be a subjective judgment, and there is no denying that the basic thrust of her convictions and values would meet with Sartre's approval. The philosopher writes that "the man who becomes aware of himself through the *cogito* also perceives all others, and he perceives them as the condition of his own existence. . . . The other is indispensable to my own existence, as well as to my knowledge about myself" (*Existentialism* 37–38).

A more material objection might be that Dolly's decision to rejoin humanity has, per se, little or no direct effect on the course of the action of the play. Dolly is Wilder's own invention; she does not appear in his source for the play, Nestroy's *Einen Jux will er sich Machen*. However, as Wilder has written, the play "is about the aspirations of the young (and not only of the young) for a fuller, freer participation in 'life' " (*AC* 110). At the end of the play, the junior clerk, Barnaby, delivers its "moral," remarking that he believes the play to be "about adventure" (401). Indeed, he and Cornelius Hackl leave Yonkers specifically to look for adventure, which they find in abundance in New York, although they hesitate to label it as such when they find it. Similarly, Minnie and Mrs. Molloy, in their trip to the restaurant; Ambrose and Ermengarde, in their flight from Vandergelder; and even Vandergelder himself and Mrs. Levi all find sufficient adventure to last them a lifetime, once they break out of their stifling, anaesthetizing daily routines and actively seek participation in life. Thus, Mrs. Levi's decision to "rejoin the human race" is entirely of a piece with the play's central concern: the desire for involvement in life, which motivates all the characters to one degree or another.

Moreover, the emphasis is found not just in this one play. Dolly herself is a reincarnation of Fanny Otcott, and the earlier play dramatizes the moment of decision that Dolly merely recounts. The Irish actress's scrapbooks, in which she is immersed at the beginning, correspond roughly to Dolly's Bible and oak leaf, which sparked her decision when she came across them one night in her seclusion, and after the Bishop leaves her, Fanny's black servant boy, Sampson, enters to announce that three gentlemen have called and been sent away by the housekeeper, in accordance with the actress's earlier instructions. Fanny commands: "Go call them back, Sampson. Tell them I have come down. . . . Bring up the best box of wine, the one with my picture painted on it. I shall be young again" (40).

It might be objected that, since the choices are in neither case accompanied by anguish, "fear and trembling," "anxiety," or "dread," they are inconsequential or trivial, but they both seem to be renewals or reaffirmations of the characters' fundamental projects, and they both propel the characters into action and involvement. Again, the "existentialist" aspects of these plays indicate no more than a general sympathy on Wilder's part with the existentialist point of view.

On the other hand, choice and anxiety—even anguish—are shown to be inextricably linked in *The Skin of Our Teeth*. In each act, the decision to go on struggling and living is shown to be preceded by a surrender to despair. In Act I, Antrobus, after seeing the mark of Cain on Henry's forehead, says that he cannot go on. He is persuaded to continue only by his children's efforts to please him by showing how much they have learned. In Act III, he tells his wife he has lost "The desire to begin again, to start building" (242). Only after he has seen Sabina's confusion and need for reassurance and found that his books have survived the war does he regain the will to renew the struggle. In Act II, his despair is due to Gladys's emulation of Sabina, but his decision to try to shepherd the family to safety is less a conscious choice to survive than an automatic, reflexive response to the threat of imminent deluge. In none of the three cases is the character's anguish elicited by an awareness of the responsibility of choosing itself—a consciousness of the infinite, vertiginous possibilities, none inherently more "correct" than any other, confronting the chooser and of the impossibility of justifying or excusing oneself once the choice has been made. Antrobus's anguish springs, rather, from his feeling that if he chooses to continue, he and his family are doomed to repeat the same or similar errors over and over. In other words, the future is not the *unknown* for him, as it is for the existentialist, but just the reverse. In any case, in coupling anguish with choice in this play, Wilder is clearly drawing near (perhaps unwittingly and independently) to the existentialist views he was to espouse and consciously promulgate in his next major work, *The Ides of March*.

Not surprisingly, the action in two of the three acts of *The Alcestiad* turns upon a critical choice made by the central character, Alcestis, and in each case, the choice does alter decisively the course of all the characters' lives and their immediate situations and relationships. In the first act, Alcestis decides after all to marry Admetus and abandon her endeavor to serve Apollo at Delphi, realizing that if it is possible for the god to assume the humblest of human shapes, that of a herdsman, and yet remain unrecognizable, then it must also be possible for there to be something of the divine about the humble, prosaic, day-to-day existence she has hitherto scorned: the existence of the ordinary wife and mother, including the ordinary royal wife and mother. This choice, then, is a momentous one which determines the entire course of her future life. Moreover, Alcestis does not waver or vacillate once her mind is made up but instead chooses with her whole self and embraces the consequences of her decision. She asks Admetus to ask her again to marry him, saying: "Ask me in pain to bear your children. . . . To live for you and for your children and for your people—to live for you as though every moment I were ready to die for you" (33). When he does ask her again, she replies, "With my whole self, Admetus" (34). Thus, her decision is plainly an authentic one.

She does not openly display any dread or anguish while she is making the decision, but in the second act, when she chooses to die in her husband's stead (a choice that necessarily involves a total commitment of self as well), she tells the herdsman who also wishes to die for his king: "You long to die: I dread, fear, hate to die. I must die from Admetus" (43). Her choice to do so is thus, again, fully authentic. Hercules then chooses to confront his deepest fears also and descend to Hades in order to fetch her back to life.

The central importance of these two choices—especially that of Alcestis—is made evident in *The Drunken Sisters*, the so-called "satyr play" designed to be performed at the conclusion of the longer work. In that brief piece, which depicts how Alcestis was presented with the opportunity of sacrificing her life for her husband, a disguised Apollo tricks the Fates by means of a ruse into sparing Admetus's life, which they consent to do (once they learn who has tricked them) only if they are given another life to take the place of the king's; Apollo believes that they can select some slave, whose death would be a blessed relief to him, and sever his thread instead of Admetus's. The three sisters are horrified that the god could think them assassins and they explain that "Someone must *give* his life for Admetus—of free choice and will. Over such deaths we have no control. Neither Chance nor Necessity rules the free offering of the will. Someone must *choose* to die in the place of Admetus, King of Thessaly" (129). In *The Alcestiad* and *The Drunken Sisters*, of course, Wilder was consciously writing under the influence of existentialist thought, so the crucial role played by choice in both plays is no accident or mere indication of unconscious existentialist sympathies.

There are, moreover, other "existentialist" aspects to Wilder's treatment of human behavior and action, especially in *The Skin of Our Teeth*. First, Sabina comments as she dismisses the audience, "The end of this play isn't written yet" (250), a statement reminiscent of Sartre's assertion that "man . . . is always in the making" (*Existentialism* 50). Also, the nature of Antrobus's original choice or fundamental project, which generates all his subsequent, specific plans, is even suggested in the play, and it is a choice consonant with existentialist values and principles. In Act II, the Fortune-teller exhorts Antrobus to "Start a new world. Begin again" (207), and in the last act he himself acknowledges, "All I ask is a chance to build new worlds and God has always given us that" (248). Thus, his original project or deepest impulse is one that propels him into creative action; it is the project to construct a suitable environment or home for the human family. This conception of humanity as builder of worlds leads Wilder toward Sartre's view that the individual "is the one by whom it happens that *there is* a world" (52) (that is, a human or "peopled" world).

On the other hand, Sartre himself would have objected to the *structure* of the basic action in *Skin*. Using Barrie's *The Admirable Crichton* as an example of the sort of bourgeois drama he deplores, Sartre writes, "The theater that presents you with these passions and shows you disturbances that have no consequences also presents you with instances of typical characters, such as the Eternal Feminine, and tells you that you can change all the circumstances without the character being changed in the slightest" (*SOT* 95). For Sartre, "to act (which is indeed the specific object of theater) is to change the world, and changing it necessarily means changing oneself. . . . [However,] what [the bourgeoisie] asks of the theater is to refrain from disturbing it by the idea of the act; the act is impossible" (94). Wilder, it is true, writes in a theoretical essay that the drama is "forward movement" (*AC* 122). However, he is arguing against a static, Maeterlinckian conception of the drama, not against the use of cyclical dramatic structures. Moreover, forward movement of a plot does not in itself entail *change* in the Sartrean sense. Sartre himself notes that bourgeois plays are characterized by complex plots and intrigue (*SOT* 94–95). All the "action" ultimately leaves things exactly as they were, though. What Wilder's play shows is precisely, in Sartre's terms, "disturbances that have no consequences," despite the references to building new worlds. The curtain falls in the final act on a repetition of the monologue by Sabina that began the first act. Although the characters change in subtle ways in the course of the play, gradually acquiring greater maturity or hardening in their depravity, one cannot deny that the play as a whole, presenting as it does such characters as "the Eternal Feminine" (in the person of Sabina), implies that "you can change all the circumstances without the character being changed in the slightest."

In the realm of ethics there is in Wilder's preexistentialist plays at least one striking echo of existentialist—specifically Sartrean—ideas. In the confrontation between Henry and Antrobus in the final act of *The Skin of Our Teeth*, the latter enunciates a fundamental (but not exclusively) Sartrean tenet when he tells his son, who wants to be free to do as he pleases without having to answer to anyone:

> I shall continue fighting you until my last breath as long as you mix up your idea of liberty with your idea of hogging everything for yourself. . . . You and I want the same thing; but until you think of it as something that everyone has a right to you are my deadly enemy and I will destroy you. (237)

The statement has an air of cliché about it, but Sartre's assertion that "I am obliged to want others to have freedom at the same time that I want my own freedom" (*Existentialism* 45) is no less straightforward and unsurprising. That the notion is not original with Sartre, Kant having made much the same assertion, does not alter the fact that Wilder (or Antrobus) sounds very much like the French thinker at this point.[3]

However, the matter is complicated by the uncanny resemblance of Henry's rhetoric in this same scene to that of the typical Sartrean hero, such as Orestes in *The Flies*. Wilder's Henry is in rebellion against all forms of authority and, like Sartre's Orestes, sounds the note of "freedom" repeatedly, like a bell. When he awakens to find his father standing before him and pointing a revolver at him, Henry invites him to shoot, saying:

> You don't have to think I'm any relation of yours. I haven't got any father or any mother, or brothers or sisters. And I don't want any. And what's more I haven't got anybody over me; and I never will have. I'm alone, and that's all I want to be: alone. (235)

Although Orestes in Sartre's play never denies that he is related to his mother and sister, he tells Zeus in the final act that when he became aware of his freedom, he knew he was "alone, utterly alone in the midst of this well-meaning little universe of yours. . . . And there was nothing left in heaven, no right or wrong, nor anyone to give me orders" (121–22). In Wilder's play, Henry proceeds to tell his father he plans to go "a long way from here and make [his] own world that's fit for a man to live in. Where a man can be free, and have a chance, and do what he wants to do in his own way" (236). Orestes, too, goes off into self-imposed exile at the conclusion of *The Flies*, seeking, as he tells his sister, "an Orestes and an Electra waiting for us" (124) beyond rivers and mountains. Later in the scene, when Antrobus tells his son he must behave in front of his mother, Henry shouts "Nobody can say *must* to me. All my life everybody's been crossing me,—everybody, everything, all of you. I'm going to be free, even if I have to kill half the world for it" (238). Although Sartre would, of course, regard this last outburst as evidence of "bad faith," there is no denying that Henry is simply, in this scene, a distorted or deformed and simplified version— almost a parody—of

Orestes. The course of action Orestes follows in Sartre's play, from uncommitted drifting in the stream of life to active involvement with humanity and his own destiny, resembles that followed by Dolly Levi, rather than the pattern of Henry's life, but the parallels in the two characters' utterances and attitudes are undeniable. It is as if Wilder split Orestes—or, at least, one facet of Orestes—into two characters, Henry and Antrobus, letting each voice half of the feelings and convictions of Sartre's hero on the subject of freedom. The fact that the rebellious, self-assertive, antiauthoritarian Henry is presented as unambiguously evil suggests that Wilder himself harbored ambivalent feelings toward the point of view he was later to recognize as Sartre's, and indeed, Sartre's atheism proved repugnant to Wilder and he turned instead (or returned) to Kierkegaard, whose conception of freedom, although an important element in his thought (e.g., *Fear* 162; and *Dread* 99), is less sweeping and obsessive than Sartre's. Even Sartre began, in his later writings, to recognize the limits of human freedom, although he remained fundamentally antiauthoritarian in his orientation.

Another significant existentialist aspect of Wilder's drama is his advocacy of an intensification of consciousness or awareness, especially such as can be evoked by an individual's sudden confrontation with his or her own (or another's) mortality. In his recognition that everyday existence tends to involve a "tranquilizing" or "anaesthetizing" of the consciousness, an evasion of deeper or more painful truths, and an absorption in "idle talk" or trivialities, he resembles Heidegger and Kierkegaard, especially the latter in his observation that "the majority of men live without being thoroughly conscious that they are spiritual beings—and to this is referable all the security, contentment with life, etc., etc., which precisely is despair" (*Fear* 159).[4] However, this theme in Wilder's drama may with equal justice be termed a "Proustian" or "Maeterlinckian" element, as well as an "existentialist" one. In fact, inasmuch as he conceives of the realm beneath everyday appearances as "too wonderful for anyone to realize," rather than as a meaningless, terrifyingly amorphous void such as Sartre describes in *Nausea*, Wilder is closer to the Platonist Maeterlinck and to Proust than he is to the existentialists.

It has already been pointed out that a confrontation with death is usually, in Wilder's work, the event that occasions a character's intensified awareness and appreciation of the wonders hidden beneath life's mundane surface. This perceived association may also be encountered in existentialist (although, again, not only existentialist) writing, primarily that of Heidegger (109–16). Even Sabina in *Skin* utters a simplified Heideggerian axiom when she states, "In the midst of life we are in the midst of death, a truer word was never said" (112), and the very precariousness of human existence, as it is presented in Act I, calls to mind Heidegger's emphasis on death as an ever-present possibility, the full recognition of which is a necessary condition for authentic existence (109–16). However, the *appreciation* of apparently insignificant moments and presences in one's life is a relatively passive response to the sudden recognition of human mortality, whereas the response called for by Sartre, Heidegger, and Kierkegaard, the total commitment of one's being to a project, is an entirely active one.

Finally, one other aspect of Wilder's drama that is almost completely in harmony with existentialist teachings is his minimalist theatrical style. Although one cannot properly speak of an "existentialist style" of theatre or an "existentialist aesthetics," as one can of a naturalist, symbolist, or expressionist style and aesthetics, Sartre wrote and lectured extensively on the theatre, and he and Wilder share a number of general opinions regarding specific stylistic questions and fundamental theoretical concerns. First of all, Sartre agrees with Wilder that the theatre tends to generalize any action or character it shows. Sartre states:

> The problem of the individual case seems to be material for the novel. I don't think that there are individuals in theater. Hamlet is an individual, of course, but he is primarily a myth, the myth of the individual at a particular moment. But the playwright cannot undertake an investigation in depth that would produce such a very complex character as one of Proust's heroes, for example. (*SOT* 280)

Sartre's reference to myth recalls Wilder's fondness for myth as a foundation for such plays as *The Skin of Our Teeth* and *The Alcestiad*, *Proserpina and the Devil*, *Childe Roland to the Dark Tower Came*, and even *The Flight into Egypt*, and his fascination with myth itself, as it appears in the work of other authors. Sartre is not advocating a drama, like Wilder's, which incorporates or is founded upon great, time-honored myths, and in 1944, he even explicitly criticized such a drama, despite his own venture into that territory in *The Flies* (15). He is simply noting the capacity of the theatre "to raise the exhibited individual action into the realm of idea and type and universal" (*AC* 108), as Wilder puts it. Nevertheless, Wilder's explicit recognition in his essays of the theatre's universalizing power reveals his fundamental agreement with Sartre on this point.

Next, Sartre (like Wilder and in opposition to Brecht) believed that the spectator's emotional "participation" in a dramatic action or identification with a character was preferable to his or her detachment or "alienation" (*SOT* 9–10, 115–20, 140–41, 283). In his early writings, conversations, and lectures, Sartre argues that the aesthetic distance between actor and spectator must be preserved in the theatre, but he remained ignorant at that period of Brecht's aesthetic theories and was not advocating a Brechtian theatrical style in any case. More to the point, "aesthetic distance" included, for him, physical separation of actors from audience. Sartre looked with disfavor on attempts to undermine the theatrical illusion, especially by bringing actors and audience into physical proximity with one another, allowing the dramatic action to spill over into the auditorium (12). Wilder's "Pirandellian" use of the theatre aisles in *Our Town* and *The Skin of Our Teeth* and his incorporation of actors pretending to be spectators in the former play would have met with Sartre's disapproval, at least at this stage of the latter's career. Sartre came to recognize the power and usefulness of Brecht's "alienation techniques," even terming Brecht's theatre "the essential modern development and fully in tune with our times" (183), but he himself preferred to see audiences "participating" in the action of his plays—that is, identifying with the characters and becoming personally, emotionally involved in the conflict presented.

In this respect, of course, he resembles Wilder, but there is one major area of disagreement between the two playwrights. That area concerns the acceptable techniques for *achieving* or *generating* this emotional involvement. Sartre is more consistent than Wilder, for he argues:

> There is no longer any call to work with the indeterminate and confused principle of the playwright and the director of the past or the philosopher of the theater of the past, who held . . . that a mirage presented and accepted as mirage necessarily appeals to the real feelings of an audience. (149)

Noting the "innocence" of turn-of-the-century playwrights and directors, he writes:

> They simultaneously held that the place called the stage was an illusory place, a mirage, and that the character who was to get to the stage by way of the aisles would convince the audience of the reality of the performance because he brushed against them as he passed. But now all the dramatists of our generation no longer believe that theater is realistic. . . . For either you want reality, and if so, you must carry it through to the end, there's nothing for it but that—you evoke real feelings by real events; or you recognize the totally illusory character of dramatic representation, but if so, you have to exploit it as such—as a denial of reality . . . and not as an imitation of it. (149–50)

Wilder began experimenting with anti-illusionistic techniques in order to evoke his audiences' belief in the truth of the action he set before them, although perhaps not in its "reality." All the same, Sartre would doubtlessly consider Wilder naïve or "innocent" because of the latter's attempts to use antirealistic techniques to bolster his audiences' belief; and Wilder's notion that a nonillusionistic style in the theatre can cause spectators to "pay [more] deeply from [their] heart's participation" in the drama goes counter to Sartre's views as expressed in the passages cited here. The root of the disagreement, again, seems to be Wilder's Platonist belief in a higher, essential reality beyond that accessible to the senses. For Sartre, in contrast, the dimension beyond phenomenal reality is *le néant*.

On the other hand, at least one anti-illusionistic feature of Wilder's dramatic technique fits in closely with Sartre's thought in that very matter and might loosely be characterized as "existentialist" in a general sense.

That feature is his use of the bare stage and other minimalist devices. The bare or nearly bare stage called for by Wilder in *Our Town*, *The Happy Journey*, *Pullman Car Hiawatha*, *The Long Christmas Dinner*, *Childhood*, and *Infancy* is an appropriate symbol or representation of the void.

However, the minimalist "setting" for these plays of Wilder's is not so much a featureless void as a wholly concrete, anti-illusionistic, undisguised *stage*, complete with "dusty flats" leaning against the back wall. Moreover, insofar as Wilder might conceive of his bare stage as a symbol of the void, it would almost certainly be a "void that contains the Infinite," such as Mallarmé envisioned, rather than the utter nothingness perceived by Sartre or Heidegger. Wilder clearly states in his theatre essays that one important purpose of the absence of scenery in his plays is "to raise the exhibited individual action into the realm of idea and type and universal" (*AC* 108) or "from the specific to the general" (124). Wilder's bare stage is thus not meant to imply that human life occurs within a spiritual or existential void—especially since the spiritual realm is brought directly on to the bare stage in *Pullman Car Hiawatha* and the audience at *Our Town* is reminded by the Jane Crofut letter, at the end of Act I, that the Infinite in fact contains the apparent "void" in which the play occurs.

However, there is, according to Wilder, a second purpose to his use of the bare stage and other minimalist conventions: to provoke "the collaborative activity of the spectator's imagination" (*AC* 124). Explaining the manner in which the absence of scenery in *Our Town* contributes to the restoration of significance to "the smallest details of daily life," the playwright asserts that "The spectator through lending his imagination to the action restages it inside his head" (101). Wilder, in fact, perceives all nonrealistic conventions—especially those involving suggestion—as functioning in this way, as is apparent in his analysis of the original Greek audience's decoding of the "signs" presented to it by Euripides's *Medea*. The sort of imaginative involvement he describes clearly entails more than a simple identification with the drama's characters on the part of the spectator or an emotional participation in the action, such as both Wilder and Sartre endorse and seek to encourage in their audiences. The latter form of "participation" may, of course, be called forth by a conventionally realistic play, and according to Brecht, is more likely to be called forth by such a play than by a "presentational" one. However, the creative or re-creative imaginative participation at which Wilder aims, with his minimalist techniques, also may, without great difficulty, be linked to general existentialist values and beliefs.

Wilder's interest in provoking this active participation may have been aroused, ironically, by his association with Gertrude Stein. In his Introduction to Stein's *The Geographical History of America* (1936), the playwright discusses Stein's aversion to punctuation and quotes from her writings the following explanation of that aversion:

> A comma by helping you along holding your coat for you and putting on your shoes keeps you from living your life as actively as you should live it. . . . A long complicated sentence should force itself upon you, make yourself know yourself knowing it. (*AC* 191)

The lack of punctuation is clearly, in this respect, the literary counterpart of the bare stage. However, Stein's basic perspective is Platonist rather than existentialist. Active involvement of the spectator was, of course, one of the aims of the futurists, too; the symbolist poets also wanted their readers to participate more actively than was customary in experiencing their poems (Cornell 55, 59). Thus, there is nothing exclusively existentialist about this particular artistic aim or impulse.

At the same time, it is connected, for a number of different reasons, with basic existentialist principles, and the connection may be readily perceived. First, the bare stage allows each spectator greater leeway than usual in assigning subjective meanings and applying subjective interpretations to the action and objects on stage. In undermining the visual "authority" of the scene designer, the playwright demonstrates to the spectator that—in the theatre, at least—the individual can to a certain extent determine the meaning and "essence" of the material objects he or she sees before him or her. That meaning is a function of the way in which the objects are used by the actors—in other words, of the purpose they serve and the role they play in the actor's "fundamental project" on stage. A plank laid across the backs of two chairs can "mean" or "signify" a counter at a drug-store soda fountain. A ladder can "mean" the upper story of a house; four chairs, an automobile; and low stools or chairs, a row of bushes. The stage itself can "mean" whatever the Stage Manager says it means—Main Street, a church, or a hillside cemetery. Thus, the spectators, following the example of the actor, may to a degree create for themselves the reality of place and objects and—in the case of *The Long Christmas Dinner*—the age of a character and even the very supernumeraries, the family's servants. The *basic identity* of any given object or gesture or area of the stage is determined not by the spectator or even the actor, of course, but by the dramatist. Nevertheless, in general, meaning on Wilder's bare stage is conferred by *human action* or *choice*, whether that of the actor, playwright, or spectator. It is significant, too, that the dramatist's primary purpose in utilizing a minimalist approach was to convey a sense of the value of things and persons ordinarily taken for granted. The bare stage and all the Wilderian conventions associated with it can thus be seen to demonstrate the existentialist axiom that values are subjectively assigned to phenomena and other people through the individual's active choice and involvement.

It should not be surprising, then, to learn that Sartre recognized that material objects are, to some extent, unnecessary on stage and that he appeared fascinated—in the abstract, at any rate—by the expressive power and flexibility of pantomime. He writes: "The object is not needed in theater.

It is superfluous. The gesture engenders it simply by being gesture, by using the object" (*SOT* 264). For instance, "the gesture of stabbing brings the dagger into being" (103). It seems that Wilder and Sartre are clearly of one mind on this topic. However, Sartre also later modified some of his more categorical earlier pronouncements, stating, "there's no question, of course, of doing away with properties altogether; for there is no particular need to require an audience to make an effort to accept a further superfluous illusion by having a clenched fist stand for a dagger" (103). At the same time, such active involvement by the audience is, of course, theoretically in harmony with Sartre's own emphasis on action and involvement in general, as well as with all the existentialists' assertion of the authority of subjectively assigned meanings and values. Sartre continues, moreover:

> the fact remains that you can reduce properties to practically nothing. We saw that very well demonstrated by the Chinese Opera a few years ago. With almost nothing you can conjure up a river and a boat. (103)

Thus, Wilder's use of pantomime in his minimalist plays constitutes a definite link between his theatre and Sartre's views on the nature of the art form. Sartre's views are somewhat contradictory to be sure, and in his own plays he calls for no wholesale elimination of properties from the stage, but the link is nevertheless a solid one.

In Sartre's terms, moreover, the spectators at Wilder's plays are "freer" than the spectators at a wholly realistic or illusionistic play, since they are forced to become conscious of their freedom to assign meanings to phenomena. One may deny that such a spectator actually "restages [the action] inside his head," as Wilder claims he does, but one cannot deny that Wilder himself *believed* his bare stage would evoke this response from the spectator, and this belief in and respect for subjective interpretations indicates definite existentialist sympathies on his part. Sartre, too (once again contradicting one of his earlier statements), when asked by an interviewer, "Do you think that it is better to present a fully finished work, or should the audience be left a margin for infiltrating a whole dimension of its own?" replied, "I think the audience should be left a margin." He added later: "an audience should be left some freedom. It should not be crushed under multiple and unduly pure characters" (283–84). However, here Sartre is referring to the audience's freedom to determine for itself the attitude it takes toward complex, ambiguous characters and not to its freedom to perceive empty air as an object of some sort or one object as something else. On the other hand, the actor in Wilder's minimalist plays is certainly demonstrating for the more passive spectator the existential truth that the meaning or "essence" of the world and its phenomena is assigned by individual human beings through their actions.

Thus, although Wilder can legitimately be said to have harbored existentialist convictions and even to have formed an acquaintance with existentialist thought, from the very outset of his career, his Platonist prejudices and presuppositions prevented him from espousing in any of his plays an entirely consistent existentialist point of view. Even his view of the individual as individual—his conception of the rights, prerogatives, potentialities, and responsibilities of the particular human being—deviates from that of the existentialists. He never comes to the point of asserting, with Kierkegaard, that in the field of morality (or even faith), "the individual as the particular is higher than the universal, is justified over against it, is not subordinate but superior" (*Fear* 66), except in relatively inconsequential or noncontroversial matters. In fact, such existentialism as there is in his view of the individual is entirely in harmony with conventional American values, such as respect for diversity of opinion, recognition of everyone's right to the (active) pursuit of a subjectively chosen happiness, reverence for individual liberty and a hostility toward any unjust authority that threatens it, and admiration for inventiveness, community involvement, and committed, goal-oriented activity. Perhaps the bulk of Wilder's "existentialism," then, is simply "Americanism."

NOTES

1. A reference in one of Wilder's later essays (*AC* 144) shows him to have acquired at least a rudimentary knowledge by that time (1949) of the German philosopher's work, and unpublished letters and lecture notes show that he was familiar with Nietzsche's thought as early as 1930 (University of Chicago lecture notes on Shakespeare and the Comic Spirit, ms., Wilder papers, YCAL; postcard to Mrs. B. Artzybasheff, 2 Feb. 1943, ms., Wilder papers, YCAL; letter to S. Steward, 1 Oct. 1937, ms., Wilder papers, YCAL).
2. For a further discussion of other Kierkegaardian aspects of the play, see Haberman, *Plays* (40–53).
3. A debt that Sartre himself notes in *Existentialism* (47).
4. See also Heidegger (extract rpt. in Solomon, *Existentialism* 108–9).

Chapter 7

East Meets West: Reflections of Asian, Classical European, and Popular American Theatres in Wilder's Plays

In his own explanations or analyses of his dramatic work, Wilder most often links it with the great classical or traditional theatres of both the Orient and the Occident rather than with the theories or practices of any of the movements or playwrights examined thus far (with the possible exception of existentialism). It is the anti-illusionistic conventions of the ancient Greek, Elizabethan, Renaissance Spanish, Chinese, and Japanese theatres that he most frequently cites as precedents and inspirations for his dramatic experiments. His theatre also bears a striking resemblance in certain respects to the medieval European theatre, as well as to at least one form of American popular paratheatrical entertainment, the civic or academic pageant. This chapter thus moves the discussion closer to Wilder's own perception of his plays and of himself as a dramatist. At the same time, however, it explores important similarities of which the playwright may himself have been unaware.

Limitations of space prohibit a thorough analysis of all the traits shared by Wilder's theatre and these premodern forms. Therefore, the discussion, unlike those in previous chapters, will necessarily be abbreviated, confining itself to major resemblances or points of convergence or divergence.

Certain features of Wilder's theatre, or of individual plays, cause it to resemble more than one of the traditional forms mentioned here, so to eliminate redundancy, those features will be treated separately at the outset. The features in question are anachronism (which in Wilder's plays is really met with only in *The Skin of Our Teeth*), allegorical figures, the assumption of female roles by male actors, direct address, condensed time and space—especially in the depiction of journeys, and the mingling of actors and audience.

The traditional theatres incorporating anachronistic elements include the medieval, Elizabethan, Renaissance Spanish, and Chinese. Of these, the Chinese, Elizabethan, and Spanish Golden Age theatres are farthest from Wilder's in their use of such elements. In all three cases, the anachronism is primarily the result of a fundamental indifference to historical accuracy on the part of playwrights and performers, not of any conscious artistic choice. Wilder borrowed the scheme for *Skin* from *Finnegans Wake* and Henry James's *A Sense of the Past* rather than from any of the traditional theatres in question, but he also noted that it can be seen in *A Connecticut Yankee in King Arthur's Court*, as well (I. Wilder letter to V. Kling, 11 May 1965, ts., carbon, Wilder Papers, YCAL). In any case, in the Elizabethan and Spanish Renaissance theatres, the chief anachronistic elements were the costumes, which were almost always the same in style and period, if not in costliness, as those worn by the spectators. Lope de Vega, in his treatise, *The New Art of Making Comedies*, speaks with scorn of the anachronistic costumes used by Spanish actors (547). Elizabethan play texts, too, contain historical inaccuracies such as the famous striking clocks in the Rome of Shakespeare's *Julius Caesar*. Chinese plays abound in anachronisms as well (Arlington 29), which is not surprising considering that the playwrights' main emphasis is on the moral lesson of the story rather than on a faithful recreation of the past. Also, the *ch'ou*, or clown figure, in Chinese drama commonly injects local or topical allusions, even in plays treating supposedly historical events, into remarks he is addressing directly to the spectators (Chen 34).

In contrast to the largely contingent or unintentional anachronisms in these theatres, in *The Skin of Our Teeth*—and in that play's prototype, the three-minute play *Proserpina and the Devil*, which juxtaposes and even, as its title suggests, conflates characters from Greek myth and Christian iconography—Wilder's use of anachronism is more calculated and systematic. *The Skin of Our Teeth* appears closer to the medieval drama and theatre in this respect, since the use of anachronism on the medieval stage was, apparently, at least partially intentional, forming part of a fundamental, all-encompassing vision in the plays. In the medieval cycle plays, as Glynne Wickham notes:

> historical time was brought into conjunction with universal time and . . . both remained linked to ritual time in the new Feast of Corpus Christi. . . .
>
> In this new context of universal time where the past was reflected in the present and the future, the proper narrative environment for the depiction of all these events was fourteenth-century Europe. For the script-writers and the actors this meant

> translation of Pontius Pilate into Sir Pilate, J. P., or into a German Burgomeister, Annas and Caiaphas into Bishops of the Roman Catholic Church, the shepherds of Bethlehem into those of the Alps, the Jura or the Cotswolds. (62–63)

To cite perhaps the best-known example, the Judean shepherds tending their flocks on the night of Christ's birth in *The Second Shepherds' Play* are made to swear Christian oaths and refer to towns in the immediate vicinity of Wakefield. Anachronism in the medieval plays is certainly less studied or systematic than it is in *The Skin of Our Teeth* (or even *Proserpina and the Devil*), but Wickham's discussion of the time sense inherent in the cycles is just as applicable to Wilder's play as it is to the medieval drama.

On the other hand, there is at least one important, if subtle, difference between the function of the anachronisms in *Skin* and their function in the cycles. Since the action depicted in the medieval plays is technically remote in time from the period of the plays' composition, the anachronistic elements are all contemporary and local allusions and references. In *The Skin of Our Teeth*, however, since the action is outwardly set in the twentieth century, the anachronisms are references and allusions to other times and places. Thus, the effect of anachronism in Wilder's play is to expand the present moment outward in all directions, blurring the focus on the "here and now" so that it is seen to contain the "then and there" as well, whereas the anachronisms in the medieval cycle plays absorb the distant time and place into their present and immediate counterparts. Stated differently, Wilder's anachronisms in *Skin* make the immediate and familiar seem strange and unfamiliar or unexpectedly significant and wondrous, whereas the medieval anachronisms make the alien seem familiar and accessible. The same applies to the anachronisms in the Chinese, Elizabethan, and Renaissance Spanish theatres, and was certainly the reason for their inclusion (if they were intentional) in those traditional forms. Of course, Wilder is also implying, as were his medieval predecessors (and perhaps those in China and seventeenth-century Europe), that the past lives in the present. However, the difference in point of view is noteworthy and underscores the parochial focus on the one hand and the global one on the other.

Wilder's use of allegorical characters in *The Skin of Our Teeth* and *Pullman Car Hiawatha* links those plays with the theatres of the Middle Ages, Elizabethan England, and Renaissance Spain, but once again, the differences between his use of the device and that which is usual in the other theatres are small but definite. Allegorical figures in medieval drama and its Elizabethan descendant are almost all personified abstractions or generalities (such as "Fellowship," "Kindred," "Good-Deeds," "Discretion," or "Knowledge" in *Everyman*, "Time" in *The Winter's Tale*, "Rumor" in *II Henry IV*, or "The World," "The Flesh," "Mercy," and "Peace" in *The Castle of Perseverance*). Wilder, on the other hand, tends to employ allegorical figures to personify physical phenomena—places, communities, heavenly bodies.

The personifications of the hours in *Pullman Car* and *Skin* are partial exceptions, since they represent arbitrary, conventional divisions of the essentially indivisible flow of time. However, that flow is itself a concrete material phenomenon, artificially demarcated perhaps, but undeniably "real." More geographical, "Wilderesque" allegorical characters may be found in the Jacobean and Caroline court masques, but the aesthetic realm of the masque, with its emphasis on lavish, illusionistic spectacle and dancing, is remote from that of Wilder's theatre.

The Spanish drama of the Golden Age, in at least one instance, is closer to Wilder's in this regard than is the Elizabethan or medieval. At the end of the first act of Cervantes's play *The Siege of Numantia*, several figures representing geographical entities appear: first Spain herself, "crowned with towers" (109), then the river Duero, which flows by the scene of the action, and, accompanying it, "tributaries represented by three boys, dressed . . . in willows and white poplar leaves" (111). A similar device is used in Cervantes's *La casa de los celos* (*The House of Jealousy*), in which "Castile," with a lion and castle in either hand, rises into view through a trapdoor at one point (Shergold 232). Although Cervantes's personified geographical features are more emotionally involved with their plays' dramatic actions than are the corresponding figures in *Pullman Car*, the nature of the personifications themselves constitutes one intriguing parallel between these two Spanish plays and Wilder's one-act piece.

The other features linking Wilder's theatre with two or more of the traditional forms under consideration fall under the heading of anti-illusionistic devices, although the term is somewhat misleading in the present context. Medieval European, Chinese, Japanese, Elizabethan, Renaissance Spanish, and Greek and Roman comic playwrights frequently acknowledge and exploit the artificiality of the theatrical medium. However, that acknowledgment is not part of a concerted, systematic attempt (comparable to Wilder's), to subvert the theatrical illusion, since no illusionistic theatre in the modern sense existed at the time. The dramatists of antiquity had little choice but to write as they did, given the outdoor, daytime performances at which their works were to be presented. With all the spectators keenly, unavoidably aware of one another's presence, it would have been all but impossible to persuade them they were somewhere other than in a theatre. The same situation obtained in the Elizabethan public playhouses and Spanish *corrales*, as well as in the medieval outdoor performance venues; and the indoor performance spaces of China, Japan, and medieval and Renaissance Europe, with their inescapable reliance on shared illumination of auditorium and stage and their boisterous audiences and plentiful distractions, also prevented the creation of a complete theatrical illusion in the contemporary sense. Hence, the "anti-illusionism" in the drama of these theatres was motivated largely by pragmatic, utilitarian considerations, rather than by theoretical or idealistic ones, as Wilder's is.

Wilder, on the other hand, as something of an aesthetic reactionary, rejected the sophisticated illusionistic means at his disposal and sought to recapture the vigor and immediacy and primitive magic of earlier (and less familiar) theatrical styles and traditions. He thus gives the impression that he is *creating* or re-creating his own theatrical conventions as he works, borrowing from one source or another or simply experimenting playfully with the fundamental possibilities of the stage. Wilder's invented—or reinvented—conventions are certainly not mere arbitrary "gimmicks," but are intimately related to his favorite themes and concerns. All the same, the sense of novelty and calculated experimentation with which his drama is endowed sets it apart from that of the Middle Ages, the Elizabethans, the seventeenth-century Spaniards, and even the Chinese and Japanese, no matter how many technical or stylistic similarities there may be between them.

In fact, it might even be said that it is easier for Wilder's audiences to accept or understand his technical experiments and "innovations" because, like the dramatists of the traditions on which he drew, he has grounded his plays solidly in the dominant aesthetic mode of the age, in this case, naturalism. This circumstance would mean that Wilder's drama is essentially just as much "of its time" as the other forms are of theirs and thus, on one level—paradoxically—his style and themes are irrevocably divorced from theirs.

In any event, one of the most common theatricalist or nonrepresentational techniques employed in traditional Asian and European theatres is the casting of male actors in female roles. This practice may be met with in the ancient Greek and Roman, medieval, Elizabethan and Jacobean, Chinese, and Japanese Noh and Kabuki theatres and constitutes a link—albeit a tenuous one—between these theatres and Wilder's. In the Chinese and medieval theatres there are exceptions, and the practice was not instituted in China until the Manchu dynasty (1644–1911) (Chen 21), but in both cases the dominant convention is or was the all-male cast. Although Wilder's plays all include women's roles which he expected actresses to play, the Stage Managers in *Pullman Car Hiawatha*, *The Happy Journey*, and *Our Town* all assume, among their secondary roles, at least one woman's part, whether of one line's duration or several speeches' length. Near the beginning of *Pullman Car*, "Mr. Washburn," impersonating a woman in one of the invisible upper berths, asks if anyone will lend "her" some aspirin. In the first scene of *The Happy Journey*, the Stage Manager plays two women, "Mrs. Schwartz," the next-door neighbor, and "Mrs. Hobmeyer," both of whom bid Ma Kirby farewell and wish her a pleasant trip. In Act I of *Our Town*, finally, the Stage Manager temporarily becomes "Mrs. Forrest," who is jostled by George Gibbs while the latter's attention is directed toward a soaring baseball and who expresses her indignation with vehemence. These instances scarcely amount to a convention of the sort met with in the traditional and historical theatres listed above, but they do attest to Wilder's recognition that gender on the stage may be as much an assumed attribute as is identity. Moreover, Wilder at one point considered stipulating that all the roles in *The Skin of Our Teeth* be played by male actors, although he later dropped the idea (Harrison 217).

In almost all the traditional forms, however, the convention involves at least a degree of illusionism, as it does not in Wilder's plays. In the Greek and Roman theatres the actors' performance of female roles was facilitated by the use of masks, a device Wilder never employs. The mask itself, as used in the ancient theatre, was, in fact, both illusionistic (since it covered the entire head and allowed the actor to change his features along with his role) and anti-illusionistic (since the features were immobile).

In the medieval theatre, the use of male actors to portray female characters dates from the earliest times, when, in the Easter trope, "*Quem Quaeritis*" (tenth century), priests "impersonated" or represented the three Marys approaching Christ's tomb to anoint his body. Although women did play female characters in later plays (Wickham 92), this arrangement, again, was the exception rather than the rule.

The Elizabethan and Jacobean convention moved toward illusionism in its use of boy actors for most female roles instead of adult males, such as were used by the Greeks, and the Chinese and Japanese Kabuki theatres are, perhaps, furthest from Wilder's in this matter, since actors playing women in both forms tend to specialize in such roles, called *dan* roles in Chinese opera and *onnagata* in the Kabuki, and to practice a sophisticated and meticulously executed form of female impersonation. The Stage Managers in Wilder's plays who briefly assume women's roles of course make no attempt to produce a convincing impersonation of those characters, at least in the areas of dress and appearance, whereas the *dan* and *onnagata* actors take great pains to create a complete illusion and undergo rigorous training aimed at making them expert female impersonators. The illusion is aided in both cases by the use of makeup, wigs, and women's clothing. The Noh actor of female characters is closer to Wilder's Stage Managers who briefly assume women's roles, since, although he wears a mask and, like the *onnagata* and *dan*, women's garb, he makes no attempt to alter his voice to imitate a female register and timbre (Bowers 20).

The assumption of a variety of minor (and not-so-minor) roles by Wilder's Stage Managers in *Our Town*, *The Happy Journey*, and *Pullman Car Hiawatha* also recalls the general Greek, Roman, and Elizabethan practice of doubling or tripling an actor's roles. That the doubling or tripling or quadrupling was accomplished with the aid of a mask in the Greek and Roman theatres meant, again, that the practice, like that of having males portray female characters in those theatres, was both illusionistic and anti-illusionistic. The performance of multiple roles by Wilder's Stage Managers is more consistently anti-illusionistic in its effect, since the performers' appearance remains the same whether they attempt to endow their secondary roles with vocal and physical individuality or, as in the case of the man in *The Happy Journey*, simply read the lines without any effort at characterization.

Another common anti-illusionistic or presentational device used in nearly all traditional theatres—and used much more liberally than "female impersonation" in Wilder's—is direct address. The *parabasis* of Old Comedy; the prologues, reports of offstage actions, and concluding lines of Roman comedy; the prologues of certain Greek tragedies; and similar passages in the plays of antiquity are merely the first extant examples of the device that Wilder incorporates into nearly all his plays. Direct address was also used by the medieval playwrights, although not so frequently or pointedly as it is by Wilder, being confined chiefly, as in the Greek and Roman theatres, to prologues and epilogues, such as those framing *Everyman* and the Wakefield *Murder of Abel*. In several cycles, though, there is a narrator or expositor who, like the Stage Managers in Wilder's plays, serves as a kind of chorus, providing historical and scriptural background information and exposition, and even clarifying the action's meaning and implications after the fashion of the Greek chorus and Wilder's Stage Managers.[1] This character in the *Ludus Coventriae* is named "Contemplatio," an appellation that would admirably fit the Stage Manager in *Our Town*—and even, at certain moments, "Mr. Washburn" in *Pullman Car Hiawatha*. Many of the medieval playwrights also made use of direct address in the bodies of the plays themselves, as well as in prologues and epilogues.[2] In the Elizabethan theatre, of course, the audience was often addressed directly, whether in prologues and epilogues, such as those in *Henry V* and *The Tempest*; narrated transitions between acts, such as those in *Pericles* and *The Winter's Tale*; or in the main action itself, as in Launce's monologues in *The Two Gentlemen of Verona*. However, one distinction between the Elizabethan dramatist's use of direct address and Wilder's is that Wilder's characters tend to use the device more to meditate aloud than to deliver narration or exposition, a reversal of the situation in Elizabethan and Jacobean drama, where the device normally drives the action forward. Even Dolly Levi, addressing the audience in the fourth act of *The Matchmaker*, uses the opportunity more to "philosophize" and explain her motivations than to relate any unseen incidents in the play's main action or deliver other essential exposition. In the Elizabethan drama, of course, the soliloquy serves much the same purpose as the meditative address to the audience in Wilder's plays, but the extent to which the actors, in their soliloquies, actually employed direct address remains unknown. In general, the soliloquist should probably be regarded as oblivious of the audience's presence and engaged simply in communing aloud with his or her own bosom.

Wilder's technique of compressing space and time in the depiction of journeys has more in common with methods used in the medieval and

Asian theatres than with those typical on the Elizabethan and Spanish Golden Age stages, although all the traditional theatres accelerated fictional time in one way or another. In the Greek and Roman and English and Spanish Renaissance theatres, time and space were ordinarily condensed (if they had to be) during breaks in the action, rather than during the action itself. Actors simply exited from one fictional location and reentered in another. In the Spanish theatre, long journeys were occasionally depicted in spatially and temporally compressed form as continuous actions (Rennert 90–91), with the same few scenic properties serving in some cases to represent both the point of departure and the destination, but such instances were exceptional. In the medieval drama, on the other hand, although the characters in some cases exit and reenter to indicate that they have moved from one place to another, in other cases a journey is depicted as a continuous action, with both time and distance compressed, as in Wilder's "journey" plays. For instance, in the Brome *Abraham and Isaac*, the trek to Mount Moriah consumes some six or seven lines of dialogue, and both the rhyme scheme and the content of the lines themselves indicate that the journey was presented as a continuously visible action. Similarly, Noah's long sojourn upon the waters in the Ark and his drifting progress toward Ararat are condensed in most extant plays treating the Deluge into a few minutes of stage time, with the Ark continuously visible and even (probably) stationary, just as "Pullman Car Hiawatha" and the Kirby Chevrolet are throughout their respective fictitious journeys.[3]

In Chinese opera, the parallel to Wilder's technique is more inexact. One writer describes the Chinese technique in the following terms: "If, in a stage story, a general goes upon a journey, the scene is not changed to transport one's mind to another place, instead the soldier cracks a whip, dashes across the stage to a crash of cymbals, and announces that he has arrived" (Buss 62). This method of compressing space and time differs from Wilder's methods in that the actual journey itself is virtually omitted—as it is in the standard Elizabethan, Greek, and Spanish Golden Age method—and motion is actual, if abbreviated, rather than implied, as it is in *Pullman Car*, *The Happy Journey*, and *Childhood*.

In the Noh, however, one finds a very close parallel to Wilder's technique, and even to his intention or meaning. The stages of the journey itself are sometimes shown in Noh plays, as they rarely are in Chinese opera.[4] The primary parallel, however, lies in the fact that the journey recurs regularly in play after play in the Noh repertory, as it does in several of Wilder's dramatic works, and thus becomes an important, even symbolic, feature of those plays, rather than simply an incidental element in the narrative. The fact that the traveler is a monk and in many instances receives a supernatural revelation at the end of his journey even endows the journey itself with spiritual overtones similar to those associated with the journeys in Wilder's plays. Wilder in fact indicated in 1961 that had he known the

Noh better while he was writing his own plays, one of the features he would have borrowed from it would have been the device of the journey (letter to Miss Niemoeller, 25 July 1965, ts., Wilder papers, YCAL).

Another common anti-illusionistic tactic of Wilder's, the destruction of the physical boundary between actor and spectator—more specifically, the use of audience areas as acting spaces—is also encountered in the medieval, Elizabethan, Spanish Golden Age, and Kabuki theatres. In the medieval cycle plays, the most famous use of this device occurs in the Coventry Pageant of the Shearmen and Tailors, in which Herod, after hearing of the flight of the three kings, "ragis in the pagond [i.e., the pageant-wagon] & in the strete also" (l. 447). In plays where the Devil and his assistants appeared, they seem regularly to have mingled with the crowd, to the latter's horrified delight.[5] One cannot tell for certain whether the portion of the street or square where Herod raged or the devils sported was actually filled with spectators, but it seems most unlikely that such a splendid opportunity for performer-spectator interaction would have gone unexploited by the actors.

Wholly indisputable evidence of similar spectator-actor encounters is contained in some Tudor interludes, which were probably performed not outdoors, as the cycles and some of the moralities were, but in the Great Halls of manor houses. In nearly all of these plays, one or more characters calls for "room" as he enters, indicating that he must make his way to the primary acting area through a crowd of spectators. The earliest extant interlude, Henry Medwall's *Fulgens and Lucrece* (1497), even opens with the same device Wilder (possibly in imitation of Pirandello) uses in *Our Town*—the device of having actors pose as members of the audience.

Scholars disagree over whether the device employed by Wilder of having the actors pass through the audience at certain moments was ever used by the Elizabethans and Jacobeans. It was certainly a feature of many Spanish plays of the Golden Age. Despite Richard Southern's belief that processions that passed over the stage in the public theatres began and/or ended somewhere in the lower galleries (585–90), it seems unlikely that the "yard" was ever used as a playing space, at least in the public houses.

On the other hand, the related device used by Wilder in Act I of *Our Town* (and by Medwall, Pirandello, Ivan Goll, and the futurists), the incorporation of actors impersonating spectators, was employed by at least some English Renaissance playwrights. The most famous and elaborate use of this device by an English playwright is to be found in *The Knight of the Burning Pestle*, where the "spectators" involved include a citizen, his wife, and their apprentice, "Rafe," who becomes involved in the action as the Knight of the title. In Jonson's *Every Man Out of His Humour*, too, two "spectators" (friends of a supposed company member) are introduced in the Induction and remain at the side of the stage on stools commenting on the action from time to time throughout the performance.

In another related "Pirandellian" device, also used by Wilder (in *The Skin of Our Teeth*, primarily, but also in *Pullman Car Hiawatha*), actors pretend to be conversing spontaneously in their own persons. This sort of colloquy usually occurs at the beginning of the play in the Elizabethan examples. Asper, in the Induction to Jonson's play, is one such actor. The device is also used in the Induction to John Marston's *The Malcontent*—where, as in the *Every Man Out* Induction, it is combined with the device of an actor pretending to be a spectator—and in that to Jonson's *Bartholomew Fair* as well. In *The Malcontent*'s Induction, Will Sly, one of the King's Men, is the pretended spectator, a strutting dandy, who at once point says archly to the tiring-man, "I'll hold my life thou took'st me for one of the players" (ll. 6–7). In his character of man-about-town, he calls out the real players, who appear as themselves, and even asks to see himself, whom he knows to be one of the company. Wilder never plays this elaborately with the dichotomy between illusion and reality, but he certainly includes apparently spontaneous interjections by the actors "in their own persons" in *Skin* and *Pullman Car*. In the latter play, the girls playing "Ten O'clock" and "Twelve O'clock" drop out of character briefly to tell "Mr. Washburn" the authors of the quotations they are about to recite, and he himself alternates between his "real" identity and those of the various minor characters he temporarily impersonates.

The presence of spectators on the stage in the private playhouses also suggests a specific parallel between Wilder's theatre and the Jacobeans', since it is, essentially, the converse of the actors' intrusion into the audience's territory, which occurs in *Our Town*, *The Skin of Our Teeth*, *Infancy*, and *Childhood*. The difference is significant, however, since, when the dramatic action spills over into the auditorium, the playwright has far more precise control over the actor-audience encounter and its relation to the rest of the performance. In fact, evidence indicates clearly that the Elizabethan practice was tolerated as an inescapable evil, rather than encouraged by playwrights or theatre managers in the hope of increasing the feeling of intimacy and immediacy in the performance.

On the Renaissance Spanish stage actors utilized the audience area as a playing space chiefly for processional or spectacular entrances. For example, mounted characters often passed, on their way to the stage, through the crowd of *mosqueteros* or "groundlings" standing in the *patio*, the section of the Spanish *corral* theatre corresponding to the "pit" or "yard" in the Elizabethan public playhouses (Shergold 220–21, 228, 230–31). In one play, a ship is required to sail up to the stage. N. D. Shergold believes that "This was probably done, as in pageants, by building the ship on wheels, so that it could move through the patio" (227). In this matter, then, the evidence for the Spanish theatre is much more conclusive than that for the Elizabethan.

Furthermore, performers moved into the spectators' space on other occasions as well. Most Spanish plays in performance were accompanied by musical interludes known as *jàcaras*, which were sung between the acts. At times one or more of the singers stood to perform in one or another of the boxes located around the periphery of the *patio*, or on the risers or bleachers which fronted the boxes (Rennert 291). Although Wilder never incorporates a precisely equivalent device into any of his plays, "Mr. Fitzpatrick" in *The Skin of Our Teeth* describes a remarkably similar use of the theatre space, purportedly called for in the play's script but impossible to realize because of the sudden illness of the singers who were to portray the planets. These singers were to have been scattered throughout the theatre, with at least one of them, Mars, being placed in the auditorium aisle.

The feature of the Kabuki stage that provides for a rough parallel to Wilder's use of the auditorium, a parallel already noted by at least two commentators (Ernst 66; Pronko 144–45, quoting and commenting on Ernst) is the *hanamichi*, the runway on the left side of the auditorium, raised above the level of the spectators' heads and extending from the back of the theatre to the front edge of the stage, on the stage right side. This runway is used as an acting area for strong, processional entrances and similar exits. Although it does not actually constitute a means whereby the actor "intrudes" into the audience's traditional territory, since it is raised, it brings him into close proximity with the spectators, as do the wedding procession and recession in *Our Town* and the Antrobuses' retreat down the "pier" in Act II of *The Skin of Our Teeth*. It also allows for simultaneous staging of separate scenes (Ernst 93) and therefore links the Kabuki stage with the configuration used by Wilder in Act III of *Our Town*.

THE THEATRE OF CLASSICAL GREECE AND ROME

Wilder's lifelong interest in the theatre may originally have been sparked by his appearance, at age ten, along with his older brother, Amos, in crowd scenes in the University of California Classics Department's productions of Greek tragedies, staged in the then-new Hearst Greek Theatre on the Berkeley campus (A. N. Wilder, 9, 62; I. Wilder, Foreword 7–8). The future playwright's acquaintance with the ancient Greek and Roman theatre continued to expand in later years, especially during his stay in Rome at the American Institute of Classical Studies (A. N. Wilder 31–32), and several passages from his theatre essays attest to his familiarity with ancient Athenian staging practices and dramatic works, although some of his knowledge has been rendered obsolete by more recent scholarship.[6] Extensive unpublished lecture notes on Greek tragedy for a course he taught at the University of Chicago in 1930 show his knowledge of the entire canon to have been comprehensive (ms., Wilder papers, YCAL). His third novel, *The Woman of Andros*, was based on Terence's *Andria*, and in 1955, he wrote an introduction to an edition of *Oedipus Rex*, in a translation by Francis Storr (rpt. in *AC* 77–87). Obviously, the Greek and Roman drama and theatre were for Wilder a continuing interest—even preoccupation.

The most obvious reflection of this preoccupation in Wilder's dramatic corpus is *The Alcestiad*, which was written in the form of a Greek tragic trilogy, complete with "satyr play" at the end. The second act even follows closely the action of Euripides's *Alcestis*, on which it is based.

However, Wilder's play lacks a true chorus in the Greek sense. The character of the Watchman does assume some of the functions of the Greek tragic chorus. He enters after a "prologue" between Apollo and Death similar to that in Euripides's play and supplies the perspective of the ordinary citizen on the affairs of the great, which are the play's primary concern. However, he leaves the stage early in the act, as the Greek chorus would not have done, returning only briefly to let Teiresias into the palace and then again at the beginning of the second act, when he relates what has transpired since the end of Act I and offers some scraps of commentary on the events he recounts. In this latter appearance, then, he functions more as a messenger than as a chorus. Thereafter, he is treated as simply another character, involved in the action to the extent that his occupation dictates and permits, but without any special choric function. If he serves as the play's chorus, then, he does so only intermittently and partially. He does not appear in the final act, his office being performed by a younger man who is treated as an ordinary character. Although the first man represents the common people's point of view, he is joined in that function by the herdsmen and various townspeople who crowd the stage in all three acts during moments of public rejoicing, terror, or mourning. Finally, *The Drunken Sisters* employs no chorus whatsoever, let alone the traditional satyr chorus which gave the Greek genre its name. Nevertheless, the structure of *The Alcestiad* approximates that of the typical Aeschylean trilogy-with-afterpiece more closely than many modern adaptations of classical Greek plays, such as Sartre's *The Flies*, Giraudoux's *Electra*, or O'Neill's *Mourning Becomes Electra*. At the same time, the play's Christian overtones place it in a different moral and theological universe from that of Greek tragedy.

On the other hand, ironically, the Stage Managers in *Our Town* and *Pullman Car Hiawatha* have much in common with the chorus of Greek drama, as several critics have already pointed out (e.g., Burbank 89; Gassner xv). Oscar Brockett notes that the function of the Greek chorus is manifold. He writes:

> First, it is an agent in the play; it gives advice, expresses opinions, asks questions, and sometimes takes an active part in the action. Second, it often establishes the ethical or social framework of the events and sets up a standard against which the action may be judged. Third, it frequently serves as an ideal spectator, reacting to the events and characters as the dramatist might hope the audience would. Fourth, the chorus helps to set the overall mood of the play and of individual scenes and to

heighten dramatic effects. Fifth, it adds movement, spectacle, song and dance, and thus contributes much to theatrical effectiveness. Sixth, it serves an important rhythmical function, creating pauses or retardations during which the audience may reflect upon what has happened and what is to come. (26)

The Stage Manager in *Our Town* certainly provides numerous opportunities for the audience to reflect on what has happened and what is to come, as well as on the deeper meaning of the events it is witnessing. Although he does not himself, like the Greek chorus, constitute an "ideal audience," since he is more of a presenter than a witness, he guides the real audience in its reflections, pointing an occasional moral, clarifying the playwright's meaning, and communicating the broader implications of the action presented. He definitely "establishes the ethical or social framework of the events," in part by reminding the audience periodically of the larger community surrounding and including the characters shown, and especially in his remarks on war and its ravages. In so doing, he not only "sets up a standard against which the action may be judged," but he sets up a religious framework as well, as does the Greek chorus in such plays as *Antigone* and *Oedipus Tyrannos*. The Stage Managers in both *Our Town* and *Pullman Car Hiawatha* give advice to the characters, express opinions, and occasionally take an active part in the drama, but they also provide narrative "bridges" or exposition, as does the Greek chorus (for instance, in Aeschylus's *Persians* and *Agamemnon*, Sophocles's *Antigone*, and Euripides's *Bacchae*). The Stage Manager in *Our Town* also helps to expand the play's temporal frame of reference, just as the Greek chorus frequently does. Aeschylus's choruses, especially, recall events long past that bear on the present action, and time occasionally seems compressed during their songs, as it is in Act I of *Our Town*. However, the chorus in Greek tragedy does not ordinarily know the future, as does Wilder's omniscient Stage Manager in *Our Town*. It is more truly a witness to the events shown in the play, never a coordinator of them or a master of ceremonies. The difference is perhaps the main distinction between the two conventions, along with the obvious fact that Wilder's Stage Managers are not composite characters or social bodies, representatives of the point of view of an entire social class. They are perhaps more akin to Pirandellian or Molièrean *raisonneurs* in this regard.

In matters of staging or dramatic technique, Wilder's drama displays few exact or striking parallels with that of the Greeks and Romans. Although the Greek and Roman stages—at least in their early years, when the dramas were being written—were relatively free of scenery, they did not apparently make much use of self-consciously minimalist techniques such as those employed by Wilder. The evidence regarding scenic practices in ancient Greece and Rome is inconclusive at best, but it seems that the sheer physical size of the Greek, if not the Plautine and Terentian, theatres, militated against the use of such Wilderesque conventions as pantomime, visual metaphors or puns, and the like. Certainly properties, such as the chariot (and horse) that brings Agamemnon and Cassandra into the orchestra in Aeschylus's *Agamemnon*, the famous blood-red cloth in the same play, and the urn supposedly containing the ashes of Orestes in Sophocles's *Electra*, were all real or meant to seem so. In the area of scenery itself, too, efforts were made at concrete representation of place, and a degree of scenic illusionism even managed to find its way into performances. Scene painting dates from the time of Sophocles, if one credits Aristotle, and although it was almost certainly not illusionistic in nature but probably symbolic or partial, the *skene* or scene building itself, however primitive it might have been at first, must have constituted a reasonably convincing and realistic setting for the action of most plays. The orchestra, which was used as an acting area by both the chorus and the individual actors, must have been relatively free of scenery, but the altar at the center was probably used as a scenic element when appropriate. Moreover, for certain plays, such as Aeschylus's *Suppliants*, real statues of the gods may have been set up around its periphery, since they are referred to in the dialogue and were readily available. Finally, the cranelike structure known as the *méchané* or *machina*, although (literally) exposing the mechanics of performance to the audience's view, served a fundamentally illusionistic purpose, in that it was installed to enable gods and other supernatural or magical beings to appear to fly or hover in midair.

A degree of scenic realism or illusionism was also necessary for the performance of Roman comedy. The neighboring house façades that constitute the typical setting for the plays of Plautus and Terence certainly boasted real or realistic, operable doors that could be both barred and battered, although the houses to which they gave access might have been indicated merely by flat panels representing the façades.

One curious (and probably fortuitous) similarity between Wilder's drama and that of the Greeks (but not of the Romans—at least not in the later years) is the banishment from the stage proper in both theatres of acts of violence and deaths. Harriet in *Pullman Car Hiawatha* is the only character in Wilder's plays to die on stage. Significantly, all Henry's enormities in *The Skin of Our Teeth*—his assault on the neighbor's boy who tries to steal the wheel in Act I and his similar attack on the black chair-guide in Act II—occur offstage and are merely reported by other characters. Emily's death is not shown in *Our Town*, nor is her brother Wally's, or the baby's in *The Happy Journey*, or, predictably, those of Admetus, Alcestis, and Laodamia in *The Alcestiad*. An exception might be *The Long Christmas Dinner*, since many of its characters exist through the dark portal representing death, but the action is purely symbolic and cannot really be called a breach of classical decorum in this respect.

On the other hand, despite the similarities, both pronounced and vague, between Wilder's dramaturgy and that of the ancients, the differences are perhaps ultimately more telling. Greek and Roman theatre was "total theatre," rich in spectacle. Masks, dance, and sung or chanted dialogue, all of which were of major importance in Greek and Roman performances, count for little or nothing in the theatrical equation of Thornton Wilder. Wilder's plays are for the most part not structured as Greek plays—tragedies or comedies—were, with episodes separated by choral songs, although Act I of *Our Town* might represent a rough equivalent of the ancient form, as might *Pullman Car Hiawatha* in its entirety. The plot outline of *The Matchmaker* is certainly the same as that for any Greek New Comedy or Roman comedy, but the same could be said for nearly any Western European comedy since Menander's day, and since Wilder's play is adapted from an Austrian original, the resemblance could hardly be said to constitute a link between him and the Greeks. Taken as a whole, Wilder's theatre bears less resemblance to that of the Greeks and Romans than it does to other theatres, especially those of medieval Europe, China, and Japan.

THE MEDIEVAL THEATRE

Commentators frequently refer to George Antrobus in *The Skin of Our Teeth* as an "Everyman" figure (e.g., A. N. Wilder 27; Goldstone, *Portrait* 185), and there is some truth to the label. The critical commonplace provides a clue to the similarities between Wilder's drama and that of medieval Europe, and although Antrobus only superficially resembles the rather abstract, generalized protagonist of *Everyman, The Skin of Our Teeth* is without a doubt the most "medieval" of Wilder's plays.

To begin with, the underlying biblical *mythos* of the second act is identical with that of, perhaps, the most famous and popular episode in the medieval Corpus Christi cycles, that of Noah and the Flood. Wilder's treatment of the story in Act II of *Skin* naturally differs from the usual dramatization accorded it in the Middle Ages, since the action in *Skin* is outwardly set in Atlantic City in the twentieth century. The medieval plays, of course, adhere faithfully to the biblical account in such externals as character names, setting, and overall story line, while amplifying or embroidering upon certain incidents. Wilder's play is admittedly a "fantasia," as he terms it, on biblical and other themes, but all the same it does make use in its second act of some traditional elements of the medieval Noah plays. For instance, Wilder's treatment includes the depiction of strife between Antrobus/"Noah" and his wife prior to the deluge, although Maggie Antrobus is scarcely the stubborn, willful, witless harridan that one finds in the Noah episodes of the cycle plays. In both the typical medieval Noah play and Act II of *Skin*, though, "Noah's" wife delays the family's departure in the ark. In the Chester Noah play, she refuses to board the vessel because her gossips must be left behind. In *Skin*, her reason is less frivolous: she refuses to leave without her son, who is truly nowhere to be found and is, in fact, the one to blame for keeping them all waiting.

At least two other dramatic pieces by Wilder—the "three-minute" plays, *The Flight into Egypt* and *Hast Thou Considered My Servant Job*?—also treat biblical incidents that were dramatized in the medieval cycles as well. However, Wilder's unconventional reworking of the stories involved—his use of a talking donkey in *Flight* and his adoption of the heavenly setting and inverted ending of the Judas story in *Job*—sharply distinguish his brief playlets from the straightforward retellings in the cycle plays.

In addition to these parallels between three of Wilder's dramatic works and three individual episodes in the great medieval cycles, the entire plan of *Skin* resembles that of the entire Corpus Christi cycle. The purpose of the cycles, like that of *Skin*, was to show all of human history in a single panorama. Although in the case of the typical cycle that panorama took several days, not a few hours, to unfold, those several days, like the three acts of *Skin*, still represent a compression of the time period covered by the drama's subject matter, the period extending from the Creation to the Judgment Day. Although Wilder's play actually dramatizes a shorter span, the Creation and Fall, at least, are conjured up in allusions in Act I and in the quotation from Genesis assigned to "Midnight" in Act III. Doomsday does not fit into the pattern of "eternal recurrence" explored in *Skin*, but Wilder does treat it in *And the Sea Shall Give Up Its Dead*.

In addition, the structure of the cycles distantly resembles that of *Skin*. To the medieval dramatist, the pattern of incidents and characters that made up the Passion of Christ was prefigured in a number of Old Testament stories and personages that were brought to life in earlier episodes of the cycles. The drama of humanity's first disobedience and sin was reversed, as if in a mirror, by the world's redemption through Christ's self-sacrifice. Wickham, following V. A. Kolve, notes, "Christ replaces Adam, Mary replaces Eve, and the Cross on Calvary replaces the Tree of Knowledge in the Garden of Eden" (63). In addition, direct parallels, such as those between Noah's Flood and Doomsday and the respective lives of Moses and Jesus, were drawn. Thus, the Corpus Christi cycle was constructed on a pattern of repeated analogous actions similar to that which serves as the foundation for the action of *Skin*.

On the other hand, *The Skin of Our Teeth* is not the only play of Wilder's whose form and content show affinities with the medieval cycles or medieval drama in general. Wilder's two uncompleted one-act cycles, "The Seven Ages of Man" and "The Seven Deadly Sins," also have medieval precedents—especially the latter. The deadly sins appeared frequently on the medieval stage, primarily in the moralities. At Beverley in 1469, moreover, each sin had its own "pageant" (and presumably its own play) in a cycle of dramas reminiscent of Wilder's own projected series (Wickham 114). The seven ages of man are of slightly later provenance, but the concept—or an approximation of it—also informs medieval thought and drama. For instance, there is a late morality or interlude with the title *Youth*, concerned with the frailties and temptations associated with that period of life, and although there are no corresponding plays dealing with "Infancy" or "Dotage," the various stages of the individual's earthly pilgrimage are evoked in such works as *The Castle of Perseverance*, which follows its protagonist, *Humanum Genus*, from childhood to old age.

Besides these similarities of form and subject matter linking Wilder's drama with that of medieval Europe, there are a number of technical or stylistic resemblances between the two theatres, in addition to those discussed earlier in this chapter. One of the most interesting—and most disputed—of these parallels is the "pageant master's" or stage director's presence in the midst of the performers during performances of at least some plays. The Jean Fouquet painting depicting a play about the martyrdom of Saint Apollonia, which shows a figure in ecclesiastical garb carrying an open book (possibly the script) and pointing with a rod in the direction of some people—either spectators or performers—who appear in the background off to one side, has been variously interpreted.[7] Scholars disagree about the identity and function of this figure, but many (e.g., Wickham 83; Chambers 2:140) are convinced that he is a pageant master directing the performance in plain sight of the audience. One description of Cornish staging practices, dating from the early seventeenth century, states that the actors were followed about on stage by a person known as the "Ordinary," who fed them their lines, which they were not expected to commit wholly to memory (Wickham 83; Chambers 2:140).[8] Although most actors elsewhere were fined for failure to memorize their parts, the possibility that some types of performance were directed by on-stage pageant masters is intriguing in light of the on-stage coordination of the performance by the Stage Managers in *Our Town* and *Pullman Car Hiawatha*—and the latter's prompting of "Ten O'clock" and "Twelve O'clock"—which thus constitutes one more possible parallel between Wilder's dramaturgy and that of the medieval playwrights.

Like their Greek and Roman antecedents, medieval plays were syntheses, in performance, of many diverse constituent arts. The extent to which Wilder incorporates into his plays a variety of subsidiary, otherwise autonomous arts was discussed in Chapters 2 and 4. It is perhaps in his use of only one of these arts, song, that his theatre in any way resembles that of the Middle Ages. Occasionally, songs or verses of dialogue were set to original music in the medieval plays. The so-called "Coventry Carol" from that town's Pageant of the Shearmen and Tailors is perhaps the best—and best-known—surviving example. However, familiar hymns were also sung at times in a number of plays, the commonest being the "Te Deum," chanted by the souls released from Limbo (and presumably, by the play's spectators as well) after the episode of the Harrowing of Hell (for example, in the

Chester cycle). Wilder is thus, in a very general way, following medieval practices in his incorporation of "Bless'd Be the Tie That Binds" and "Art Thou Weary, Art Thou Languid?" into *Our Town* and "There Were Ninety and Nine That Safely Lay" into *The Happy Journey*—and even in his use of popular songs such as "Tenting Tonight" and "Jingle Bells" in *The Skin of Our Teeth* and *The Matchmaker* and "I Been Workin' on de Railroad" in *The Happy Journey*.

In scenic practices, Wilder's theatre is further removed from that of the Middle Ages than in its use of song, but there are still noteworthy parallels between the two theatrical idioms. First, the typical scenic arrangement of the medieval stage resembles that of Wilder's in certain respects. For instance, the simultaneous depiction of physically separate sites in Acts I and III of *Our Town* and, in a limited sense, in *Pullman Car Hiawatha* recalls medieval mansion staging. No "mansions" are required for these plays, however, and it is only in the most general sense that they may be said to employ "medieval" or quasimedieval methods of simultaneous staging. Certainly, the bare medieval *platea* may constitute a similarity between that era's staging practices and Wilder's. One critic, at least (Goldstein 79), has likened Wilder's bare stage to a medieval *platea*. However, Wilder's bare stage is never unlocalized, as the *platea* sometimes was. It is true that if a character emerged from a particular mansion to play a scene on the *platea*, the *platea* was then understood to represent either an area adjacent to the place represented by the mansion or an extension of that place itself. However, in other cases the location of the action was only vaguely alluded to or implied.[9] Wilder, by contrast, is always careful to specify in the dialogue where the action of his plays is set.

In addition to these differences in the use and arrangement of the stage space, there are differences in the treatment of properties and the incorporation of special effects separating the medieval theatre from Wilder's. First, pantomime in the modern sense was not a feature of the medieval theatre, as it is of Wilder's. Properties, although few, were for the most part real or realistic. Cain, in the Wakefield *Murder of Abel*, would have entered driving a team of real horses and oxen—or a team of actors disguised as such—harnessed to a real plough (Williams 98–99). He would have killed Abel with a real jawbone, after both brothers had offered sacrifices of real sheaves. The three kings in the Coventry Pageant of the Shearmen and Tailors rode real horses, and in the inventory of the Grocers' Guild of Norwich is listed "a rib, colored red" (94; Chambers 2:142), undoubtedly for use in a play depicting the fashioning of Eve.

Although audiences watching the cycles and moralities were definitely required to use their imaginations to fill in certain details, especially during episodes that depicted long journeys by land or sea, medieval artisans developed numerous sophisticated machines with a view to creating ever more perfect theatrical illusions. For instance, one witness of the Valenciennes Passion Play in 1547 described the special scenic effects in the following terms:

> The machines of Paradise and of Hell were absolutely prodigious and capable of being taken by the populace for magic. For there one saw Truth, the Angels and other characters descend from on high, sometimes visibly and sometimes invisibly and then without warning. Lucifer arose out of Hell, riding on a dragon, without anyone being able to see how it was achieved. Moses's [sic] dry and sterile rod suddenly sprouted flowers and fruit; the souls of Herod and Judas were carried up into the air by devils. (Henri d'Outreman, qtd. and trans. in Wickham 86–87)

Clearly, this sort of elaborate prestidigitation is a far cry from the simplicity of Wilder's minimalist staging—and even from the scenic "effects" in a play like *The Skin of Our Teeth*, effects that destroy the theatrical illusion and are not "tricks" at all but rather evident human errors or mechanical malfunctions.

Thus, Wilder's typical staging methods are only partially "medieval." Although his plays call for some of the same presentational techniques utilized by medieval dramatists and pageant masters, it is his use of biblical subject matter and the breadth of his vision that link his theatre most incontestably and clearly with that of the Middle Ages.

THE ELIZABETHAN THEATRE

Since many features of the Elizabethan theatre and drama have their roots in medieval practice, techniques linking Wilder's drama with that of medieval times also cause it to resemble that of the Elizabethans and Jacobeans. However, since Wilder refers far more regularly to the Elizabethan drama and theatre in his own essays, it appears that he looked more to Shakespeare and his contemporaries for inspiration and vindication than to Henry Medwall or the Wakefield Master.[10]

It is not difficult to see what he found congenial about Elizabethan theatre and drama. To begin with, the spatial and temporal scope of Elizabethan plays, especially plays like Shakespeare's *Pericles* or *The Winter's Tale*, while not generally as immense as that of an entire Corpus Christi cycle, is nonetheless vast when compared with that of the typical climactic play, whether classical, neoclassical, or Ibsenesque. However, *The Skin of Our Teeth*, the play by Wilder with the greatest temporal scope, more closely resembles the medieval cycles in its scheme and structure than it does any Elizabethan or Jacobean drama.

Wilder himself comments on the relative sparseness of scenery on the Shakespearean (and Spanish) stage, citing it as a precedent for his own experiments with scenic minimalism (*AC* 108). In principle, and in a general way, the perceived precedent is valid. The dearth of scenic elements and furniture on the Elizabethan stage must have helped to thrust the actors and the words they spoke into greater prominence, just as Wilder's bare stage does in such plays as *Our Town, The Happy Journey, Pullman Car Hiawatha,* and *The Long Christmas Dinner* (although the language in the latter three, especially, makes no claim to brilliance). However, pantomime in the modern sense, such as one finds in all Wilder's minimalist plays, was absent from the Elizabethan stage, just as it was from the medieval and Greek theatres.

Nor were visual metaphors employed to any great extent in the representation of place or object on the Elizabethan stage, as they are in *Our Town, Pullman Car, The Happy Journey, Infancy,* and *Childhood*. One possible exception, certainly, is the use of the undisguised upper stage to represent the walls of a city or ramparts of a castle. In general, though, the commonest principle governing Elizabethan and Jacobean scenic practices (except, of course, for the masques and other private or court performances) was selective realism. The Elizabethan approach to scenery, like that of the expressionists, might also be termed "synecdochic," a part of the fictional locale standing for the whole, in contrast to Wilder's "metaphoric" approach. Alternatively, in rare instances placards were set out to inform the spectators of the location represented by the stage during a particular scene (Gurr 118). To a certain extent, Wilder employs similar methods—for instance with the trellises and tables in *Our Town* that suggest entire gardens and kitchens, and with the figures representing towns and fields in *Pullman Car Hiawatha* (not to mention the Stage Manager in *Our Town*), who all constitute a form of speaking "placard." However, despite the relative absence of scenery on the Elizabethan and Jacobean stage, there was little if any reliance on techniques corresponding to those by which Wilder transforms chairs and a plank into a drug-store soda fountain in Act II of *Our Town*, a pair of ladders into upstairs bedrooms in Act I, and stools or chairs into low bushes in *Infancy* and *Childhood*. The many separate properties Philip Henslowe lists, including many representing similar things, would not have been needed had the Elizabethans' practice in this area not been basically representational. Wilder's partiality to pantomimic or metaphoric representation of place and object in his plays moves his style closer to that of the Asian theatre—especially the Chinese and Japanese.

One particular anti-illusionistic practice used by Wilder (besides those discussed in the beginning of this chapter), the visible scene shift, does find a parallel on the Elizabethan stage. The so-called "discovery space," concerning which whole seas of scholarly ink have been spilled, certainly allowed some scene changes to be accomplished out of sight of the audience. However, as Andrew Gurr notes, "So far as the evidence of stage directions enables us to judge, even the most substantial properties were likely to be carried on to the stage more often than they were discovered" (124). Such properties included the dais or scaffold, and especially the banquet table (127). Given the absence of a front or act curtain in both the public and private theatres and the shared source of illumination of both amphitheatre and stage in the public playhouses, all such changes of scene must have been accomplished in "broad daylight" and in full view of the spectators. Wilder's use of this technique of scene shifting was discussed in Chapter 4, in the section on Brecht.

In a general sense, also, Wilder's theatrical minimalism does possess a fundamental affinity with the Elizabethan style, since in both cases the emptiness of the stage allows great freedom of movement in time and space, a freedom frequently exploited. The vast spatial and temporal scope of the Elizabethan drama to a great extent assumes as a prerequisite the bare stage on which that drama unfolded. Even the rapid set changes allowed by Italianate wing-and-drop perspective scenery cannot offer the kind of freedom that a bare stage can. Similarly, although relatively substantial settings are required for *The Skin of Our Teeth*, in which a greater expanse of time is telescoped than in any of Wilder's other plays, in works such as *Pullman Car Hiawatha* and *The Happy Journey*, where both space and time are compressed, a scenery-free stage is indispensable.

THE THEATRE OF THE SPANISH GOLDEN AGE

The Spanish popular theatre of the age of Lope de Vega and Calderón de la Barca so closely resembles the English theatre of the same period, both in staging methods and conventions and in the general configuration of the stage and auditorium, that the relationship between Wilder's theatre and the Elizabethans' is, in many respects, identical to that between his theatre and that of Lope and his contemporaries. The American playwright's familiarity with the latter theatrical tradition is well documented. First, for many years he pursued the scholarly hobby of attempting to assign dates to Lope de Vega's plays. The fruits of his research were published in two articles, one of which appeared in 1952 and the other in 1953.[11] He also mentions Lope in the Preface to *Our Town*, citing as a precedent for his own approach to staging the device used in the Spanish dramatist's theatre of letting a carpet on a bare stage represent a raft at sea (*AC* 102). Apparently, his interest in Lope was first sparked by his reading a biography of the Spanish master while he was at Lawrenceville (Harrison 78).

Although the standard subject matter of most Spanish plays of the Golden Age, conflicts of love and honor, bears little resemblance to that treated by Wilder in his dramatic works, there are nonetheless a number of technical similarities between Wilder's theatre and that of Lope and Calderón, even beyond those examined in the first section of this chapter. Simultaneous settings, which are also to be found, of course, in the third act of *Our Town*, were sometimes employed in Spanish plays, according to Rennert (291). The convention was uncommon on the Elizabethan and Jacobean stage, although evidence of its use, at least in the early years of the period, may be found in Sir Philip Sidney's complaint in *The Defense of Poesy* that "you shall have Asia of the one side and Africa of the other, and so many other under-kingdoms, that the player, when he comes in, must ever begin with telling where he is." Some simple, unobtrusive visual puns, of a type perhaps also seen on Elizabethan stages, seem to have been employed as well on the Spanish stage in the representation of place and object. One such pun is the carpet mentioned by Wilder that was meant to represent a raft at sea. Moreover, the upper stage or gallery, occupying approximately the same location as its counterpart in the Elizabethan playhouse, may have served, along with the visible stairway which connected it to the stage, to represent the hill called for in numerous plays (Shergold 203, 220). It is also possible that some attempt was made at illusionism in the depiction of these hills—a painted cloth, for instance, hung from the gallery and extending to the stage floor (224). Again, any visual puns that were in use on the Spanish stage were attributable to expediency, rather than theoretical or aesthetic considerations.

In any case, as on the Elizabethan stage, the principle of "selective realism," rather than that of symbolism or visual metaphor, seems in most instances to have dictated the approach toward the representation of places and objects. There was no noteworthy use of pantomime to create objects used by the characters. Properties, although few, were always corporeal. One play required a fountain (Rennert 95; Shergold 204). In several a garden was represented, and rocks, mountains, and trees were also frequently displayed on stage to help indicate place (Rennert 95). The impulse toward realism is especially evident in the frequent—or at least widespread—use of real horses on stage (and in the *patio*). Special ramps were even built to allow horses (and humans) easier access to the stage from the *patio* and vice versa (Shergold 220–21). In addition, stage machines or *tramoyas* played an important role, especially in later years, in Spanish theatrical performances. Although their primitive character caused periodic malfunctions and thereby shattered, often in ludicrous fashion, the illusions they were designed to create (214), their illusionistic purpose is undeniable and is essentially out of harmony with Wilder's views regarding the nature and strengths of the theatre.[12] Those views and the playwright's scenic practices, again, have more in common with the Chinese and Japanese theatre traditions.

THE CHINESE THEATRE

Many critics have already remarked on the numerous remarkable parallels Wilder's drama exhibits with the traditional Chinese theatre. *Our Town*, in particular, in both initial reviews and subsequent analyses, has been regularly associated with the Chinese theatre (understood to mean the Beijing Opera). For instance, Robert Benchley, reviewing the play in the *New*

Yorker on 12 February 1938, wrote, "Frank Craven [as the Stage Manger], in the manner of the old Property Man in 'The Yellow Jacket,' moves what chairs and tables there are and draws the curtains" (26). Benchley disliked the playwright's use of pantomime, which he regarded as "suited more for charades and other guessing games" (26) than for stage plays, and he concluded:

> That several of Mr. Wilder's scenes emerge refulgent from all this sign language and wigwagging is a great tribute to his powers as a dramatist. It is all very charming when the Chinese do it, but Mr. Wilder did not write a charming play and we are not Chinese. (26)

Many other critics besides Benchley also identify the Stage Manager as a variant of the Chinese property man (e.g., Burbank 89; Eastman 944; Eaton 21), but, as Benchley indicates, there are other features of the play, such as the use of pantomime, that might be considered "Chinese" or quasi-Chinese as well. Wilder's interest in pantomime was, in fact, apparently sparked by a performance by Mei Lan-fang which the playwright was fortunate enough to witness in New York in 1930 (Haberman, *Plays* 85). While working on *Our Town*, he even explicitly described the play as "utilizing the technique of Chinese drama" (postcard to A. Wertheimer, 14 Nov. 1937, ms., Wertheimer papers, YCAL), and he admitted that the device of the two portals representing birth and death in *The Long Christmas Dinner* was derived from Chinese theatrical conventions (Simon 88). Actually, the only convention of the Chinese stage that could have suggested the device to Wilder is the invariable presence of two doorways, one on the right side and one on the left, in the upstage wall in Chinese theatres. These doorways are known as "Spirit Doors," and entrances are generally made through the stage-right opening, exits through its stage-left counterpart (Arlington 26; Chen 21). Although the portals in *The Long Christmas Dinner* correspond fairly closely in their placement ("birth" stage right, "death" stage left) to these "Spirit Doors," Wilder goes beyond Chinese practice in assigning the symbolic meanings he does to them.

In fact, although Wilder lived in China for a time as a child and attended missionary schools there, he claimed never to have seen a performance of Chinese opera (Mei Lan-fang's performance being merely a showcase of Chinese techniques) (Haberman 84–85; letter to Miss Niemoeller, 25 July 1961, ts., Wilder papers, YCAL). However, he seems early in his career to have acquired a rudimentary familiarity with Chinese theatrical conventions, whether from having seen Mei or from books and conversations. His familiarity is evident not only in his avowed transformation of the "Spirit Doors" into the portals of birth and death in *The Long Christmas Dinner*, but also in several references in his essays to the Chinese convention of having an actor indicate he is on horseback by carrying a stylized whip (*AC* 109, 123). Although in one essay his description of the convention is inaccurate, indicating an imperfect knowledge of Chinese theatre at that stage of his career, and the convention itself is frequently mentioned in other writers' accounts of the Chinese theatre and hence was relatively common knowledge, the reference itself is sufficient testimony to an interest in Chinese staging methods on Wilder's part and a recognition of the similarity of those methods to his own.

All the same, it is only in certain limited, if important, respects that Wilder's theatre resembles traditional Beijing Opera. These respects all—or nearly all—have to do with scenic minimalism or symbolism. In other areas the style of Chinese performance, with its emphasis on colorful and elaborate, stylized costumes; bizarre and unnatural make-up; abstract codes of gesture and blocking; cacophonous music and singing; dance; and acrobatic displays; is utterly unlike that demanded (or assumed) in Wilder's plays.

In structure and purpose, also, Wilder's drama differs markedly from classical Chinese drama. Unlike most Chinese dramas, Wilder's plays are not melodramas with stock heroes, villains, innocent victims, and conventionally happy endings. They are not episodic either, as are most traditional Chinese plays. The brevity and compression of Wilder's most typical dramatic works are in pronounced contrast to the length of Chinese opera plays, performances of which may last five or six hours, although within that time several shorter plays or excerpts from plays will have been presented. Finally, although there is a didactic strain in Wilder's drama, none of his plays propounds the sort of sentimental morality invariably informing the Beijing Opera, according to which villainy is always punished and virtue richly rewarded.

Bearing all these obvious (and less obvious) differences in mind, however, one can still easily discern the pronounced resemblances between Wilder's theatre and traditional Chinese opera. In the first place, the Chinese stage, which is devoid of nearly all scenery and properties, is emphatically anti-illusionistic. Objects are frequently conjured up entirely through pantomime, as they are in Wilder's plays. For example, as was evident in one of the passages from Sartre's writings on the theatre quoted in the previous chapter, a common technique of the Chinese actor is to suggest, solely through pantomime, that he is in a boat on a river. A chariot in Beijing Opera is suggested by a pair of flags with wheels painted on them, borne by two supposedly invisible stage assistants, between whom the actor playing the character riding in the "chariot" walks (Chen 28; Arlington 46). Wilder's technique of representing vehicular travel in his plays is close to both these Chinese practices. Finally, in order to show that he is entering (or leaving) a house, the Chinese actor will perform a gesture imitating the drawing back of a bolt and will then move forward, lifting first one foot and then the other, as he steps over the (imaginary) high threshold that was a feature of all Chinese houses in former times (Chen 39; Pronko 55). Obviously, any character in *Our Town* who passes through the doors to the Gibbs or Webb kitchens—as George does in Act II, for instance—must perform a similar sequence of pantomimic movements. Wilder's extensive use of pantomime in his other plays, too, requires no further comment here.

Similarly, visual puns or metaphors are frequently employed on the Chinese stage. A table and two chairs are almost the only stage properties needed, and they are utilized in a variety of ingenious ways and arranged in a wide array of configurations to represent the places and objects required for the action. For instance:

> A chair can serve as a "prison." The imprisoned actor stands behind it and looks through barred windows by peering through the back supports. A chair can be a "well." If an actor, depending on the play's context, jumps upon it and then down on the other side and then makes a hurried exit—all this is prefaced with the gestures indicating a fatal decision—then he has jumped down a well and drowned himself. (Chen 28)

Wilder's use of similar visual puns in *Our Town*, *Pullman Car Hiawatha*, and his other minimalist plays, like his use of pantomime, needs no further comment here.

Other anti-illusionistic techniques are shared by Wilder's theatre and its Chinese counterpart, too. The most immediately obvious and perhaps the most important of these techniques is the visible scene shift, accomplished in the Chinese (and Japanese) theatres by the technically "invisible" property man. The critics who refer to the Stage Manager in *Our Town* as a form of Chinese property man are only partially correct, however. At least one of them (Eaton 21), in terming the Stage Manager a "vocal Chinese property man," touches on a crucial distinction, but the distinction is merely glanced at and glossed over. The difference lies in the respective functions of Wilder's Stage Manager and the property man. The latter essentially "disappears" while he is on stage, the audience being only marginally aware of his presence. His task is to assist with the mechanical aspects of the performance, efficiently and, above all, unobtrusively. Although the Stage Manager in *Our Town* does periodically rearrange the furniture on the stage, he is meant to be anything but an invisible, self-effacing assistant to the other performers. He not only serves as chorus and bit player, but he also determines the pacing and overall shape of the performance, responsibilities far beyond those assigned to the Chinese property man. The Stage Manager in *The Happy Journey* is perhaps closer to the property man in this respect, but he, too, participates directly in the fictional action presented, as the latter does not. "Mr. Washburn" in *Pullman Car* is furthest of all from the Chinese stage assistant, since he does not even rearrange the stage properties (although he does draw a chalk outline of the car itself on the stage at the beginning of the play).

At the same time, Wilder does employ in *Our Town* a reasonable facsimile of the Chinese property man—namely, the stage assistants who, while the

Stage Manager is meditating aloud to the audience about the wider significance of the action, accomplish the more extensive scene changes (the introduction of the ladders to represent upstairs bedrooms in Act I and the change from Main Street to the interior of the church in Act II).

Also exposing the mechanics of performance in Chinese opera is the visible orchestra, for which, however, there is no close analogue in Wilder's drama. One other convention of the Chinese stage that does find a close parallel in Wilder's plays, though, is the explicit differentiation, at certain moments, of actor from role. The actor is not assumed to be in character when he first appears. One writer describes in the following terms the sequence of events following an actor's entrance:

> As he approaches the centre of the stage after his entrance, the actor faces slightly to the right, raises his left hand to the level of his chin, while, with his bare right hand, he holds the lower corner of the left sleeve. In this position, "the introduction sleeve," he sings the prologue of the next action. It indicates that he is "still" an actor. As he finally announces the name of the character he is to play, he lowers his arm slightly and thus shows that he is "in character." (Chen 38)

In this distinct transition from real to fictional identity, the Chinese performer resembles not only the fictitious "actors" and theatre personnel in *The Skin of Our Teeth*—"Miss Somerset," "Mr. Fitzpatrick," "Fred Bailey," "Ivy," "Hester," and the actors playing Henry and Antrobus—but also the Stage Managers in *Our Town*, *Pullman Car Hiawatha*, and *The Happy Journey*, who assume their various minor roles without the least attempt (except perhaps in the case of the minister in *Our Town*) to create an illusion that they actually *are* the characters they are impersonating. In this and other respects, then, Wilder's theatre and the Chinese are indeed close relatives, and not only or always in the ways perceived by early critics of *Our Town*.

THE JAPANESE THEATRE

Because many Japanese theatrical conventions resemble or were derived from Chinese practices, most of the elements in Wilder's drama that cause it to seem "Chinese" also cause it to resemble the Japanese Noh and, to a lesser extent, Kabuki theatres. Even the ways in which it differs from Chinese drama are similar or identical to the ways in which it differs from one or both major Japanese forms. Nonetheless, there are certain unique features linking Wilder's theatre with the Noh and Kabuki, and the relationship therefore deserves to be investigated separately.

Wilder developed a strong interest in the Noh late in life and was influenced early on by Paul Claudel's account of a Noh play in *L'oiseau noir dans le soleil levant*, but he was able to read examples of the drama, in the volume compiled by Ezra Pound and Ernest Fenollosa, only after he had written his major plays. As late as 1961, he wrote to a student that he had never seen a Noh or Kabuki performance (letter to "Miss Niemoeller," 25 July 1961, ts., Wilder papers, YCAL), and he first witnessed a Noh performance by a Japanese company at the Yale School of Drama, apparently in the late 1960s or early 1970s (letter to Dennis M. Cunningham, n.d., ts., Wilder papers, YCAL). However, he himself clearly recognized the aesthetic affinity between his theatre and the Noh. In the Preface to *Three Plays* (1957), he refers to the Noh device of the condensed or accelerated journey as a precedent for and parallel to his own anti-illusionistic practices (*AC* 109), and his continuing fascination with the Japanese form is itself evidence of a strong perceived kinship.

The affinity is perhaps most immediately discernible in the minimal settings employed in the Noh, but both the Noh and Kabuki are essentially anti-illusionistic theatres. Kabuki plays, it is true, are performed with often spectacular, semi-illusionistic settings. The illusion is undermined in several ways, though, as Earle Ernst points out in his comprehensive study of Kabuki (127–36).

A clearer and more important parallel between Wilder's theatre and that of Japan lies in certain motifs shared by him and the Noh dramatists. One such motif, that of the journey, was mentioned by Wilder himself. The other motif shared by Wilder's drama and the Noh is that of the return to earth of a ghost or spirit—especially a spirit tied to a particular patch of ground. In most Noh plays, the central character is a specter who at first appears to the secondary character, a monk or other traveler, in the guise of an ordinary inhabitant of the region where the traveler has stopped. After telling in the third person his or her tale of woe, the ghost leaves but then reappears to reenact or recollect in the first person the tale just related.[13] This particular pattern of character and incident finds a marked parallel, of course, in the last act of *Our Town,* in Emily's return to life for her twelfth birthday. Not only is Emily irresistibly drawn, like the ghosts in the Noh, to the familiar scenes of her earthly existence, but her overpowering urge to reexperience or relive a special occasion in her life, although it is not a crucial or climactic occasion, closely resembles the compulsion of the Noh ghosts to reenact or recount the decisive moments of their lives. The Noh convention stems from the playwrights' Buddhist faith, especially its emphasis on nonattachment to earthly life, but one need not therefore conclude that Wilder wrote *Our Town* under the influence of Buddhist precepts.[14] The resemblance between this one incident in the play and similar occurrences in Noh drama is perhaps fortuitous, but nonetheless suggestive. Wilder deviates from Noh practice by presenting the incident largely from the ghost's point of view, but the deviation is minor in comparison with the similarities.

In addition to these motifs linking Wilder's drama with the Noh, there are numerous technical and stylistic parallels between his dramaturgy and both Noh and Kabuki staging practices. First, pantomime is commonly used to suggest or indicate objects in performances of the Noh.[15] On the

Kabuki stage, real or realistic properties are generally employed. However, one exception, a convention borrowed from the Noh, involves the principle of visual metaphor, the most significant use of that principle in the Japanese theatre. The property employed is the fan, which, depending upon how it is handled and how far it is opened, may represent a teacup, a sword or knife, whip, pipe, tray, bottle, or lantern (Ernst 161). It has an even wider range of possible significance in the Noh, in keeping with the less realistic, more symbolic staging principles followed in the older form.

Other visual puns are occasionally employed in the Noh as well. For instance, a cloth is used in one play to represent a heap of stones and earth covering a dead character, and in another a similar cloth represents a clump of grasses from which a ghost emerges. At the same time, however, scenic practices in the Noh, while minimalistic and austere, governed by the principle of ascetic restraint, tend to fall under the heading of "selective realism" or partial representation rather than symbolic substitution or visual metaphor. Although the bareness of the Noh stage brings the form itself closer visually than Kabuki to Wilder's minimalist dramas, the few stage properties used suggest, at least, the true, complete outlines of the objects they are supposed to represent. More to the point, they are obviously expressly constructed as theatrical properties, not "found" objects that in another context perform a different function. Huts or cottages are represented by small bamboo frameworks, but the bell in the famous play *Dojoji* is normally a realistic, full-size papier-mâché or cloth reproduction. Thus, except for the various uses of the omnipresent fan, visual puns are rare on the Noh stage, in contrast to Beijing Opera practices.

Other Japanese performance conventions are equally anti-illusionistic, however. The visible musicians are one such convention. In addition, as in the Chinese theatre, scene shifts and other necessary adjustments in both the Noh and Kabuki are made in plain sight of the audience by visible, if unobtrusive, stage assistants, although a front curtain is used to mask some changes in Kabuki performances. At times, the Kabuki actor draws attention to the fact that he is an actor by referring to himself by his real name while still supposedly in character (Ernst 80; Bowers 193). In some instances, the juggling with illusion and reality becomes even more involved—and playful—than that in *The Skin of Our Teeth*. One actor in a Kabuki play is required, while still in character, to assert at one point that he is his character's favorite actor (Ernst 80). Similar witticisms may be found in other plays, or at least in stories of remarks improvised by certain celebrated actors during the playing of particular roles. In one play several characters are frightened by a red object they see in the distance, only to breathe a collective sigh of relief upon recognizing it as the carpet in the theatre balcony (81). Actors themselves actually drop entirely out of character periodically during Kabuki performances, whether to sip a cup of tea, have perspiration wiped off their brows, or have their costumes adjusted

(189). The resemblance of all these practices to Wilder's anti-illusionistic techniques in *The Skin of Our Teeth*, *Our Town*, *Pullman Car Hiawatha*, and *The Happy Journey* should require no comment. It is important to note, again, however, that Wilder's characters in *Skin* only give the *illusion* of dropping out of character, whereas the Kabuki actor actually does the deed: and furthermore, he remains mute while doing so, unlike them.[16]

The chorus in the Noh and the narrator occasionally used in Kabuki are both anti-illusionistic devices that bear a resemblance to Wilder's choral Stage Manager/narrators.[17] However, the former especially differs in important respects from the Stage Managers in Wilder's plays. It does function as a narrator at times, as do the Stage Managers in *Our Town* and *Pullman Car Hiawatha*, and it occasionally provides commentary on the action or the characters' plight, pointing out any especially poignant or subtle aspects to the given circumstances. Moreover, it frequently utters the central character's thoughts aloud, as "Mr. Washburn" directs the passengers to do for themselves in *Pullman Car*. However, in contrast to the two Stage Managers in the Wilder plays mentioned, fundamentally it is not a character at all. It speaks the central character's lines for him or her on occasion, but the character is on stage at the time. The Noh chorus resembles Wilder's Stage Managers less than it does a motion picture sound track, with the latter's capacity to permit an actor to voice his or her character's "inner monologue" or to allow an anonymous narrator to deliver exposition directly. The narrator in Kabuki is not a true character either, and therein also differs from Wilder's Stage Managers. Like the Noh chorus, he, too, can relate a character's thoughts while the latter performs in silence, but he functions primarily as an anonymous, featureless narrative voice. Such distinctions, however, while not insignificant, are ultimately of less moment than the resemblances enumerated here, which together point to a profound sympathy between Wilder's theatrical vision and that of the Japanese.

AMERICAN CIVIC AND ACADEMIC PAGEANTS

There are also noteworthy similarities between at least two plays of Wilder's, *Pullman Car Hiawatha* and *The Skin of Our Teeth*, and a formerly popular, if minor, form of American theatrical entertainment: the civic, religious, or academic pageant. This exceedingly widespread form of theatrical activity flourished in schools and communities during the early decades of the twentieth century, growing in popularity from 1910 to 1920, while Wilder was still a student (Clark; Brown). The playwright himself makes reference to a variant of the form in one of his stage directions. He calls in *Pullman Car Hiawatha* for Grover's Corners, Ohio, to speak "in a foolish voice as though he were reciting a piece at a Sunday School entertainment" (59).

One of the most common devices of the pageants was the introduction of allegorical and human figures, living and dead, who recited quotations or sang songs. The pageant format usually entailed a series of such recitations, although there were also episodes of longer duration than the brief cameos in *Pullman Car* and *Skin*, featuring some minimal dramatic development. Figures in actual civic pageants frequently included the personified spirit or "genius" of the town or community (e.g., "Jose," the central character in San Jose, California's "Historical Community Pageant" of 1917; see San Jose Community Pageant, program, Bancroft Library, University of California, Berkeley), personifications of the seasons (Blomquist 410), allegorical figures representing such entities as Labor and Management (Chicago, 1913; see "Chicago Pageant" 346), the months (Chicago, 1913; see "Chicago Pageant" 345), the years since the city's founding (Savannah, 1919, see Taft 159, frontispiece), and legendary and historical figures from the community's past. The similarity between all these conventions or practices and the presence and behavior of the towns, fields, planets, and hours of *Pullman Car* is self-evident. Even the overall form of the play—or at least of its second half—resembles that of the pageants. Pageants usually concluded with a grand finale in which all the participants appeared on stage at once (Taft 101), as happens in the climax of *Pullman Car*. The Stage Manager even corresponds in some measure to the Pageant Master, who generally had to be on hand in the orchestra pit during the performance to cue musicians and actors (14–16).

In addition, the aim of the civic pageant was to augment civic pride through the presentation of as complete a picture as possible of the communal life, past and present. As such, it was an expression of that generalized truth that constitutes one-half (perhaps the dominant half) of Wilder's theatrical vision. In the words of one enthusiast of the times, pageantry

> is the drama of community life. . . . [T]he modern pageant is drama in which the place is the hero and the development of the community is the plot. In direct contrast to the regular drama of the theatre which . . . traces the development of individual life, the purpose of the pageant is through the sequence of the generations to trace the development of community life. (Langdon 407)

Our Town partially fits this description and shares this purpose on one level, but the civic pageant also provided a suitable format and suitable techniques for Wilder to use in portraying the broader contexts in which the main action of a play like *Pullman Car* occurs, the general, universal Truth of which it is merely an illustration. Furthermore, since the development of the human community is the plot of *The Skin of Our Teeth*, pageant techniques were also suitable for the passage at the end of that play in which the cosmic and universal implications of the action are revealed by the Hours of the night. The standard practice at civic pageants was to include as many local residents as possible in the various tableaux, episodes, musical interludes, and pantomimes presented, and Wilder does essentially the same thing in *Skin* when he has the theatre staff take over the roles of the Hours. In using techniques similar to those of the pageant writers in his play, the dramatist simply expands the focus from the individual, geographical community to the universal, cosmic one.

There is no "hard" evidence that Wilder attended or participated in a particular pageant during the genre's heyday, but a widely publicized one was held in 1910, at the MacDowell Colony in Peterborough, New Hampshire, where Wilder stayed for periods of time beginning in 1924 to work on a number of his plays and novels. He almost certainly would have heard references to it during his stays there, since the pageant stage was made a permanent feature of the colony grounds (Mackaye 137). Moreover, pageants were so common at the height of their popularity (during Wilder's secondary and undergraduate school days) that it would have been well-nigh impossible for anyone as aware and inquisitive as he was to be ignorant of their existence and format. The form of *Pullman Car* itself is the best evidence of his familiarity with the genre. The similarities are too obvious to be fortuitous or coincidental. In the case of this play, then, and the device of the Hours in *Skin*, Wilder's "world theatre" returns to his native country, with the use not only of ordinary contemporary American lives as subject matter, but also of a popular, familiar, although not indigenous, form of American "folk theatre" as a formal and stylistic pattern.

Even this array of foreign and domestic and historical theatrical traditions and forms does not entirely exhaust the sources—both merely possible and indisputable—of elements in Wilder's theatre. Some of the more self-evident sources have not been treated for the very reason that they are self-evident. First, *The Matchmaker* was an acknowledged adaptation of Johann Nestroy's nineteenth-century Viennese satire *Einen Jux will er sich machen*, and much of the unsentimental comedy and freewheeling theatricality of Wilder's play is traceable to the Austrian original.[18] As was stated in the first chapter, also, Wilder lifted almost an entire scene of the same play from Molière's *L'avare*.[19] Wilder also contended that both *The Matchmaker* and *The Skin of Our Teeth* were modeled on the old-fashioned American touring stock company productions he had seen as a boy at Ye Liberty Theatre in Oakland, California. *The Matchmaker* is indeed—on the surface at least—the sort of frothy romantic comedy that would have fit into the repertory of an early twentieth-century touring stock company. Elements in *The Skin of Our Teeth* derived from the stock-company "style" include the missed cues and unpredictable scenery in Act I, the two-dimensionality or cartoonlike quality of the settings in Act II (and perhaps in the other acts as well), "Miss Somerset's" refusal to play one scene in Act II, and the disruption of the performance in Act III due to the sudden sickness of some of the actors, along with the impromptu rehearsal and substitution of the theatre's auxiliary personnel for the stricken thespians, although these latter occurrences were clearly not everyday events in touring stock companies but represent exaggerations of the kinds of minor catastrophes with which any such company would regularly have had to contend. Additionally, the device of having a servant (Sabina) deliver exposition at the beginning of Act I is a dramaturgical cliché as typical of nineteenth-century melodrama as it is of Ibsen. Wilder himself, finally, provides a clue to the ways in which the play reflects the touring stock-company style of production when he writes:

> the walls are frankly "flats" that ripple when a draft hits them. To be consistent, I should be willing that the Atlantic City boardwalk be one of those vaudeville drops. (qtd. in Haberman, *Plays* 69)

There are, moreover, a number of extra-theatrical influences on several of the plays. The extent to which *The Skin of Our Teeth* is indebted to *Finnegans Wake* has already been noted. Wilder also confessed that Emily's farewell "to clocks ticking . . . and Mama's sunflowers. And food and coffee. And new-ironed dresses and hot baths" (99)—and presumably Harriet's farewell to earth as well—was inspired by a passage in *The Odyssey* (Modic 60). Finally, the playwright admitted that the idea for the graveyard scene in *Our Town* came to him from a canto of Dante's *Purgatorio* (*AC* 109), and his brother later revealed that one of Blake's engravings was perhaps an even more important source of inspiration for the scene (A. N. Wilder 69). In any case, there are truly echoes or reminiscences of a world of theatre—and of art and literature—within the relatively few plays produced by Thornton Wilder.

NOTES

1. Typical cycles include the Chester cycle and the *Ludus Coventriae*.
2. For instance, in the Wakefield *Murder of Abel*, Cain turns belligerently to the audience to justify himself immediately after slaying his brother. Similarly, in the same cycle's *Noah and His Sons* or *Noah's Deluge*, Noah's wife and Noah himself both address the audience, each one in turn, soliciting support for their respective sides in their domestic brawl (ll. 377–92).
3. With respect to this point, it should be noted that one particular form of medieval drama, the *stationendrama* (which influenced Strindberg and the expressionists), has already been discussed in Chapter 4, along with the extent to which certain of Wilder's journey plays may or may not legitimately be classified as representatives of the genre. For the most part, again, they may not.
4. Such Noh plays include *Kagekiyo*, by Zeami, and *Motomezuka* (*The Sought-for Grave*).
5. A good example of this sort of action occurs in the twelfth-century Norman-French *Play of Adam*, a forerunner of the cycle plays (e.g., ll. 223–25, 263, 745).
6. For example, he states in "Some Thoughts on Playwrighting" (*AC* 123) that in the mask worn by the actor who originally played Medea was "an acoustical

device for projecting the voice" and that the actor wore "shoes with soles and heels half a foot high." Scholars now unanimously recognize that the superb acoustics of the ancient Greek theatres made any hidden voice-projection devices unnecessary and that the *cothornos* or "tragic buskin" was not worn by Greek actors until the Hellenistic period (336 B.C.–31 B.C.).

7. The painting is frequently reproduced as, for example, in Taylor and Nelson (85).

8. Such a person is still employed for rehearsals in modern European theatre productions.

9. For instance, in the Shearmen and Tailors' Pageant, the three kings simply meet somewhere, probably in the desert (ll. 240–82), and agree to follow the star they see above. They are definitely in a strange land, since two of them comment that they have lost their way and know not what country they are in, but the location or nature of that strange land remains undisclosed (and is, indeed, irrelevant). In the Brome *Abraham and Isaac*, also, the two title characters are revealed at first praying somewhere near their home, although the exact location is never specified.

10. For instance, in the Preface for *Our Town* (*AC* 102), Preface to *Three Plays* (*AC* 108), "Some Thoughts on Playwrighting" (*AC* 116, 120, 124, 126).

11. "New Aids toward Dating the Early Plays of Lope de Vega," *Varia Variorum: Festgabe für Karl Reinhardt* (Münster and Cologne: Böhlau Verlag, 1952), rpt. in *AC* (257–66); "Lope, Pinedo, Some Child Actors, and a Lion," *Romance Philology* (Aug. 1953), rpt. in *AC* (267–77).

12. Some of the commoner *tramoyas* included machines for making objects and persons appear to fly, such as clouds containing apparitions, which floated horizontally above the stage; pulleys and chains or ropes for raising and lowering gods or angels to and from the stage; devices enabling actors to make sudden appearances and exits; and techniques for allowing books or other objects to burst into flame as if by magic.

13. Such is the action of such Noh plays as *Matsukaze*, *Nonomiya* (*The Shrine in the Fields*), *Komachi and the Hundred Nights*, *Atsumori*, and *Nishikigi* (*The Brocade Tree*).

14. A. N. Wilder (64) cautions against this conclusion.

15. For instance, in *The Melon Thief* (a *kyogen* or short comic interlude performed between separate Noh plays), a vagrant is tantalized by the sight of ripe melons in a farmer's field and decides to steal as many as he can. Climbing over the fence, he proceeds to harvest them until he is temporarily taken aback by the sight of a previously unnoticed scarecrow, which in the darkness he mistakes for a man. In this play the scarecrow is real and the vines and melons, imaginary. Similarly, in *Motomezuka (The Sought-for Grave)*, two characters act out in pantomime the gathering of herbs, and in *Komachi at Sekidera*, a child performs in pantomime the action of serving wine.

16. Wilder reportedly did approve of director Alan Schneider's decision to have Mary Martin and other actors in his 1955 production of *Skin* call one another by their real names when they were "out of character" and refer to roles they had really played in other productions (Schneider 213). However, even this refinement fails to move the device or the play out of the realm of illusionism, since the lines spoken remained Wilder's.

17. In a previously cited letter to Miss Niemoeller, Wilder states that one thing he would have borrowed from the Noh, had he been more familiar with it at the

time he was writing his own plays, was "the relation of protagonist and chorus observer," along with "the two-part drama—real, then supernatural," the device of the journey, "the entrance of the spirit across a 'bridge,' " the "ideal spectator seated in the audience," and "perhaps the use of quotations from classic poetry" (letter of 25 July 1961, ms., Wilder papers, YCAL).

18 For a thorough comparison of the two plays and a discussion of Wilder's borrowings and modifications, see Littman (139–55).

19. For a comparison of the scenes in the two plays, see Haberman, *Plays* (127–36).

Chapter 8

The Unique Character of Wilder's Theatre

Despite the vast aesthetic scope of Wilder's plays and despite the myriad echoes and resonances they contain of other playwrights' work and of larger theatrical traditions and movements, together they constitute a personal artistic statement unlike that of any other contemporary dramatist, and each work—at least each of the major works—bears the unmistakable stamp of its author's singular vision. Each possesses a peculiarly "Wilder-esque" flavor or quality that clearly marks it as a product of one playwright's fertile and genial imagination. All the same, when one attempts to define that flavor or quality, to identify the attributes that set Wilder's drama apart from that of all other playwrights, one finds it difficult to pinpoint them precisely.

There are, of course, a number of trademarks, special devices that reappear in several of the plays. The Stage Manager is perhaps the first of these to spring to mind, followed closely by the combination of a scenery-free stage and imaginary properties indicated through pantomime. To these might readily be added the compression of time and space, especially in the continuous depiction of long journeys, and the evident fondness for repetition of both words and phrases of dialogue and incidents and patterns of action.

However, these four technical and formal hallmarks do not by themselves fully explain or establish the special, distinctive quality of Wilder's drama. An examination of the ways in which each individual device is used can bring one closer to an understanding of that quality, though. All are employed in characteristic ways, endowed with characteristic properties, and made to serve particular ends. For example, the Stage Managers are unique in several respects. Of the numerous analogues to them in the Greek, medieval, Japanese, Brechtian, and Pirandellian theatres, no single one performs as many *different* functions as do "Mr. Washburn" in *Pullman Car Hiawatha* and his counterpart in *Our Town*. Only in Wilder's plays do these figures serve as chorus, bit player, narrator, and omniscient coordinator of the performance. Only in these two plays (and in *Tonight We Improvise* and perhaps some of Brecht's works) are they characters in their own right. Moreover, their respective characters or personalities are themselves distinguishing features. "Mr. Washburn" is a bustling, earnest, efficient administrator who is well-meaning and conscientious—in short, a recognizable type of American executive or manager. The Stage Manager in *Our Town*, similarly, is a typical laconic, unflappable, rural New Englander, who is sparing of word and gesture, even-tempered, given to rumination, and imbued with a wry, subtle sense of irony. Even the Stage Manager in *The Happy Journey* may be said to possess a distinct, if only partially revealed, personality. Like the man in *Our Town*, he accomplishes his assigned tasks with economy and deliberation, without unnecessary comments or gestures, and without haste. All these personality traits endow the individual Stage Managers—and the plays in which they appear—with a "family resemblance," a peculiarly American and specifically Wilderesque air or character. In watching these plays, one feels reassured, if only intermittently, that even if all does not go smoothly at every moment in the performance, at least there is a responsible, capable, adaptable person on stage to help surmount any difficulties, someone to draw the auditor's attention to important matters or perhaps only to make sure the properties are correctly arranged. This sense of security—a critic might call it complacency—that is communicated to the spectator is one ingredient in the distinctive flavor of Wilder's drama, or at least the flavor of some of his most characteristic plays.

Like his Stage Managers, the other three technical "trademarks" of Wilder's theatre are also used in unique ways. Wilder's use of scenic minimalism is highly idiosyncratic. As was noted by the playwright himself, minimalism in the theatre has a long and venerable history. However, Wilder's use of scenic minimalism, in combination with pantomimically implied properties, sets him somewhat apart from many Western theatrical traditions and movements, if not from Asian theatre forms. Furthermore, his use of these minimalist techniques in plays with naturalistic dialogue and action and naturalistically drawn characters distinguishes those plays from their counterparts in the Oriental theatres, as well. His compression of space and time links his plays with futurist theatrical experiments as well as with the Japanese, Chinese, medieval, and Elizabethan theatres, but the spiritual aspects of his "journey" plays—as, indeed, of all his plays—clearly differentiate them from the futurist *sintesi*, and his uninterrupted depiction of the journeys themselves—and of the passage of the years in *The Long Christmas Dinner*—goes beyond the accelerated journeys and telescoped time encountered in the other traditional theatrical forms mentioned here. Finally, the playwright's use of verbal repetition and cyclical structure, although not without parallels and precedents in the works of other dramatists—and novelists, as well—is distinctive, if not unique, in that it occurs, again, in the context of comparatively naturalistic dialogue and action.

Beyond this combination of naturalistic techniques and clearly artificial formal patterning lies another important distinguishing feature of Wilder's drama: its subject matter and manner of presenting it. The characters in his plays, with the exception of those in *The Alcestiad* and the "three-minute" playlets, are all ordinary people—primarily, ordinary Americans—and the activities in which they engage are, for the most part, unheroic and unexceptional. The secondary role played by anecdote in Wilder's drama was noted in Chapter 2. *The Matchmaker*, with its incident-laden farce action, may be an exception, as may *The Skin of Our Teeth*, but in the former play, one of the central points (and an important source of the play's humor) is that the incidents—a trip from Yonkers to New York City, an encounter between two young men and a pair of shop girls, a meal at a fashionable restaurant—are in themselves thoroughly commonplace and insignificant but are invested with meaning by the participants, who perceive them as either "adventures" or debauchery. In *The Skin of Our Teeth*, on the other hand, the incidents are so generalized that very little in the way of a "dramatic event" (death, desertion, imprisonment, exoneration, birth, conversion, banishment, marriage, divorce, and the like) can be said to occur in the play, although there is one mainstay of dramatic plots, a seduction, in Act II. The missing element in Wilder's drama is not, in fact, events or incidents per se, but rather, directly dramatized interpersonal struggle and conflicts of will.

This emphasis on uneventful actions and ordinary characters does not set Wilder's drama wholly apart from that of other dramatists. The concentration on ordinary characters is a naturalistic attribute, as is, to a lesser extent, the focus on mundane, insignificant activities. The static, "undramatic" quality of the plays causes them to resemble, not only the symbolists' dramatic works, but Beckett's and a host of other modern playwrights' as well. However, the comparatively muted conflicts in Wilder's plays, the relative ease with which harmony is restored and equilibrium regained—even in the final act of *The Skin of Our Teeth*—gives all the playwright's dramatic works a "family resemblance" and, along with the other characteristic technical elements, helps to endow them with their own unique personality.

An even more significant thread uniting all—or nearly all—Wilder's plays is the dramatist's determination to undermine or destroy the theatrical illusion. Of course, he creates secondary illusions in the process of shattering the primary one (as was pointed out in the discussions of the Brechtian and Pirandellian dimensions of his drama), and, again, this anti-illusionism does not in itself distinguish his theatre from that of other ages, countries, and playwrights. Wilder might be said to employ a more complete arsenal of anti-illusionistic techniques than any other playwright—with the possible exceptions of Pirandello, in *Tonight We Improvise*, and Brecht—and perhaps in no single play by another writer are so many different anti-illusionistic techniques used so frequently as in *Our Town*, *Pullman Car Hiawatha*, and *The Skin of Our Teeth*. However, it is not simply or primarily the quantity and variety of such techniques employed by Wilder that distinguishes his dramaturgy from that of the majority of other playwrights. As was pointed out in Chapter 7, Wilder's systematic, purposeful use of non- or anti-illusionistic devices imparts a slightly polemical or subversive quality to his theatre, a quality only reinforced by his incorporation of numerous elements taken from naturalism, the aesthetic mode against which he was rebelling. Again, his theatre is not utterly unique in this respect, since both Brecht and Pirandello, not to mention the futurists and expressionists, introduced anti-illusionistic elements into their plays in reaction against the prevailing theatrical naturalism of the period in which they wrote, and Pirandello's style, at least, is also grounded in naturalistic principles and practices, even in his most anti-illusionistic plays. Brecht's drama, too, is infused with naturalistic philosophy to a degree.

Wilder's uniqueness as a dramatist might be said to lie in a combination of all the factors discussed thus far, and there would be some truth to the assertion. His theatre is a theatre of balanced polarities or equilibrium. The Western naturalism is a counterweight to the Eastern scenic and performance conventions. The American setting, characters, and outlook are complemented by European cosmopolitanism and philosophical speculation and by Asian austerity. Polemical or "subversive" anti-illusionism is counterbalanced by the reassuring manner and presence of the Stage Managers and by the careful authorial control of the secondary illusions, not to mention the dramatist's reverence for humanity's past achievements and his fundamentally accepting attitude toward the world. Platonic idealism coexists with existential empiricism and with pragmatism. Individuality and generality offer equally valid and, ultimately, interdependent truths to the observer's eye.

Above and beyond these considerations, though, Wilder's theatre is distinguished to some extent by its identifiably "American" character. Of course, because this is by definition a cultural, rather than an individual, trait, it cannot be the sole—or even the primary—basis of the plays' uniqueness, but many of the unique aspects of Wilder's drama are also recognizably and quintessentially American. To begin with, the utilitarian and pragmatic spirit of Wilder's peculiar brand of scenic minimalism, with its exploitation of "found" objects in the representation of locales and its refusal to attempt to mask the mechanical realities of the theatre space, is a thoroughly American spirit. Wilder's fondness for compressing and accelerating dramatic time mirrors the national obsession with speed, whether in the factory, the food industry, or on the highway, just as his fascination with journeys mirrors the country's restless temperament (as well as his own). His "Americanism" is evident also in his recurring focus on, and idealization of, the nuclear (and, in *The Long Christmas Dinner*, the extended) family. The Kirbys, Webbs, Gibbses, and Antrobuses are all homogeneous units, which are symmetrically balanced from the standpoint of gender, except for the odd extra daughter (there is never an extra son) or maid. In their "normalcy" and averageness, they might have been made to order for a Madison Avenue executive—at least one of the era in which they were composed. What is more, the composition of Wilder's invented dramatic families remains remarkably consistent, even as late as *Childhood*. It is perhaps not surprising or unique to choose a family to symbolize the human race, as Wilder does in *The Skin of Our Teeth*, but it is noteworthy that the family depicted in that play is an "average" (in 1930s, 1940s and 1950s terms), two-generation, somewhat idealized, American household.

The playwright's sympathetic depiction of "average," ordinary people is another "American" characteristic of his drama and, of course, a manifestation of an egalitarian, antielitist bias. That bias is also apparent in the affectionate exploitation of popular culture in *The Skin of Our Teeth*. In fact, much of Wilder's dramatic work could be regarded as an endeavor to make "difficult" or obscure ideas, such as those of Joyce and the existentialists, accessible to the multitudes, which is a characteristically American undertaking. Finally, the playwright's fundamental optimism—his belief in progress, however limited or qualified—is an undeniably American attitude, recalling the Enlightenment roots of American culture and society.

However, Wilder's theatre is unique, even among American playwrights. Moreover, there is perhaps one other, larger consideration that holds the key to understanding and appreciating Wilder's unique place in the modern (and premodern) theatre. That consideration is the very aesthetic scope of the plays themselves, a feature that paradoxically may also be regarded as "American" in character. Other playwrights, it is true, and especially American playwrights, experimented with a variety of styles in the early decades of the century, moving from naturalism to expressionism and back and even dabbling in symbolism on occasion, all with remarkable facility if not always with clear comprehension. O'Neill is, of course, the best-known example, but Elmer Rice—and even Theodore Dreiser—also fit the description. Strindberg, too, passed from a naturalistic phase to a symbolist and then an expressionist or protoexpressionist period. Ibsen, also, after beginning his career as a writer of poetic historical tragedies, moved on to lengthy dramatic poems with distinctly existentialist—and especially Kierkegaardian—overtones, and then to naturalistic drawing-room tragicomedies before concluding his career with quasisymbolist works such as *The Master Builder* and *When We Dead Awaken*.

However, Wilder differs from these other dramatists in at least two important respects. First, he cannot be said to have passed through successive phases as a playwright—except for his existentialist phase, which nevertheless did not materially affect his dramaturgical *style*. *The Alcestiad*, although unlike his other major plays in many respects, still exhibits the characteristic features of compressed time, anti-illusionism, and repetitive—but, in this case, only vaguely cyclical—structure. For the most part, then, Wilder's theatrical vision, and even his typical thematic concerns, were fixed at an early stage of his career. Many of the "three-minute" plays bear witness to this fact, as has been demonstrated, and several recurring devices—the Stage Managers in *Pullman Car Hiawatha*, *Our Town*, and *The Happy Journey*; the bare stage and imaginary properties in these three plays and *The Long Christmas Dinner*; and the parade of philosopher/Hours in *Pullman Car* and *The Skin of Our Teeth*—testify to it as well.

Perhaps the absence of "phases" in Wilder's career as a dramatist is due to the fact that he wrote far fewer plays than any of the other playwrights just mentioned. Perhaps had he been exclusively a playwright, his work might fall into more clearly defined stages of development (although Strindberg was a novelist as well as a playwright and still passed through definite phases in the latter capacity). The fact remains that the aesthetic scope of Wilder's drama, instead of being spread out over a series of separate plays, is for the most part compressed and channeled into each of the few major, characteristic works he wrote for the stage. *Our Town* contains naturalistic, existentialist, symbolist, Brechtian, Pirandellian, futurist, Chinese, Noh, medieval, Elizabethan, and Greek elements. *The Skin of Our Teeth* contains all of these (except Chinese, Noh, and Greek elements), and expressionist and civic pageant features as well. Similar lists could be assembled for each of the major one-act plays and, to a lesser extent, for *The Matchmaker* and *The Alcestiad* also.

It is not simply the stylistic and thematic heterogeneity of Wilder's plays, however, that sets them apart from the works of the other playwrights mentioned here, since their total dramatic output also exhibits broad aesthetic or stylistic scope. The aesthetic scope of Wilder's plays is, in fact, greater. For instance, although all the other dramatists wrote one or more nonrealistic plays, none experimented as freely with anti-illusionistic techniques as Wilder. None of them employed quasifuturist methods of compressing time and space, as does Wilder (although perhaps the acceleration and ultimate reversal of time in the second scene of Strindberg's *A Dream Play* constitutes an exception). Wilder's theatre even includes stylistic elements not found in the work of the two modern dramatists with whom his dramatic universe has the closest affinities, Brecht and Pirandello. The latter makes relatively little use of scenic minimalism or quasi-Oriental visual metaphors, and Brecht, although keenly interested in the Chinese and Japanese theatres, has very little if anything in common with the symbolists. Thus, the very variety of aesthetic movements and idioms with which Wilder's theatre exhibits parallels distinguishes it from that of almost any other playwright.

Perhaps such a distinction seems relatively insignificant, something of a dramaturgical stunt or technical tour de force without any real substance behind it. It is true that Wilder's plays—with the possible exception of *The Alcestiad*—are not notable for any great philosophical complexity or depth. Perhaps the power they do possess, aside from their immediate emotional impact, is due largely to the novelty and variety of the stylistic and technical experiments they contain. However, this astonishing profusion of echoes, recollections, and resonances from a world of theatre forms and theories is not arbitrarily imposed on his plays by Wilder with the aim of calling attention to them. Rather, it is intimately and organically connected to his unique, individual character and concerns. Not only does it spring from his extraordinarily restless and inquisitive—and extraordinarily absorptive and retentive—intellect, but it mirrors his central thematic concern in the plays, which is implicitly or explicitly evident in nearly all of them: the problem of the individual's apparent insignificance within the endless expanses of space and time and humanity. It is this integral connection between the aesthetic "immensity" of Wilder's plays and the spatial, temporal, and social scope of his fundamental concern that constitutes perhaps the most important and unique aspect of his dramaturgy. Although his dramatic work serves as a point of intersection for an incredibly vast array of tendencies, impulses, and currents from both the modern and the ancient theatres, those currents and impulses are all, not only assimilated by the playwright, but also pressed into the service of his one perennial, overriding interest—or obsession. Even when his theatre borrows from or resembles that of playwrights, theorists, and theatre artists who sought to break away from earlier forms and dominant aesthetic conventions, he manages, by subtle inversions of the elements borrowed or careful provision of new contexts for them, to suggest the essential oneness or, at all events, interconnectedness of all theatrical styles, forms, and modes of expression in all lands and in all ages. Although he himself, too, wished to break away in his plays from an established set of theatrical conventions—that of naturalism—he even succeeded in linking his dramatic work with that aesthetic movement as well, absorbing its techniques and aims into his total vision and subsequently transcending them.

This perceived aesthetic interconnectedness of all world theatre is only part of the correspondence, though, between Wilder's primary thematic concerns as a dramatist and the aesthetic mode in which he gives them expression. The paradoxical situation of a uniqueness founded on extensive links with other people's work has its complement, which is also rooted in Wilder's fundamental concern. His drama maintains its own individuality and uniqueness in spite of the aesthetic immensity in which it exists, and to which it makes continual reference. It is difficult to say or see precisely how this feat is accomplished, but the result undeniably bears the dramatist's personal stamp, the mark not only of his philosophical concerns but of his personality and vision as well. This result may be achieved in part by the inversion of borrowed elements and their removal from their original contexts, but the individuality of Wilder's theatre cannot be entirely or satisfactorily explained as the result of an exceptional skill in the techniques of collage or pastiche. It is true that the borrowings and coincidental resemblances are integrated into the plays with great art, so that the spectator—even the educated spectator—is unaware of many of the aesthetic resonances while watching the plays. Even the playwright was doubtlessly unaware of several of them, however. It was perhaps his own profound sense of personal connection to a multitude of human cultures that enabled him to synthesize all the voices and visions that find a meeting place in his drama and with them to forge a theatre idiom that reflects the manifold cultural traditions and legacies—the miniature cosmos—that each individual carries within him- or herself (whether knowingly or unknowingly).

In seeking to define how he differed from the dramatists who were his contemporaries, Wilder wrote that he seemed exceptional in just one respect: he gave the impression of enjoying his work "enormously" (*AC* 111). Certainly that work is unique in a number of other ways. However, aside from all the technical considerations examined here, it is perhaps Wilder's geniality and ebullience, his affirmative outlook, and his compassionate—but not wholly uncritical—acceptance of the world and of individual people, combined with a certain restraint or delicacy—a reluctance to uncover or dwell on the sordid, grim, or horrifying aspects of life—that gives his work its particular personality or "atmosphere." Many have perceived that atmosphere as old-fashioned, outmoded, not of its time. Stylistically, of course, the plays are as fully "of their time" and place as they are of countless other times and places. If philosophically the playwright's Neoplatonism places him outside the main currents of contemporary thought, the naturalistic and existentialist overtones in the plays keep him firmly in contact with those currents. Thus, it would be an oversimplification to contend that the uniqueness of his drama lies in a combination of contemporary, innovative stylistic experimentation with an old-fashioned philosophical outlook or set of assumptions. If his theatre is not wholly of its time, that is because it is, in one way or another, of all times and all places.

Bibliography

WORKS BY THORNTON WILDER

Plays and Novels

The Alcestiad, or A Life in the Sun. With a Satyr Play, The Drunken Sisters. New York: Harper and Row, 1977.

The Angel That Troubled the Waters, and Other Plays. New York: Coward-McCann, 1928.

Childhood. Atlantic Monthly 206 (Nov. 1960): 78–84.

Infancy. New York: Samuel French, 1961.

The Long Christmas Dinner and Other Plays in One Act. New York: Coward-McCann, 1931. (Includes *The Long Christmas Dinner, Queens of France, Pullman Car Hiawatha, Love and How to Cure It, Such Things Only Happen in Books*, and *The Happy Journey to Trenton and Camden*.)

Three Plays: Our Town, The Skin of Our Teeth, The Matchmaker. New York: Harper and Bros., 1957.

The Woman of Andros. New York: Albert and Charles Boni, 1930.

Other Works by Wilder

"American Characteristics" and Other Essays. Ed. Donald Gallup. New York: Harper and Row, 1979.

"Goethe and World Literature." *Perspectives USA* (Fall 1952). Rpt. in *AC* (137–48).

"Homage." In *Hommage â Maurice Maeterlinck* (Brussels: Brochure-Program de L'Institut National Belge de Radiodiffusion, 1949) 78–79.

Introduction. *The Geographical History of America or, The Relation of Human Nature to the Human Mind*. By Gertrude Stein. New York: Random House, 1936. Rpt. in *AC* (187–92).

The Journals of Thornton Wilder: 1939–1961. Sel. and ed. Donald Gallup. New Haven, Conn.: Yale University Press, 1985.

Preface to *Three Plays*: *Our Town, The Skin of Our Teeth, The Matchmaker*. New York: Harper and Bros., 1957. Rpt. in *AC* (104–11).

"Some Thoughts on Playwrighting." In *The Intent of the Artist*. Ed., with intro., Augusto Centeno. Princeton, N.J.: Princeton University Press, 1941. Rpt. in *AC* (115–26).

"Thoughts for Our Times." *Harvard Alumni Bulletin* 53 (7 July 1951): 779–81.

"Toward an American Language." *Atlantic Monthly* 190, no. 1 (July 1952): 29–37. Rpt. in *AC* (3–33).

"The Turn of the Year." *Theatre Arts Monthly* 9, no. 3 (March 1925): 143–53.

With Isabel Wilder. "Playgoing Nights: From a Travel Diary." *Theatre Arts Monthly* 13, no. 6 (June 1929): 411–19.

Unpublished Materials

Wilder, Thornton Niven. Papers. Yale Collection of American Literature, The Beinecke Rare Book and Manuscript Library, Yale University Library, New Haven, Conn.

WORKS BY OTHERS

Arlington, L. C. *The Chinese Drama from the Earliest Times until Today*. Shanghai, China: Kelly and Walsh, 1930.

Aurier, G.-A. "Le symbolisme en peinture: Paul Gauguin." *Le Mercure de France* [sér. moderne] 2 (March 1891): 155–65.

Balakian, Anna. *The Symbolist Movement: A Critical Appraisal*. New York: New York University Press, 1977.

Baudelaire, Charles. "Richard Wagner et 'Tannhauser.' " *Oeuvres complètes*. Édition établie et annotée par Y. G. Le Dantec; revisée, completée, et presentée par Claude Pichois. Paris: Gallimard, Pleiade, 1968, 1210–11.

Beckett, Samuel. *Proust. The Collected Works of Samuel Beckett*. 1957. Reprint, New York: Grove, 1970.

______. *Waiting for Godot: A Tragicomedy in Two Acts*. New York: Grove, 1954.

Benchley, Robert. "Two at Once" [Review of *Our Town* by Thornton Wilder]. *New Yorker* 13, no. 4 (12 Feb. 1938): 26.

Bentley, Eric. *The Playwright as Thinker: A Study of Drama in Modern Times*. 1946. Rpt. New York: Meridian, 1955.

Block, Haskell. *Mallarmé and the Symbolist Drama*. Detroit: Wayne State University Press, 1963.

Boccioni, Umberto. "The Italian Futurist Painters and Sculptors." In *Catalogue de Luxe of the Department of Fine Arts Panama-Pacific International Exposition*, ed. John E. D. Trask and J. Nilsen Laurvik. 2 vols. San Francisco: Paul Elder, 1915, 1:123–27.

Bowers, Faubion. *Japanese Theatre*. New York: Hermitage House, 1952.

Brecht, Bertolt. *Brecht on Theatre: The Development of an Aesthetic*. Ed. and trans. John Willett. New York: Hill and Wang, 1964.

———. *The Jewish Wife and Other Short Plays*. Trans. Eric Bentley. New York: Grove Press–Evergreen, 1965.

Brockett, Oscar G. *History of the Theatre*. 6th ed. Boston: Allyn and Bacon, 1991.

Brockett, Oscar G., and Robert R. Findlay. *Century of Innovation: A History of European and American Theatre and Drama since 1870*. Englewood Cliffs, N.J.: Prentice-Hall, 1973.

Brown, Frank Chouteau. "The 'Book of the Pageant' and its Development." *The Drama* 18, 5 (May 1915): 269–83.

Burbank, Rex. *Thornton Wilder*. Twayne's United States Authors Series 5. New Haven, Conn.: College and University Press, 1961.

Buss, Kate. *Studies in the Chinese Drama*. Boston: Four Seas, 1922.

Campbell, Joseph, and Henry Morton Robinson. "The Skin of Whose Teeth? The Strange Case of Mr. Wilder's New Play and *Finnegans Wake*." *Saturday Review of Literature* 25 (19 Dec. 1942): 3–4.

Carter, Lawson A. *Zola and the Theater*. New Haven, Conn.: Yale University Press, 1963.

Cary, Joseph. "Futurism and the French *Théâtre d'Avant-Garde*." *Modern Philology* 57 (Nov. 1959). Rpt. in *Total Theatre: A Critical Anthology*, ed. E. T. Kirby. New York: E. P. Dutton, 1969, 99–114.

Castronovo, David. *Thornton Wilder*. New York: Ungar, 1986.

Cervantes Saavedra, Miguel de. *The Siege of Numantia*. Trans. Roy Campbell. In *Six Spanish Plays*. Vol. 3 of *The Classic Theatre*, ed. Eric Bentley. 4 vols. Garden City: Doubleday-Anchor, 1959, 3: 101–60.

Chadwick, Charles. *Symbolism*. The Critical Idiom 16. London: Methuen, 1971.

Chambers, E. K. *The Medieval Stage*. 2 vols. London: Oxford University Press, 1903.

Chen, Jack. *The Chinese Theatre*. New York: Roy, 1951.

"Chicago Pageant." Editorial. *Journal of Education* 78 (9 Oct. 1913): 346.

Clancy, James H. "Beyond Despair: A New Drama of Ideas." *Educational Theatre Journal* 13 (Oct. 1963): 157–66.

Clark, Lotta. "Pageantry in America." *English Journal* 3 (Mar. 1914): 146–53.

Clough, Rosa Trillo. *Futurism: The Story of a Modern Art Movement, A New Appraisal*. New York: Philosophical Library, 1961.

Cornell, Kenneth. *The Symbolist Movement*. New Haven, Conn.: Yale University Press, 1951.

Corrigan, Robert W. "Thornton Wilder and the Tragic Sense of Life." *Educational Theatre Journal* 13 (Oct. 1961): 167–73.

Cubeta, Paul M. *Modern Drama for Analysis*. New York: Holt, Rinehart and Winston, 1955.

Driver, Tom F. *Romantic Quest and Modern Query: A History of the Modern Theatre*. New York: Delacorte Press, 1970.

Eastman, Fred. "The Pulitzer Prize Drama." Review of *Our Town*, by Thornton Wilder. *Christian Century* 55 (3 Aug. 1938): 943–44.

Eaton, Walter Prichard. Review of *Our Town*, by Thornton Wilder. *New York Herald Tribune Books* 14 (1 May 1938): 21.

Ernst, Earle. *The Kabuki Theatre*. Honolulu: University of Hawaii Press, 1974.

Esslin, Martin. *Brecht: The Man and His Work.* Rev. ed. Garden City, N.Y.: Doubleday-Anchor, 1971.

Fergusson, Francis. "Three Allegorists: Brecht, Wilder, and Eliot." *Sewanee Review* 64 (Autumn 1956): 544–73.

Firebaugh, Joseph J. "The Humanism of Thornton Wilder." *Pacific Spectator* 4 (Autumn 1950): 426–38.

Frenz, Horst. "The Reception of Thornton Wilder's Plays in Germany." *Modern Drama* 3 (Sept. 1960): 123–37.

Fulton, A. R. "Expressionism—Twenty Years After." *Sewanne Review* 52 (Summer 1944): 398–413.

Fussell, Paul. "Thornton Wilder and the German Psyche." *Nation* 186 (3 May 1958): 394–95.

Garten, H. F. *Modern German Drama.* London: Methuen, 1964.

Gassner, John. "The Two Worlds of Thornton Wilder." Introduction to *The Long Christmas Dinner and Other Plays in One Act.* By Thornton Wilder. 1959. Reprint, New York: Avon/Bard, 1980, vii–xx.

Gilman, Richard. *The Making of Modern Drama.* New York: Farrar, Straus, and Giroux, 1974.

Gold, Michael. "Wilder: Prophet of the Genteel Christ." *New Republic* 64 (22 Oct. 1930). Rpt. in *Years of Protest*, eds. Jack Salzman and Barry Wallenstein. New York: Pegasus, 1967, 237.

Goldberg, RoseLee. *Performance: Live Art 1909 to the Present.* New York: Harry N. Abrams, 1979.

Goldstein, Malcolm. *The Art of Thornton Wilder.* Lincoln: University of Nebraska Press, 1965.

Goldstone, Richard H. "Thornton Wilder." In *Writers at Work: The Paris Review Interviews*, ed. Malcolm Cowley. New York: Viking, 1958, 99–119.

———. *Thornton Wilder: An Intimate Portrait.* New York: Saturday Review Press/E. P. Dutton, 1975.

Gurr, Andrew. *The Shakespearean Stage: 1574–1642.* Cambridge: Cambridge University Press, 1970.

Guthrie, Tyrone. "The World of Thornton Wilder." *New York Times Magazine*, 27 Nov. 1955: 26–27.

———. *A Life in the Theatre.* New York: McGraw-Hill, 1959.

Haberman, Donald. *The Plays of Thornton Wilder: A Critical Study.* Middletown, Ohio: Wesleyan University Press, 1967.

———. *Our Town: An American Play.* Twayne's Masterwork Studies 28. Boston: Twayne, 1989.

Harrison, Gilbert A. *The Enthusiast: A Life of Thornton Wilder.* New Haven, Conn., and New York: Ticknor and Fields, 1983.

Heidegger, Martin. *Being and Time.* Trans. John Macquarrie and Edward Robinson. London: SCM Press, 1962. Extract rpt. in *Existentialism*, ed. Robert C. Solomon. New York: Random House/Modern Library, 1974, 94–116.

Jasper, Gertrude R. *Adventure in the Theatre: Lugné-Poë and the Théâtre de l'Oeuvre to 1899.* New Brunswick, N.J.: Rutgers University Press, 1947.

Jones, W. T. *A History of Western Philosophy.* New York: Harcourt, Brace, 1952.

Kierkegaard, Søren. *Philosophical Fragments or, A Fragment of Philosophy*. Trans. David F. Swenson. Rev. Howard V. Hong. Princeton, N.J.: Princeton University Press, 1936. Reprint, 1962.

———. *Fear and Trembling and The Sickness unto Death*. Trans. Walter Lowrie. Princeton, N.J.: Princeton University Press, 1941. Reprint, 1954.

———. *Concluding Unscientific Postscript*. Trans. David F. Swenson and Walter Lowrie. Princeton, N.J.: Princeton University Press, 1941. Reprint 1969. Extracts rpt. in *Existentialism*, ed. Robert C. Solomon. New York: Random House/Modern Library, 1974. 17–24.

———. *The Concept of Dread*. Trans. Walter Lowrie. Princeton, N.J.: Princeton University Press, 1944.

Kirby, Michael. *Futurist Performance*. New York: E. P. Dutton, 1971.

Kuner, Mildred Christophe. *Thornton Wilder: The Bright and the Dark*. Twentieth-Century American Writers Series. New York: Crowell, 1972.

Langdon, William Chauncy. "The Festal Drama." *Drama* 7, no. 27 (Aug. 1917): 404–25.

Lewis, Flora. "Thornton Wilder at 65 Looks Ahead—And Back." *New York Times Magazine*, 15 Apr. 1962, 28–29.

Littman, Mark Evan. "Theme and Structure in the Plays of Thornton Wilder." Dissertation, Northwestern University, 1969.

London, Jack. *The Sea Wolf*. New York: Grosset and Dunlap, 1904.

Macgowan, Kenneth, and Robert Edmond Jones. *Continental Stagecraft*. New York: Harcourt, Brace, 1922.

Mackaye, Hazel. "The Peterborough Pageant." *Drama* 1, no. 1 (Feb. 1911): 136–47.

Maeterlinck, Maurice. *The Treasure of the Humble*. Trans. Alfred Sutro. New York: Dodd, Mead, 1900.

Mallarmé, Stéphane. "Crise de vers." *Divagations*. Paris: Fasquelle, Club français du livre, 1961.

———. *Selected Poetry and Prose*. Ed. Mary Ann Caws. New York: New Directions, 1982.

Marinetti, F. T. *Selected Writings*. Ed. R. W. Flint. Trans. R. W. Flint and Arthur A. Coppotelli. New York: Farrar, Straus, and Giroux, 1972.

Matthaei, Renate. *Luigi Pirandello*. Trans. Simon and Erika Young. World Dramatists Series. New York: Ungar, 1973.

Modic, John. "The Eclectic Mr. Wilder." *Ball State Teachers College Forum* 1 (Winter 1960/61): 55–61.

Norris, Frank. "Zola as a Romantic Writer." *Wave* 15 (27 June 1896). Rpt. in *The Literary Criticism of Frank Norris*, ed. Donald Pizer. Austin: University of Texas Press, 1964, 71–72.

Olson, Robert G. *An Introduction to Existentialism*. New York: Dover, 1962.

Oppel, Horst. "Thornton Wilder in Deutschland: Wirkung und Wertung seines Werkes im deutschen Sprachraum." *Abhandlungen der Klasse der Literatur/Akademie der Wissenschaften und der Literatur*. Jg. 1976/77, no. 3, Mainz, 1977. 1–31.

Papajewski, Helmut. *Thornton Wilder*. Trans. John Conway. New York: Ungar, 1968.

Parmenter, Ross. "Novelist into Playwright." *Saturday Review of Literature* 18 (11 June 1938): 10–11.

Pascal, Blaise. *Pascal's Pensées*. Trans. W. F. Trotter. New York: Dutton, 1958.
Pirandello, Luigi. *Naked Masks: Five Plays*. Ed. Eric Bentley. New York: E. P. Dutton, 1952.
———. "On Humor" [excerpts]. Trans. Teresa Novel. *Tulane Drama Review* 10, no. 3 (Spring 1966): 52.
Porter, Thomas E. "A Green Corner of the Universe: *Our Town*." In *Myth and Modern American Drama*, ed. Thomas E. Porter. Detroit: Wayne State University Press, 1969: 200–224.
Pronko, Leonard C. *Theater East and West: Perspectives Toward a Total Theater*. Berkeley: University of California Press, 1967.
Rennert, Hugo Albert. *The Spanish Stage in the Time of Lope de Vega*. New York: Hispanic Society of America, 1989.
Ritchie, J. M. *German Expressionist Drama*. Twayne's World Authors Series 421. Boston: G. K. Hall, 1976.
Robichez, Jacques. *Le symbolisme au théâtre*. Paris: L'arche, 1957.
Robinson, Henry Morton. "The Curious Case of Thornton Wilder." *Esquire* 47 (March 1957): 70–71, 124–26.
Rudlin, John. *Jacques Copeau*. Directors in Perspective Series. Cambridge: Cambridge University Press, 1986.
Sartre, Jean-Paul. *The Flies*. Trans. Stuart Gilbert. In *No Exit and Three Other Plays*, by Jean-Paul Sartre. New York: Random House/Vintage, 1955: 49–127.
———. *Existentialism and Human Emotions*. New York: Philosophical Library, 1957.
———. *Being and Nothingness: A Phenomenological Essay on Ontology*. Trans. Hazel E. Barnes. 1956. Reprint, New York: Washington Square Press, 1966.
———. *St. Genet: Actor and Martyr*. Trans. Bernard Frechtman. New York: George Braziller, 1963. Extract rpt. in *Existentialism*, ed. Robert C. Solomon. New York: Random House/Modern Library, 1974, 237–40.
———. *Sartre on Theatre*. Ed. Michel Contat and Michel Rybalka. Trans. Frank Jellinek. New York: Random House/Pantheon, 1976.
Sawyer, Julian. "Wilder and Stein." *Saturday Review of Literature* 26 (17 Apr. 1943): 27.
Schneider, Alan. *Entrances: An American Director's Journey*. New York: Viking, 1986.
Schopenhauer, Arthur. *Schopenhauer: Selections*. Ed. DeWitt H. Parker. New York: Scribner's, 1928.
Shattuck, Roger. *The Banquet Years: The Origins of the Avant-Garde in France, 1885 to World War I*. Rev. ed. New York: Vintage, 1968.
Shergold, N. D. *A History of the Spanish Stage from Medieval Times until the End of the Seventeenth Century*. Oxford, U.K.: Oxford University Press, 1967.
Simon, Linda. *Thornton Wilder: His World*. Garden City, N.Y.: Doubleday, 1979.
Sokel, Walter H. *The Writer in Extremis: Expressionism in Twentieth-Century German Literature*. Stanford, Calif.: Stanford University Press, 1959.
Solomon, Robert C., ed. *Existentialism*. New York: Modern Library, 1974.
Southern, Richard. *The Staging of Plays before Shakespeare*. London: Faber and Faber, 1973.
Strindberg, August. "Author's Note on *A Dream Play*." *Six Plays of Strindberg*. Trans. Elizabeth Sprigge. Garden City, N.Y.: Doubleday-Anchor, 1955, 193.

Styan, J. L. *Expressionism and Epic Theatre*. Vol. 3 of *Modern Drama in Theory and Practice*. Cambridge, U.K.: Cambridge University Press, 1981.

______. *Symbolism, Surrealism, and the Absurd*. Vol. 2 of *Modern Drama in Theory and Practice*. Cambridge, U.K.: Cambridge University Press, 1981.

Symons, Arthur. *Studies in Seven Arts*. New York: Dutton, 1907.

Taft, Linwood. *The Technique of Pageantry*. New York: A. S. Barnes, 1925.

Taylor, Jerome, and Alan H. Nelson, eds. *Medieval English Drama: Essays Critical and Contextual*. Chicago: University of Chicago Press, 1972.

Tritsch, Walter. "Thornton Wilder in Berlin." *Living Age* 341 (Sept. 1931): 44–47.

Valgemae, Mardi. *Accelerated Grimace: Expressionism in the American Drama of the 1920's*. Carbondale: Southern Illinois University Press, 1972.

van Gelder, Robert. "Interview with a Best-Selling Author: Thornton Wilder." *Cosmopolitan* 124 (Apr. 1948): 18+.

Vega Carpio, Lope Felix de., *The New Art of Making Comedies*. Trans. Olga Marx Perlzweig. Excerpts rpt. in *Literary Criticism: Plato to Dryden*, ed. Allan H. Gilbert. Detroit: Wayne State University Press, 1962, 541–48.

Waxman, Samuel Montefiore. *Antoine and the Théâtre-Libre*. Cambridge: Harvard University Press, 1926.

Wescott, Glenway. "Conversations with Thornton Wilder." *Images of Truth: Remembrances and Criticism*. New York: Harper and Row, 1962, 242–308.

Wickham, Glynne. *The Medieval Theatre*. New York: St. Martin's, 1974.

Wilder, Amos Niven. *Thornton Wilder and His Public*. Philadelphia: Fortress Press, 1980.

Wilder, Isabel. "Foreword." In *The Alcestiad, or, A Life in the Sun, with a Satyr Play, The Drunken Sisters*, by Thornton Wilder. 1977. Reprint, New York: Avon/Bard, 1979, 7–19.

Willett, John. *The Theatre of Bertolt Brecht: A Study from Eight Aspects*. London: Eyre Methuen, 1977.

Williams, Arnold. *The Drama of Medieval England*. East Lansing: Michigan State University Press, 1961.

Wilson, Edmund. "Thornton Wilder: The Influence of Proust." *New Republic* 55 (8 Aug. 1928): 303–5.

Wixson, Douglas Charles, Jr. "The Dramatic Techniques of Thornton Wilder and Bertolt Brecht: A Study in Comparison." *Modern Drama* 15, no. 2 (Sept. 1972): 112–24.

Zola, Émile. "Proudhon et Courbet." *Mes haines*. Paris: Faure, 1866. Rpt. in *Les Oeuvres complètes*. Notes et commentaires de Maurice LeBlond, texte de l'édition Eugène Fasquelle. Paris: François Bernouard, 1927–29, 25: 21–34

______.*The Experimental Novel and Other Essays*. Trans. Belle M. Sherman. New York: Cassell, 1893.

Index

About the Author

PAUL LIFTON is Assistant Professor of Theatre Arts at North Dakota State University.